Exchange-Traded Funds and the
New Dynamics of Investing

FINANCIAL MANAGEMENT ASSOCIATION

Survey and Synthesis Series

CONTENTS

Oxford University Press is a department of the University of Oxford. It furthers
the University's objective of excellence in research, scholarship, and education
by publishing worldwide. Oxford is a registered trade mark of Oxford University
Press in the UK and certain other countries.

Published in the United States of America by Oxford University Press
198 Madison Avenue, New York, NY 10016, United States of America.

© Oxford University Press 2016

CIP data is on file at the Library of Congress
ISBN 978-0-19-027939-4

9 8 7 6 5 4 3 2 1
Printed by Sheridan Books, Inc., United States of America

Exchange-Traded Funds and the New Dynamics of Investing

ANANTH N. MADHAVAN

This book is about the quiet transformation of asset management through the rise of passive investing. Passive managers seek to replicate a benchmark while active managers look for outperformance. The growth of passive investing is closely related to the innovation of exchange-traded funds (ETFs). ETFs cover all regions and asset classes, including most interestingly fixed income and alternatives. Assets in ETFs are rapidly growing, typically at the expense of traditional active mutual funds. These trends have generated considerable interest, especially from retail and institutional investors and increasingly from academics, regulators, and the press. But the book is really not an ETF book per se; rather it is about a style of investing that is passive or model-based in nature and a vehicle (or wrapper) that can help investors achieve that objective effectively. A recurrent theme is the notion that passive investing involves active choices, and that the ETF wrapper, while an elegant and simple way to gain exposure, requires education.

There are many first-rate books and online resources about ETFs aimed at general audiences that describe the basics of how ETFs work and can be used by individual investors to build core portfolios and express tactical views. An excellent read that is differentiated from more basic introductions is Koesterich (2008), who presents an ETF strategist's viewpoint. Another set of books (e.g., Gastineau 2010; Abner 2010) offer a wealth of institutional detail on how index mutual funds and ETFs are constructed, launched, and traded. The CFA Institute's book on ETFs by Hill, Nadig, and Hougan (2015) is an outstanding source of current information.

Several investment books (e.g., Schoenfeld 2004) discuss passive investing in more detail. Ang (2014) provides an extremely comprehensive and highly readable book that covers all aspects of factor based investing, focusing on the drivers of returns over the long horizon. In general, books on investment—including those that are the core of many MBA classes—do not focus on the vehicles with which investors can actually implement their desired exposures. By contrast, this book offers complementary content and perspectives by showing how ETFs and their close cousins, index mutual funds, could be used to gain factor exposures.

In terms of scope, the book covers the reasons for the rapid growth of passive investing and why ETFs are the preferred vehicle for such investors. The book highlights how ETFs differ from traditional open-end mutual funds, and how they can be used to achieve a variety of investment objectives. Both academics and practitioners can use this book as a reference and guide, with numerous current examples drawn from the real world. Although the underlying structure is analytical, much of the content is intuitive in nature and the more technical or mathematical aspects can easily be skipped. While this book is not written for the average individual investor, the advisors who represent them (e.g., large advisory firms serving thousands of individuals) will likely find much of interest. For academic audiences, undergraduate and graduate students in finance and economics and students in professional credential programs such as the CFA can use the book to supplement a standard investments course. Sophisticated investors such as hedge funds, pensions, endowments, sovereign wealth funds, and other institutional investors who trade in size and seek to learn more about ETF pricing and trading will also find this book of interest. Finally, the book deals in depth with public policy questions including systemic risk and the possible detrimental impacts of passive flows on the underlying markets, so is highly relevant for regulators and policymakers.

The book is organized as follows: Part I provides the required institutional background necessary to understand the operation of ETFs and their growth as part of an ongoing rise in passive investing. ETFs have elements of both open-ended mutual funds and closed-end funds, and understanding the mechanics of how they are priced and are regulated is critical. Part II develops a framework to analyze ETF premiums and discounts, price discovery, volatility, liquidity, and transaction costs. I present empirical evidence on the pricing of ETFs and their performance in stressed markets. Having established the basics, Part III discusses practitioner applications, and extensions beyond equity to other asset classes such as fixed income, commodities, foreign exchange, and volatility. I discuss the important category of liquid alternatives—which often cross asset classes—and the opportunity they offer for future growth of the industry. Part IV examines issues related to active ETFs and so-called "Smart Beta." I argue that active ETFs will grow considerably in coming years, although the use of the ETF wrapper presents several interesting challenges from an operational and regulatory viewpoint. Part V considers current regulatory and public policy issues including the impact of ETF flows on underlying markets, sources of systemic risk, the Flash Crash of May 2010, and leveraged and inverse ETFs. In many cases, a better understanding of the structural differences between ETFs and other investment vehicles mitigates these concerns. I conclude that ETFs have extended significant benefits to investors and to the functioning of markets that meaningfully outweigh any perceived or actual weaknesses.

ACKNOWLEDGMENTS

I owe a big debt of gratitude to many colleagues in academia and industry over the years for their insights, knowledge, and mentorship. Minder Cheng sparked my early interest in ETFs and was co-author on the first academic work to look seriously at leveraged and inverse products, one that had a real influence on public policy. My coworkers over the years have been a great source of encouragement and inspiration, including Daniel Gamba, Ravi Goutam, Steve Laipply, Matt Tucker, Scott Williamson, and Mark Wiedman. I am especially grateful to my co-authors in recent BlackRock Institute Viewpoints articles, especially Ben Golub, Barbara Novick, and Ira Shapiro, who helped shape my thinking on many of the critical issues considered here.

The book also reflects joint efforts with my co-authors including Donald Keim, Ian Domowitz, Chris Downing, Daphne Du, Terrence Hendershott, Daniel Morillo, Aleksander Sobczyk, and many others. Ronald Kahn's seminal work on active management was influential in my thoughts about the future of the industry. I would also express my thanks to John McConnell and Erik Lie for encouraging me to pursue a book project and my editors at Oxford University Press, Scott Parris and Cathryn Vaulman. Finally, this is a 5–9 project meaning it takes place beyond the traditional work day. I thank my family (Rachel, Sophia, and Daniel) for their understanding and patience of many nights and weekends spent on this effort. Of course, any errors are entirely my own, and all views represented here are mine alone.

A.N.M.

Passive Investing

The Current Landscape

1.1. INTRODUCTION

Recent decades have seen a surge in interest in passive investing, where investors try to track a benchmark market index, in contrast to active management that seeks to outperform the market. The innovation of the exchange-traded fund (ETF) is a critically important element in this global trend. An ETF is an investment vehicle that trades intraday and seeks to replicate the performance of a specific index. In industry parlance an ETF is simply a "wrapper," a vehicle for investors to gain their desired exposures just like more conventional mutual funds. The fund managers who create ETFs, like Vanguard or WisdomTree, are not actually in the ETF business. Rather, they are in the *exposures* business.

ETFs have grown substantially in size, diversity, and market significance in recent years. In 2015, for the first time ever, assets in global ETFs exceeded $3 trillion passing the amount in hedge funds. As a consequence, there is increased attention by investors, regulators, and academics seeking to assess and understand the implications of this rapid growth. I view ETFs as a genuine financial innovation as opposed to the chimeras marketed prior to the financial crisis. The innovative element is that ETFs offer clients exposures that were previously unavailable or very expensive, such as certain hedge fund strategies. They also have the power to be a *disruptive* innovation to today's asset management industry. This is because many traditional active managers and hedge funds deliver a significant fraction of their active returns via static exposures to factors like value or growth that can be offered at low cost via index funds and ETFs.

The common characteristic of ETFs is that they are traded intraday on an organized exchange. Although simple, this description ignores many important differences between ETFs and other investment vehicles, including individual securities like stocks or bonds. These differences have important implications for investors. In my view, open-ended mutual funds and ETFs are likely to displace these vehicles over the coming years. Indeed, while US inflows to ETFs were 25% and above annually in the past decade, traditional active mutual funds experienced a −3% decline each year in the same period. Growth is especially evident in actively managed ETFs and in segments such as fixed income where active management was traditionally the norm. Both index funds and ETFs also have significant advantages over closed-end mutual funds.

This book provides a framework to address questions about ETFs and, more broadly, passive indexing. We begin with an overview of the drivers of passive investing where I highlight the idea that passive investing involves active choices such as the benchmark index, universe, and weighting schemes. One of the most exciting developments in this area is the rise of factor based investing that explicitly departs from traditional market capitalization weighted schemes. This sets the stage in chapter 2 for a more in-depth discussion the advantages and disadvantages to open- and closed-end mutual funds relative to ETFs. As we shall see, ETFs offer some significant advantages over these more familiar investment vehicles but also some important caveats.

1.2. ACTIVE AND PASSIVE INVESTING

1.2.1. Rise of Indexing

Passive investing, where investors typically seek to match broad market indexes, has grown tremendously in the past few decades. Sullivan and Xiong (2012) note that while passively managed funds represent only about one-third of all fund assets, their average annual growth rate since the early 1990s is 26%, double that of actively managed assets. Meanwhile, traditional active mutual funds have experienced single-digit declines over the past decade. In part, this growth reflects the establishment of modern financial economics including the value of broad portfolio diversification and the concept that prices are informationally efficient. Other important considerations in the growth of indexing include growing awareness of transaction costs, taxes, and lower fees and turnover relative to active management.

By contrast, active investing, as defined here, requires an investor to depart from market capitalization based weighting and requires a conscious decision on what securities or asset classes to over- or under-weight relative to the broader market. Active management is thus a zero sum game absent fees. Further, there is little evidence that skilled active managers can be identified easily. Index investing, through the wrappers of index mutual funds and ETFs, offers low-cost, diversified exposure to various market segments.

1.2.2. Investment Strategies

An important theme and an organizing principle is that the range of investing strategies from passive to active is, as illustrated in table 1.1, a continuum of exposures and different degrees of transparency into the underlying holdings. Passive strategies require active choices in most cases. I distinguish between passive/ exposure based funds (against a benchmark or without an index), transparent active funds (where the weighting scheme is not market capitalization based but portfolio construction is model based), and active funds which are nontransparent, including fundamental funds.

Table 1.1 CONTINUUM OF INVESTMENT STRATEGIES

Exposure Based		Transparent Active		Nontransparent Active
Pure index	**Exposure without an index**	**Alternatively weighted index**	**Model-driven**	**Fundamental**
Reflects the performance of an asset class using a market cap index.	Passively reflects the performance of an asset class without using an index process.	Delivers on a specific enhancement strategy expressed as an alternative weighted index.	Seeking to generate alpha or controlled risk exposures using quantitative models.	Seeking to generate alpha without explicit portfolio formation rules.
The majority of stock and bond index funds and ETFs exactly replicating the index.	Optimized for tax efficiency or other goals; custom index or no index.	Fundamental indexes based on earnings, etc. that are not market capitalization weighted.	Minimum Volatility Funds; Factor Funds; risk-weighted funds.	Either bottom up security selection or liquidity selection.

Most index-tracking ETFs and open-ended funds mimic standard indices that weight components based on their market capitalization. This weighting scheme is sensible offering lower turnover than many alternatives. In equity space, this has traditionally meant stock exposures across two dimensions: regions (e.g., Europe, Brazil) and focus (e.g., utilities, small-cap equity). In fixed income space, the corresponding exposures are across the dimensions of geography (e.g., UK gilts), rates (e.g., intermediate treasuries), and credit (e.g., high-yield bonds).

Traditional market capitalization weighting schemes can be expanded in several dimensions. First, while most ETFs are unlevered, fully collateralized exposures, some funds offer embedded leverage with higher returns on the upside but lower returns on the downside. I will discuss leveraged products (which include equities and other asset classes) later in the book. Second, it is increasingly common for ETF managers to use currency hedging to separate out foreign exchange and underlying asset return exposures. For example, a Japanese equity fund might hedge the yen offering a US-domiciled investor a "pure play" on Japanese stocks without any risk the dollar may appreciate against the yen. Finally, by altering an index's weighting scheme, semi-active strategies can be implicitly embedded into an ETF structure that is transparent and passive in nature. These funds track benchmarks that are themselves expressions of active investment strategies based on model-driven rules. So-called "Smart Beta" includes several important subcategories, as discussed below.

1.3. EVOLUTION OF INVESTMENT IDEAS

1.3.1. Benchmarks

Pure active managers seek to outperform a benchmark. Active managers expend considerable resources to discover alpha. Historically, the idea of passive index investing was viewed with skepticism and, until the late 1970s, was largely unavailable to the average investor. Today, index funds (mutual funds and ETFs) account for 35% of all domestic equity fund assets in 2014, up from just 20% in 2006. Assets in US ETFs rose from $70 billion in 2000 to $2.1 trillion by the end of 2015 (BlackRock 2016) with worldwide totals in all asset classes at $3.0 trillion.

In a well-known *Newsweek* column in August 1976 titled "Index-Fund Investing," Professor and Nobel winner Paul A. Samuelson noted[1] that: "As yet there exists no convenient fund . . . that apes the whole market, requires no load, and that keeps commissions, turnover and management fees to the feasible minimum. I suspect the future will bring such new and convenient instrumentalities." Although Samuelson's prediction was eventually proven accurate (Vanguard launched the first index fund available to individual investors that year), there was considerable

---

1. Samuelson had actually made the point in a column earlier in April 1975 and had championed indexing in a *Journal of Portfolio Management* article in 1974 where he asked those who did not believe a passive index would outperform the vast majority of active managers to produce "brute evidence to the contrary."

skepticism about the idea of indexing in general. Edward C. Johnson III, the Chairman of Fidelity Investments and a promoter of active management, famously commented at the time: "I can't believe that the great mass of investors are going to be satisfied with receiving just average returns." John C. Bogle[2] of Vanguard reports a fund manager questioning, "Who wants to be operated on by an average surgeon?" Ironically, Fidelity is one of the largest index managers in the world today and also offers its clients easy access to ETFs.

A very common perception is that active management is better suited to less liquid asset classes such as small-cap stocks or fixed income. As noted by Sharpe (1991) in his well-known article on the arithmetic of active management, the investment style is zero-sum if one ignores fees: Collectively active bets (defined as a deviation from cap weighting) must sum to zero, so in aggregate, active management cannot outperform an index. Logically, over any specified time period, the market return is a weighted average of the returns on the securities within the market, using beginning market values as weights where I ignore any intra-period trading activity for simplicity. So a passive manager will earn the market return, before costs. As the market's return is an equal-weighted average of the returns on the passive and active dollars managed, it follows that the average actively managed fund will also earn the market return. Further, if markets are informationally efficient (Grossman and Stiglitz 1980), there is no incentive to acquire information at cost.

Of course, this argument ignores the fact that many active positions are not conscious decisions by professional managers. For example, retail investors chasing hot stocks may have active bets on certain industries or sectors like social media. Similarly, many workers are required to hold stock in the companies that employ them, hence having an active bet that they cannot easily lay off. So, it is possible for professional active managers (mutual funds, hedge funds, etc.) to outperform as a group. Indeed, professional active managers and institutional investors are large and operate in scale, conferring considerable cost advantages. They engage in repeated games with their clients (meaning they are held accountable for long-term performance) and are typically overseen by investment professionals such as consultants.

Even pure passive indexing against a common benchmark such as the S&P 500 requires active decisions on the part of the investor and index provider. For example, index membership is selected by a committee chosen by Standard & Poor's based on a variety of criteria, both objective and subjective, and the investor needs to consider whether to also allocate funds across other capitalization segments or asset classes, and if so in what proportions. The choice of benchmark is the key. For example, if we restrict our benchmark to say US large-cap stocks, a particular fund may look quite passive. If the benchmark is broadened out to world equity (or even to include fixed income instruments such as sovereign bonds, credits, etc.) as in figure 1.1, that same manager may appear to have a considerable active tilt to the United States.

---

2. See John C. Bogle, "The First Index Mutual Fund: A History of Vanguard Index Trust and the Vanguard Index Strategy," 1997, available at http://www.vanguard.com/bogle_site/lib/sp19970401.html.

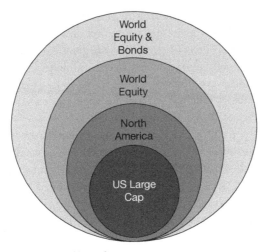

Figure 1.1 Possible equity benchmarks.

Indexes may differ significantly in their composition, and selection among them requires some form of active choice. Indeed, S&P Dow Jones calculates more than 1 million indexes a day, meaning that fund managers have many choices of benchmark.[3] For example, investors seeking growth have strong interest in emerging markets (Karolyi [2015] provides a very complete review of emerging market research and many valuable investing insights) because these markets represent a little less than 50% of global GNP yet only 9% of world equity. Investors have many choices of indexes for emerging markets that differ in what they include in the category. Different benchmarks mean that not all emerging market funds are alike.

CHOICE OF INDEX CAN MATTER

Consider the two largest emerging markets ETFs. The iShares Emerging Markets ETF (EEM) has the MSCI Emerging Markets Index as benchmark. MSCI includes South Korea as an emerging market and (as of January 2016) EEM had a 16.1% weight on that country with a 3.4% of Samsung Electronics, its largest position. By contrast, the largest emerging market fund, the Vanguard Emerging Market Stock Index Fund (VWO) is benchmarked against the FTSE Emerging Index. FTSE considers South Korea to be a developed market and therefore it is excluded from the index. VWO's largest position as of January 2016, was Taiwan Semiconductor Manufacturing, with a 3.4% weight. Both MSCI and FTSE are well-established index providers with clear guidelines for selection of benchmark weights. Ultimately, the choice of index depends largely on the investor's views about what countries constitute "emerging markets."

---

3. *Financial Times*, August 16, 2015.

Yet, numerous studies (see, e.g., Wermers 2000) have shown that despite evidence of alpha generation, active managers as a group underperform index funds. If one factors in sample selection bias, the differences from index funds are even larger. Specifically, active funds that perform poorly often exit or are liquidated/merged. These funds are often not represented in the usual reporting of fund performance, although they are part of the investable universe at the time of investment decision.

The SPIVA® US Scorecard[4] published by S&P Dow Jones Indices (2014) reports that as of December 31, 2014, the majority (82.1%) of large-cap active managers failed be beat their benchmark over a 10-year period, as did mid- and small-cap managers. This is not a recent phenomenon as shown by this quote from *Forbes* of September 3, 1990 (also cited by Sharpe 1991): "Today's fad is index funds that track the Standard and Poor's 500. True, the average soundly beat most stock funds over the past decade. But is this an eternal truth or a transitory one?"

1.3.2. Determinants of Active Performance

Active managers have underperformed passive benchmarks in 2010–2014 (US large-cap mutual funds) with fewer than 10% beating the benchmark in 2014. There is no evidence either that active managers systematically do better in "less efficient" asset classes such as emerging markets, municipal bonds, or small-cap stocks. Even winners do not persist. Of the top quartile funds in 2010, fewer than 50% were in the top quartile the next year and just a few persisted through 2014. Industry participants typically provide explanations for active underperformance in recent years based on exceptional considerations such as style rotation, increased correlation among securities, or market dynamics. Academic research (see Ang 2014), however, provides several explanations including:

- **Higher management fees**—active research is costly relative to a passive index that replicates a public benchmark;
- **Higher transaction costs**—spreads and market impact are larger for active managers whose trades convey information; managers seeking to trade quickly may also pay higher commissions and spreads; and
- **Higher turnover**—index products based on market capitalization automatically reweight given price changes, but active managers may have to rebalance deliberately and also typically have higher portfolio turnover as they seek alpha opportunities.

Some illustrative figures can highlight the performance drag an active fund faces. In table 1.2, trading costs are one-way expressed as a percentage of transaction

---

4. Available at http://www.spindices.com/documents/spiva/spiva-us-mid-year-2014.pdf. The SPIVA figures adjust for survivorship bias, as well as subtleties like weighting and manager appropriate benchmark. In the five-year period ending December 2014, SPIVA estimates 24% of domestic and international equity funds were merged/liquidated highlighting the importance of survivorship bias in mutual fund performance analysis.

Table 1.2 TRANSACTION COST AND FEE IMPACT ON RETURNS

	Active Manager (%)	Passive Manager (%)
Commissions	0.10	0.05
Spread/Impact	0.55	0.10
Total trading cost (one way)	0.65	0.15
Portfolio turnover		
Sales	80.00	4.00
Purchases	80.00	4.00
Total turnover (two way)	160.00	8.00
Transaction costs (% of portfolio value)	1.04	0.01
Management fees	0.36	0.10
Total expenses (annual)	1.40	0.11

value, and figures for management fees and turnover are typical of actively managed mutual funds.[5] The value added required to offset the costs of active management is 1.29%, which is relatively high. For higher turnover and cost funds, it can be substantially larger.

1.3.3. Purity Hypothesis

While academic evidence suggests that active managers as a group tend to underperform passive benchmarks, there are a few points that need to be kept in mind. First of all, keep in mind that indexes are not directly investable, so the appropriate benchmark return is a comparable index fund or ETF. Second, in many markets, there are extended periods of time when active managers do beat their index counterparts. In the past this often reflected poor benchmarks, where, say, a US equity growth-oriented fund was naïvely compared to a broad index such as the S&P 500 that includes both value and growth stocks. As index providers have provided more refined definitions of styles, benchmarking has improved in precision, making it easier to understand when managers truly add value.

So when do active funds outperform index funds? A valuable insight is offered by a phenomenon termed the *Purity Hypothesis* that is also known as *Dunn's Law*. This practitioner maxim states that active funds *outperform* when a particular style (e.g., US equities, large-cap value) actually performs relatively *poorly* relative to all other styles, and vice versa. This empirical regularity appears to be borne out by the data. For example, the 2014 SPIVA US Scorecard (by S&P Dow Jones Indices) finds that for domestic equities in the decade prior to December 31, 2014, mid-cap growth was the best performing equity style with the S&P MidCap 400 Growth

5. Morningstar.com. Mutual funds can charge distribution and service (known as 12b-1) fees of up to 100 basis points annually.

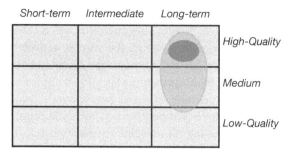

Figure 1.2 Fixed income style box and active manager target.

returning 10.03% per annum. In this period, mid-cap growth was also the one with the highest percentage (91.8%) of managers who underperformed. Conversely, large-cap value had the *lowest* relative return across styles of 6.7% a year over the decade ending December 31, 2014, but had the best performance by active managers. Only 58.8% of managers lagged the benchmark in this style category.

While the Purity Hypothesis seems puzzling at first, the logic is straightforward. Benchmark indexes are constructed to be pure plays (e.g., US large cap), but active managers typically have the flexibility to select securities outside that style, say foreign securities or mid- or small-cap stocks. This leads to better performance for the active funds when a particular style is underperforming. Consider a fixed income example. Shown in figure 1.2 is a style box for, say, US corporate bonds across two dimensions: Interest rate sensitivity (duration) and credit risk (quality or rating). For equity funds, the corresponding style boxes cut across capitalization (large, mid, and small) and across the value dimension (growth, blend, value). In figure 1.2 the darker circle shows the target style for a fundamental active manager who invests primarily in long-duration, high-quality bonds. But while the active fund may target high-quality long bonds, the manager often has some discretion in security selection, unlike an index fund. For example, a bond manager may choose to add some lower quality bonds to the mix to—on average—earn a credit risk premium.

Across all active managers targeting a particular style (long duration, highly rated bonds), there is a range of possible active investments (shown in the lighter shade) that goes into medium or even low credit quality bonds. Such style drift benefits the active manager relative to an index-tracking fund targeting that style when higher quality, long duration bonds do less well compared to other, lower quality bonds. Conversely, if a particular style does better than other segments of the corporate bond universe, index funds that are tracking precisely that style will generally outperform active funds that are blending styles. Indeed, in 2013, active managers did well against benchmarks in long duration bonds, but suffered in 2014 when yields moved lower and the style rallied.

In an equity example, active managers targeting large capitalization value stocks may put a fraction of the portfolio in medium or even small capitalization stocks. If large cap value does well, index funds and ETFs targeted against just that segment will do well; if it underperforms relative to other capitalization ranges, active managers who are not using pure style plays will do better.

The cyclicality behind the purity hypothesis is evident in the data, but it does not mean that an investor can predict a segment that will do well in advance. As Sharpe (1991) notes: "Properly measured, the average actively managed dollar must underperform the average passively managed dollar, net of costs. Empirical analyses that appear to refute this principle are guilty of improper measurement." Ultimately, the true measurement of active performance comes with precise, accurate benchmarks. Factor based benchmarks correctly capture differences in style across managers, including tilts to value, momentum, size, credit, and other drivers of returns. We will consider factors in more detail in Part IV of the book.

1.4. INVESTMENT VEHICLES

1.4.1. Exchange-Traded Funds and Other Fund Structures

So far, I have discussed investment strategies in terms of the continuum from passive to active without an explicit differentiation among the types of funds (or "wrappers") used to achieve these objectives. Exchange-traded funds are an important financial innovation and a key part of the passive investing trend. The success of the first such fund, the Standard and Poor's Depositary Receipt (SPDR), in 1993 led to the introduction of several new basket products for other actively traded indexes including the Dow Jones Industrial Average, Nasdaq 100, S&P MidCap 400 indexes, and S&P 500 sectors. New products structured in a similar manner are now offered to investors as alternative investment vehicles to traditional mutual funds and as tactical trading vehicles.

Exchange-traded funds now account for significant trading volumes on organized exchanges, presently just under a third of US equity volumes. They possess several unique features that distinguish them from other fund structures. In particular, ETFs share elements of both open- and closed-end mutual funds. ETFs are like open-ended mutual funds in that shares can be created or redeemed at the end of the trading day for the current per share net asset value (NAV) of the fund. Unlike open-ended funds, however, ETFs issue and redeem shares at NAV only in a minimum size (creation unit) and only with entities that have a legal contract with an ETF distributor to create and redeem shares, known as Authorized Participants (APs).

Unlike open-ended funds, but similar to closed-end funds, ETFs are tradable intraday on an exchange in the secondary market at prices that can and often do vary from NAV. However, closed-end funds lack the ability to force price to value through arbitrage because there is no mechanism to force the operator of a closed-end fund that is trading at, say, a steep discount to sell its holdings and give back the cash to shareholders.

1.4.2. Advantages of the ETF Structure

Relative to index open-ended mutual funds, ETFs offer significant tax advantages that derive from the ability to use in-kind transfers to reduce capital gains distributions, as explained in detail in Madhavan (2014). An ETF investor, unlike a traditional mutual fund investor, can short shares, lend shares, and can buy on margin as with equity to gain leverage. Most actively traded ETFs have options traded on them, allowing the ETF investor to use various strategies (collars, call writing, hedging with puts, etc.) to shape the desired return distribution.

The ETF structure also enables lower fees than traditional active mutual funds. First, unlike ETFs, mutual funds interact directly with investors and hence accrue distribution and record-keeping costs. By contrast, for an ETF these costs are borne by the investor's brokerage firm. Mutual funds may levy fees (such as transfer agency fees or 12b-1 fees that compensate the fund for distribution and service) that ETFs do not, raising the cost of ownership. Second, since mutual funds, through their structure, must interact with the market when faced with a net inflow or outflow, they can incur trading costs and cash drag if they cannot immediately put inflows to work. How big are these effects? A recent study estimates such avoidable costs in excess of 75 basis points annually.[6] Given the advantages of exchange-traded funds, it is possible that these instruments might eventually displace more traditional investment alternatives.

Another advantage of ETFs, one often singled out by commentators, is the ability to trade intraday versus only at the close with open-ended mutual funds (see Antoniewicz and Heinrichs 2014). This is certainly attractive for traders who wish to quickly put on or take off exposures or to transact in related securities such as options. But intraday tradability is really a byproduct of having the price of the fund determined by the market through the interaction of buyers and sellers. One could imagine, for instance, a once a day call auction where the ETF is priced versus continuous intraday trading. Many ETFs have low intraday volumes, but buyers and sellers are able to transact in size, as discussed in depth later on. In other words, the ETF as an investment vehicle allows investors to reap the benefits of lower costs and taxes.

1.4.3. Asset Classes and Diversity of Exposures

The term "asset class" is often used loosely to refer to a set of financial assets with common characteristics in payoff structure or trading. It is useful to distinguish between real and financial assets. Real assets, either tangible (e.g., planes, computers) or intangible (e.g., patents, brand) produce a stream of income over time. Typically that income is risky, as payoffs are not certain. A financial asset is a claim to a real asset, such as a stock or a bond. By contrast, a derivative (e.g., a call option) is a side bet on the value of a financial asset. Collectively, derivatives are in zero net supply, unlike financial assets. With this distinction in mind, it is clear that ETFs and other related vehicles such as mutual funds are not derivatives at

---

6. Navigate Fund Solutions, "Avoidable Structural Costs of Actively Managed Mutual Funds," November 2014, available at http://www.nextshares.com.

all, but rather wrappers of financial assets. Some industry professionals still get this wrong though. Jacobsen (2015) notes: "An ETF is a derivative. It is not regulated as a derivative, but technically, an ETF's market price is derived from the market price of a basket of securities." Clearly, equities and fixed income are asset classes, and some would argue that commodities, volatility, and foreign exchange are asset classes too.

Exchange-traded products provide exposure to a wide range of asset classes (e.g., equities, fixed income commodities, and currencies), strategies (e.g., passive index, model based), and regions. Global ETP assets under management (AUM) amounted to $2.9 trillion in 5,497 products as of March 2015. By way of comparison, a decade back in 2005, global AUM was $428 billion with 87% in the "Developed Markets Equity" category.

The growth of nontraditional asset classes including emerging markets equity, fixed income, commodities, and currencies (in figure 1.3 Alternatives and Asset Allocation funds are included in this category too) over the decade has been especially dramatic. Figure 1.4 shows the regional breakdown of global ETP assets. While the majority is still in the United States, other regions are growing. The Middle East, Africa, and Latin America clearly represent a large opportunity for future growth with collective assets of just 2% of the world total.

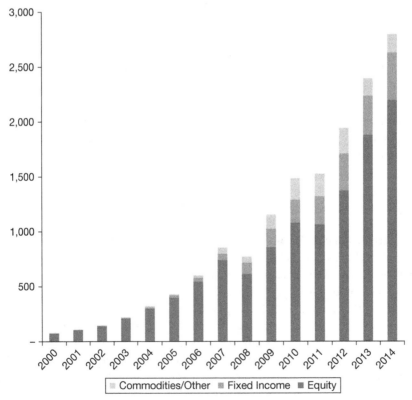

Figure 1.3 Global ETP assets in USD billions, January 2015.
SOURCE: BlackRock ETP Landscape, based on data as of January 2015.

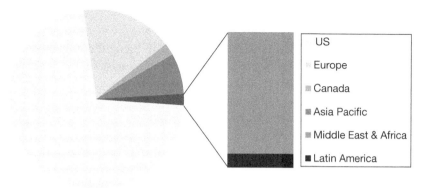

Figure 1.4 Global assets share by region in percentages, March 2015.
SOURCE: BlackRock ETP Landscape, March 2015.

1.4.4. Criticisms of Passive Indexing and ETFs

The rise of passive indexing and ETFs has not been without controversy. Critics of passive indexing argue that passive flows distort markets, create bubbles, and impair market efficiency and liquidity in individual securities.[7] We will address these broader policy questions in the latter chapters of the book, focusing now on suitability for the average investor. As passive investment vehicles, ETFs have obvious advantages for some, but they are not ideal for every investor. Some commentators are also skeptical about whether they represent a true innovation or not for the average investor.

To be an ETF investor requires making a trade. That in turn means having a brokerage account and incurring commission costs with every investment or divestment, as well as basic trading knowledge such as when to use limit versus market orders, stop loss orders, and so on. Individual investors may find investing with ETFs on a regular basis, especially in smaller amounts, to be difficult and expensive, whereas mutual funds can automate a monthly savings plan. Investors in mutual funds also incur no commission costs and do not need to trade on an exchange. In defined contribution retirement accounts (e.g., 401(k) accounts in the United States), regular contributions into mutual funds at relatively low amounts can easily be accommodated with fractional holdings, and these accounts are not typically set up for brokerage transactions. Retirement accounts also do not necessarily benefit from the tax advantages offered by ETFs and are typically not traded intraday, obviating some of the most visible benefits of ETFs.

---

7. See, e.g., John Authers, "Indexing: The Index Factor," *Financial Times*, August 16, 2015. The article notes: "How deeply the indices warp markets remains hotly disputed. . . . Most indices are weighted according to market capitalisation. That means that the more a company's price grows, the more index-trackers will be required to buy it, opening them up to accusations that they help inflate bubbles."

WHO INVENTED THE ETF?

Nathan Most (1914–2004) is widely credited with being the originator of US exchange-traded funds. He had a background as a physicist and engineer in the US Navy during World War II, and later traded commodities such as safflower seed and coconut oil. Most was 73 when he first developed a commercial version of an exchange-traded fund for the American Stock Exchange (AMEX), proving there is no age limit to innovation.

The major criticism of ETFs, however, comes from John C. Bogle, the founder of Vanguard, who has long championed index mutual funds for the ordinary investor. He declined on philosophical grounds[8] the early opportunity pitched by financial innovator Nathan Most to have the first ETFs traded against the Vanguard Index 500 fund saying that the notion was "anathema." Nathan Most then pitched the concept to State Street, which launched the SPDR S&P 500 ETF (SPY) in 1993. That fund is now the largest ETF in the world with assets of $185 billion as of April 2015. With an expense ratio of 0.09% or 9 basis points, that translates to gross revenues of about $167 million annually.

Bogle views ETFs with skepticism because of the plethora of choices (in the United States as of April 2015, there were 1,700 ETFs on 1,300 distinct indexes), with offerings in narrow subsectors such as wind energy, social media, chain restaurants, or nanotechnology. In Bogle's view, these choices can overwhelm an ordinary investor, in turn leading to greater turnover and undiversified positions. The intraday liquidity provided by ETFs could induce greater trading activity by ordinary investors in turn would ultimately be detrimental to performance.

Indeed, ETF investors do have greater turnover than mutual fund investors, facts that are supported by the current evidence. For example, the SPDR ETF (SPY) has annual turnover of 2,700% versus 12% in the Vanguard Index 500 mutual fund. However, the clienteles of ETFs and index funds are quite different. Buy and hold investors often hold index mutual funds while many diverse investors—including hedge funds, traders, and institutions—with higher turnover use ETFs. Indeed, about 65% of ETF ownership is institutional.

PUREFUNDS ISE CYBER SECURITY ETF (HACK)

The Purefunds ISE Cyber Security ETF (HACK) tracks an index of companies actively providing cyber-security (anti-viral and anti-malware) technology and services. The index it tracks comprises firms in two segments: (1) Cyber-security hardware and software, and (2) those that provide cyber-security as a service. Each segment is weighted by market capitalization, but within each segment,

---

8. See John Bogle, "Father of Passives has Doubts about ETFs," *Financial Times*, March 15, 2015. An earlier version of the ETF was also tried on the Toronto Stock Exchange, but suffered regulatory challenges.

firms are weighted equally. Given rising concerns over cyber-security, HACK outperformed broader market and technology sector funds from its inception on November 12, 2014, to June 6, 2015, gathering almost $867 million in assets.

As for the proliferation of ETFs, asset managers do not create ETFs unless they have conviction that these funds will ultimately meet a minimum threshold for success in terms of asset gathering. The reason is that starting a new fund is quite costly—it requires *exemptive relief* from regulators that can be time-consuming and other costs such as seed capital, plus marketing efforts during their incubation period. Ultimately, the number of ETFs reflects investor demand for exposures as opposed to conscious choice by asset managers. It is also worth noting that the ETF structure is also not conducive to certain active strategies because they face more stringent regulatory constraints on concentration in the securities they hold, use of leverage, and liquidity of underlying assets than do hedge funds. That said, many model-driven (or quantitative) strategies could be housed in a transparent ETF structure. I discuss such Smart Beta products later in the book.

Recent industry trends may obviate these traditional drawbacks. For instance, many companies now offer commission free brokerage trades for investments into their sponsored ETFs. New firms termed "Robo-advisors" (also known as digital advisors) automate investing, typically using a menu of low-cost index-tracking ETFs, again overcoming behavioral biases that may inhibit the use of ETFs by ordinary investors. The structure and operation of ETFs requires investor education, especially as funds increasingly move out of equities into fixed income and factor based investing. Such education and marketing efforts are costly, but for ETF managers it is a struggle to identify the distributors who are most effective. By contrast, traditional mutual funds can charge a front-end load to incentivize sales, an especially effective tool with retail investors. In Europe and elsewhere, regulatory movements against retrocessions (where brokers receive a commission for selling a fund) level the playing field for ETFs against traditional fund structures.

1.5. CHAPTER SUMMARY

Passive investing is here to stay, with considerable potential for upside growth given that two-thirds of assets are still in active vehicles such as traditional mutual funds or hedge funds that seek to outperform their benchmark. More important than the numbers though is the change in mind-set from the late 1970s when index funds first became widely available. While once viewed with disdain as settling for mediocre or average returns, passive investing has been recognized for its cost-efficiency and diversification. This is not to say that there is no room for active management. Quite the contrary, investors who are not representative of the market (e.g., a sovereign wealth fund or endowment with a decades' long horizon) may well seek active returns by departing from traditional market capitalization weighting.

The innovation of the ETF wrapper has played a major role in this trend with growth typically at the expense of the traditional active mutual fund. These fund structures have many advantages over other investment vehicles, including intraday pricing, transparency, and low cost. The advantages of ETFs are relatively clear, but some drawbacks should be noted. While the vast majority of ETFs are physically backed index trackers, investors do need to be aware of the differences in types of ETFs, particularly notes/synthetics.

Further, ETFs have been criticized as their numbers and complexity grows and as they seek to target niche sectors or geographies. That said, it is important to distinguish between the wrapper or choice of investment vehicle and the style of investing, and ETFs are popular with a diverse clientele precisely because they offer choices that traditional fund constructs do not. But what makes the ETF vehicle special and why does it have some advantages over other more established fund structures, at least for certain types of investors? To answer that question, it is useful to review a few use cases before delving into the details of how fund types can differ and their relative advantages.

2

Structure and Mechanics

2.1. INTRODUCTION

The common characteristic of ETFs is that they are traded intraday on an organized exchange.[1] Although simple, this description ignores many important differences between ETFs and other pooled investment vehicles.[2] In particular,
ETFs share elements of both open- and closed-end mutual funds. For an open-
ended mutual fund, transactions occur only at the end of the day and only at net
asset value or NAV. In contrast to open-ended mutual funds but like closed-end
funds, ETFs trade during the day in the secondary market at prices that can deviate from NAV. Further, unlike open-ended mutual funds, ETFs issue and redeem
shares only in a minimum size (creation unit) and only with market-making firms
known as Authorized Participants (APs).

The creation/redemption mechanism in the ETF structure allows the number of
shares outstanding in an ETF to expand or contract based on demand from investors.
The process of arbitrage means that liquidity can be accessed through primary market transactions in the underlying assets, beyond the visible secondary market. This
additional element of liquidity means that trading costs of ETFs are determined by
the *lower bound* of execution costs in either the secondary or primary markets, a factor
especially important for large investors.

2.2. ETF STRUCTURE

2.2.1. Authorized Participants

In economic terms, APs are liquidity providers who can interact directly with the
fund. These firms are typically large financial institutions such as Goldman Sachs or

---

1. The ETF sponsor originates the fund and selects its investment objective. The great majority
of ETFs are index-based, where the sponsor chooses both an index and a method of tracking its
target index. See Gastineau (2010) for a detailed description.

2. ETFs are a subset of a broader group of investment vehicles termed exchange-traded products
(ETPs). In an ETF, the underlying basket securities are physically represented with the objective of mimicking the performance of a broad market index.

more specialized market makers. The asset manager designates the APs before the fund is launched; they are given exclusive rights to alter the ETF's outstanding shares through creation or redemption. APs thus play a critical role in liquidity provision, linking the primary markets, where the fund's underlying assets are traded, with the secondary exchange-traded market for the ETFs shares. A large ETF may have dozens of APs, but narrower, niche funds (e.g., frontier markets) may have only a few APs with specialized trading skills in countries such as Sri Lanka.

Note that APs do not receive compensation from the ETF sponsor and are not legally obliged to create or redeem the ETF's shares. Rather, most APs are compensated for their market-making activities in the secondary market. Some APs, however, are simply clearing brokers who are paid directly for processing creations and redemptions as an agent for others.

2.2.2. Creation/Redemption Mechanism

Transparency is the key to pricing. Current fund holdings and the basket of securities the ETF is willing to accept for in-kind creations or redemptions the next business day are published at the end of each trading day. The transactions between an ETF manager and an AP are typically either for cash or "in-kind" where the AP delivers or receives a basket of securities identical (or very similar) to the ETF's holdings.[3] Like other investors, APs can buy or sell ETF shares in the secondary market exchange, but they also can purchase or redeem shares directly from the ETF if they believe there is a profit opportunity.

ETFs have evolved from open-end mutual funds and closed-end funds, and their architecture represents elements of both structures. In an ETF, unlike a mutual fund, interactions between the investor and the fund do not necessarily result in creations or redemptions. Investors can trade directly with each other or with APs and other liquidity providers. Ultimately, if there is net demand for new ETF shares, the AP will deliver the underlying securities to the asset manager in return for ETF units.

An example of ETF architecture is shown in figure 2.1.

By contrast, in an open-end mutual fund structure, liquidity is available at the end of the day and at NAV. Any net flows result in the fund manager interacting with the capital markets directly, versus the possibility in an ETF that trades occur in the secondary market without primary market activity (figure 2.2).

In a closed-end fund, capital is invested during the initial offering period and there is no subsequent opportunity for redemption. An investor who buys a closed-end fund does so by buying from a market maker or other investors in the secondary market, with no interaction with the fund post-offering (figure 2.3).

---

3. In the case of cash redemptions, transaction charges resulting from investing or raising the cash are absorbed by the AP and not the ETF, unlike open-ended mutual funds. Cash redemptions may be required because some ETF holdings, such as certain emerging market stocks, are subject to legal restrictions that prevent in-kind transfers.

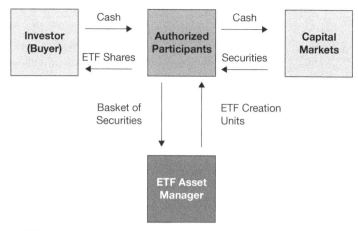

Figure 2.1 ETF creation/redemption mechanism.

Figure 2.2 Open-end mutual fund architecture.

Figure 2.3 Closed-end fund architecture.

A very large academic literature has documented the existence of economically significant discounts in most closed-end funds. There are many theories for why closed-end funds tend to trade at a discount to NAV, but the absence of a mechanism to force liquidation is thought play a major role.

A common source of confusion is that ETF managers are required to publish NAV for their funds. In reality, unlike for mutual funds, NAV is not an equivalent concept for ETFs. Although ETF shares are created or redeemed at the end of each trading day, this is largely an accounting issue because the AP will typically lock in its profits intraday by selling the higher priced asset while simultaneously buying the lower priced asset. For example, when an ETF is trading at a premium to an AP's estimate of value, the AP may choose to deliver the creation basket of securities in exchange for ETF shares, which in turn it could elect to sell or keep. The creation-redemption mechanism works through arbitrage to keep the ETF's price close to the intrinsic value of an ETF's holdings in the underlying market. The arbitrage mechanism also encourages APs to provide offsetting liquidity when there is an excess of buying or selling demand for ETF shares.

Secondary market liquidity is another distinguishing feature of ETFs relative to mutual funds that offer liquidity only at the end of the day. Unlike traditional open-end mutual funds where investors interact directly with the fund when buying or selling shares, ETF shares can be traded intraday by investors on exchanges creating an additional layer of liquidity for buyers and sellers. Secondary market trading does not necessarily lead to transactions in the underlying securities allowing for the externalization of the majority of transaction costs that result from investors redeeming from the fund. The secondary market (exchange-traded) trading volume for most ETFs is typically a multiple of the volume of creation/redemption activity. According to Investment Company Institute statistics for 2014, this ratio is about 4:1 over all ETFs.

CASE STUDY: VOLUMES AND CREATION ACTIVITY

For many ETFs, investors can buy or sell the fund in the secondary market without any creations or redemptions. Consider the iShares Emerging Markets ETF (EEM), whose constituents are often illiquid and difficult to access, but is among the most liquid US listed equities with average daily dollar volume of about $2.2 billion (or 52 million shares a day) in the last six months of 2014. Yet, in the period November 10 to December 9, 2014, about $50 billion of EEM was traded in the secondary market with zero redemptions or creations.

The traded volume of an ETF can be a misleading metric of its true liquidity as it overlooks the liquidity of the underlying constituents of the ETF, as we will see later.

2.2.3. Arbitrage: Value and Price

Deviations of price from NAV do not necessarily imply the existence of arbitrage opportunities. The ETF provider contracts with market data vendors (or other third-parties) to calculate and publish NAV based on past prices. Market data vendors can adjust last prices/quotes for new market information.[4] For example, they may make adjustments to prevent "market timing" in international and fixed income funds where previous prices or quotes may be recorded with a substantial delay. Approaches to fair valuation vary and there is no accepted standard to adjusting stale prices. Indeed, Grégoire (2013) finds evidence that mutual funds do not fully adjust their valuations to reflect fair value and returns remain predictable.

Vendors also provide an Intraday Indicative Value (IIV) that is disseminated at regular intervals during the trading day, typically every 15 seconds.[5] This value is usually based on the most recent (possibly stale) trade, and not on the midpoint

---

4. There is a further subtlety for fixed income funds where industry convention is to value using the bid price, a point I return to later.

5. This estimate also is rather confusingly referred to as an intraday Net Asset Value (INAV) or Intraday Optimized Portfolio Value (IOPV).

of the current quote on each portfolio component. So, if the fund holds Japanese stocks, say, the closing price (or quote) from Tokyo is used throughout the US trading day and a foreign exchange adjustment is made for any change in the yen/dollar relationship since the Tokyo markets are closed. For fixed income funds, IIV can often be quite misleading it does not necessarily fully update the prices of securities that do not trade or include adjustments for accrued fees or liabilities that vendors usually reflect in their end-of-day NAV at 4.00 p.m. EST.

Veteran's Day

US bond markets are closed on Columbus Day, Veteran's Day, and some other days even though equity markets are open. Many large bond ETFs, however, actively trade on such days with very tight bid-ask spreads. For example, Veteran's Day, November 11, 2014, fell on a Tuesday and equity markets were open. Although there was no trading in their underlying bonds, the iShares iBoxx High-Yield Corporate Bond ETF (HYG) and iShares iBoxx Investment Grade Corporate Bond ETF (LQD) together had volumes of approximately $350 million. Further, IIV is available for fixed-income ETFs even though their underlying securities did not trade or quote. Jacobsen (2015) notes the circularity evident in these cases: "It seems that pricing services, which take responsibility for calculating IVs for ETF sponsors, use ETFs to price the underlying securities. This is a bit like a snake eating its own tail."

For this reason, IIV is not useful for APs and arbitragers for trading purposes. Rather, these market participants will use their own proprietary models and data to estimate the underlying value of the ETF. Large institutions, market makers, and proprietary traders will incorporate information from a variety of sources in their proprietary evaluations. In the case of an international fund holding Japanese stocks, for example, this may include Japanese ADRs and the Nikkei futures in the United States. For bond funds, information on key interest rates and spread changes are relevant, as well as transaction data from sources such as TRACE.

Market makers can use the current bids and offers for portfolio securities, rather than the last sales in their calculations of an ETF's current portfolio value. More important, they have proprietary knowledge of the size and side of much of the current order flow in the ETF. Proprietary traders (including the Authorized Participants who actually execute creation/redemption transactions) often work with market makers in their joint risk management. In conclusion, the price and NAV of an ETF are distinct values, and both may differ from the expected intrinsic value of the portfolio for the reasons discussed earlier. In what follows, I lay out a simple framework that captures these elements.

2.2.4. In-Kind Transactions and Tax Efficiency

Most ETFs are considerably more tax efficient than traditional mutual funds. Indeed, the majority of ETFs do not pay out capital gains and if so, in typically small amounts. I estimated the average capital gains as percentage of NAV based on Morningstar data to be 1% in 2013. By contrast, the corresponding figure for mutual funds was 4%, with 56% of the top 100 funds making a distribution.

As noted above, unlike ETFs, traditional open-ended mutual funds are forced to interact with the market by selling securities to meet investor withdrawals or by purchasing securities when faced with inflows. These transactions can result in a taxable gain for the mutual fund investor. By contrast, ETF transactions in the secondary market typically do not result in a creation or redemption as the asset manager and APs can use the in-kind process to exchange ETF shares for the basket of underlying securities. These transactions can be managed in such a manner that the lowest cost basis securities are swapped out in a redemption, leaving the highest cost basis securities in the ETF. These transactions are not taxable to the end investor, producing the tax efficiency.

To see how this works, note that every security that is delivered into a fund is assigned a particular tax lot as shown below in table 2.1. Shown here are four transactions in XYZ stock totaling 39,010 shares for an average cost basis of $15.20, while the current price of $14.32. Faced with a redemption that amounted to, say 5,000 shares of XYZ stock, the fund manager would deliver out 5,000 shares from lot 406, which has the lowest cost basis and the most in capital gains. The fund would then own 34,010 shares with a higher average cost basis of $15.49 than before. Should the fund need to sell to raise cash, the manager would want to sell the highest cost basis lots and trade lot 77, which has an unrealized loss.

Any creations would occur at the current price $14.32. This constant "cleansing" of average cost basis is the source of the tax efficiency of ETFs versus traditional funds.

___

FRONTIER MARKETS AND UNEXPECTED TAXES

The iShares MSCI Frontier 100 ETF (FM) seeks to track the investment results of an index composed of frontier market equities in countries such as Nigeria and Kazakhstan. The fund was launched in September 2012 and quickly attracted assets as investors sought exposure to newly emerging markets. In May 2014, the index provider MSCI announced the promotion of Qatar and United Arab Emirates (UAE) from "frontier" to "emerging market" status. The promotion meant that FM needed to sell 22 securities from those two countries, representing 35% of its holdings. Local regulations prohibit in-kind transactions in Qatar and UAE securities, so FM had to physically sell the stocks it held in those two countries on the exchanges, incurring capital gains. Unlike other ETFs, the majority of FM's creations and redemptions are in cash. A further challenge was that the MSCI Qatar and MSCI UAE and indexes were up 46% and 153%, respectively, from FM's launch date through November 2014. The fund had received mostly inflows, offering few chances to reduce the cost basis via redemptions with dealers. Investors incurred capital-gains distribution estimated to be as high as 7.6% of NAV. Of this distribution, over 40% was in short-term capital gains taxed as ordinary income. The previous year, FM did not distribute any gains.

___

Table 2.1 STRUCTURAL EFFICIENCY AND TAX LOT MANAGEMENT EXAMPLE

Ticker	Trade Date (2015)	Lot Number	Quantity (Shares)	Current Price of Stock ($)	Cost Basis Per Share ($)	Unrealized Gain Per Share ($)
XYZ	April 3	77	1,120	14.32	16.03	−1.71
XYZ	November 14	102	30,000	14.32	15.67	−1.35
XYZ	December 4	333	2,010	14.32	13.50	0.82
XYZ	December 20	406	5,880	14.32	13.22	1.10

In exceptional circumstances, however, ETFs can have significant capital-gains distributions. For example, some ETFs use derivative contracts to hedge interest rates or currency returns. These transactions are not entitled to in-kind tax benefits and furthermore maturing contracts force ETFs to book gains. An example is the WisdomTree Japan Hedged Equity ETF (DXJ) that had an estimated capital gain of 7.4% at year-end 2014. Potential capital gains are not a reason to avoid these types of ETFs but investors need to recognize that more complex ETFs or funds that hold securities where in-kind transactions are not permitted (e.g., many emerging or frontier markets) may be less able to enjoy the benefits of tax efficiency.

2.3. NOMENCLATURE

The industry has generally been loose with naming conventions, which has caused confusion among investors. There are important differences in fund structure among exchange-traded products, so nomenclature is actually quite important. Of course, any attempt at trying to create a system of names is arbitrary, but nonetheless can help in practical investment decisions and also in a regulatory context. Exchange-traded funds (ETFs) are a subset of a broader umbrella group of investment vehicles termed exchange-traded products (ETPs), a catch-all or generic term for portfolio exposure products that trade intraday on an exchange. The primary distinction is between debt-instruments (or IOUs) and funds that are backed by assets, either physical or otherwise. Specifically, exchange-traded notes (ETNs) are senior, unsecured (either collateralized or more likely uncollateralized) debt securities that are exposed to the credit risk (solvency) of the issuer, typically an investment bank. Only about 2.3% of global assets are held in ETNs.

The vast majority (representing 92.5% of global assets) of non-debt instruments are traditional ("plain vanilla") ETFs that typically hold a physical portfolio of securities (stocks or bonds) that closely resembles, but need not necessarily fully replicate, their benchmark index. The goal of these funds is to provide *one-to-one* exposure to the index, usually broad market gauges offered by index providers such as Morningstar. Accordingly, they do not use derivatives or structural features (e.g., embedded leverage or caps on returns) to alter the returns of the basket of securities they hold. They also hold assets that are traded on exchanges with similar settlement cycles to the ETF itself, meaning that an ETP on private equity or bank loans would not fall into this category. Such ETFs are increasingly active meaning they attempt to outperform an index, track custom indexes, or be based on narrow sectors/strategies such as dividend yield.

So-called "synthetic" funds, a type of ETF, track an index by holding derivatives or swaps to replicate the performance of their benchmarks.

There is a further category of exchange-traded commodity funds (ETCs) that refers to funds that hold physical commodities such as silver or gold. Figure 2.4 illustrates a standardized classification scheme for the global assets under management (AUM) of $3 trillion in ETPs as of June 2015.

LEHMAN BROTHERS, SEPTEMBER 2008

Of course, keep in mind that ETNs—which are senior, unsecured debt securities—pose special risks. They are not insured in any way and assets are not segregated. Owners of Lehman Brothers Opta ETNs stood to lose a large portion, if not all, of their principal when Lehman declared bankruptcy in September 2008. The courts treated their investment as if it were an unsecured loan to Lehman, along with other creditors.

The value of such a schema is to highlight the structural differences among funds for both investors and regulators. Interestingly, the source of a lot of recent regulatory concern is actually a relatively small subset of total assets in ETPs including ETFs that are not backed by publicly traded holdings (e.g., bank loans, about $7bn or 0.2% of total assets) and leveraged/inverse products (LETPs) which are only 1.3% of global assets.

Some ETPs contain embedded leverage via swap contracts and are thus quite different from conventional, physically based ETFs offering one-to-one exposure to an index. The exchange-traded instruments category includes these types of funds, which for the most part are leveraged/inverse funds. Leveraged and inverse

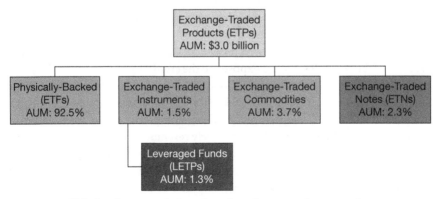

Figure 2.4 Global exchange-traded product classification and assets under management.

exchange-traded products (LETPs) may hold the individual index stocks too and thus have elements of physical-backing. Since they obtain leverage through swaps, they are correctly termed ETPs, not purely physically backed ETFs, and are included in the exchange-traded instruments category.

A logical classification scheme such as this helps distinguish among different kinds of exchange-traded products and highlights that the regulatory concerns around ETFs—such as those with embedded leverage or non-traded underlying assets such as bank loans—center very much on structures that collectively account for a small fraction of global assets.

2.4. GOVERNANCE, MANAGEMENT STRUCTURE, AND LEGAL ASPECTS

2.4.1. Fundamentals of Regulation

The governance, management, and legal structure of ETFs have some special attributes. Since the United States accounts for the great majority of global assets under management and much of the recent innovation in fund structures (e.g., active ETFs), I will focus on the US regulatory and legal environment, noting global exceptions where applicable. The regulatory framework matters quite a bit, especially as regards the future growth of ETFs in the active space where the legal basis for such funds is still in evolution.

Corporate governance seeks to alleviate and manage conflicts of interest that arise among fund owners, managers, and stakeholders. Like mutual funds or closed-end funds, most US ETFs are regulated investment companies subject to supervision by the Securities and Exchange Commission (SEC) under the Investment Company Act of 1940 (the "1940 Act"). The 1940 Act essentially authorizes three broad types of investment funds to be offered to the general public:

- unit investment trusts;
- open-end funds; and
- closed-end funds.

The 1940 Act requires mutual funds to sell or redeem shares of the fund to investors each business day in cash at a price equal to the current value of the fund's underlying holdings divided by the number of outstanding shares (the net asset value per share, or NAV), plus or minus any applicable sales charges. Mutual funds sell or redeem shares directly with investors through broker-dealers or transfer agents, and do not typically permit a secondary market for their shares. The 1940 Act essentially prohibits a closed-end fund from selling or redeeming shares after the fund's initial launch, except in a few narrow circumstances. After the initial sale of shares to investors for cash, a closed-end fund's shares are typically bought and sold in the secondary market and not directly with the fund.

2.4.2. Exemptive Relief

Because ETFs combine elements of open- and closed-end funds in ways not contemplated by the authors of the 1940 Act, the statute does not technically allow them to exist. Rather, ETFs must be granted an exemption by the SEC from complying with certain sections of the statute. The existence of ETFs today stems from an exemption granted by the SEC in 1992 to permit the first ETF, the SPDR S&P 500 ETF (SPY). Over the subsequent years, many more exemptive orders have been given, each of which permits a single ETF sponsor to issue one or more ETFs subject to specific conditions specified in the exemptions. However, despite the proliferation in ETF numbers, it is still necessary to obtain exemptive relief to launch an ETF. The SEC staff is charged with determining whether an application would be "necessary or appropriate in the public interest and consistent with the protection of investors." A major consideration is that the application does not involve self-dealing. Beyond this, the SEC considers other factors including most importantly whether the asset class represented by the index is appropriate for an ETF and would likely result in tight tracking to NAV.

A few large ETFs (e.g., SPDR S&P 500 ETF [SPY] and PowerShares QQQ Trust [QQQ] that are set up as unit investment trusts) are required by law to be "unmanaged"—that is, they may make changes to their underlying holdings only to the extent necessary to reflect changes in the underlying index. Most important (unlike open-end investment companies), unit investment trusts may not (1) hold securities that are not in the index (e.g., securities received in corporate actions) or equitize cash; (2) reinvest cash received as dividends; or (3) engage in securities lending or other "managed" activities. Generally, only US ETFs formed prior to 1996 (when the SEC first permitted "open-end" ETFs) that invest in large or mid-capitalization US stocks are organized this way. More recent launches use the open-end structure because of its flexibility.

CASE STUDY: S&P 500 INDEX FUNDS AND THE SUBTLETIES OF STRUCTURE

Index funds are not all alike even if they share a common index. In theory, the tracking difference of the ETF to its underlying index should equal the total expense ratio. Both the SPDR S&P 500 ETF (SPY) and the iShares Core S&P 500 ETF (IVV) seek to track the S&P 500® index, which measures the performance of the large-capitalization sector of the US equity market. In 2014, the fees of SPY and IVV were quite similar, 0.09% and 0.07%, so the two should have very similar tracking. But the more recent IVV, incepted on May 15, 2000, is structured as a 1940 Act open-end fund; whereas, SPY, which incepted on January 22, 1993, uses an older fund structure, namely a unit investment trust (UIT). This difference, which sounds quite technical, actually has a material impact. As a UIT, SPY cannot reinvest dividends and incurs a significant lag of about 45 days between ex-date and pay date. This induces a cash drag that can improve performance in down markets but reduce it in up markets. By contrast, IVV is permitted to reinvest dividends as received and its gap between ex-date and pay date is just 5 days.

The UIT structure also does not allow SPY to conduct securities lending, unlike IVV, to offset fees. These factors can generate performance and tracking error differences especially in years with large returns. Based on Morningstar data, for example, the annual excess returns for SPY and IVV were −0.18% and −0.08%, respectively, for the full-year 2013, a banner year for the index with total returns of 32.39%.

Elton et al. (2002) provide a more detailed analysis of the impact of these factors.

There is one other relevant regulatory element facing ETFs that complicates the process for bringing them to market. All US ETFs are also regulated under the Securities Exchange Act of 1934 (the "1934 Act") in a manner that is different from mutual funds. The 1934 Act (no-action relief) regulates securities exchanges and secondary market trading. Under the 1940 Act, the ETF is viewed as an investment company. Historically, this has meant that regulators have focused on whether an ETF will trade close to NAV in their evaluation of investor protection. By contrast, the 1934 Act stresses protection against market manipulation of the underlying holdings, and the regulatory framework and mindset is parallel to that of index options and other derivatives.

Unlike ETFs, US mutual funds are generally not subject to the 1934 Act. This is because their shares are not traded on an exchange or otherwise in a secondary market. Closed-end funds are subject to the 1934 Act, but in a manner that is less intrusive than for ETFs. Aside from relief from rules about short-selling and market manipulation that might impede market-making activity, ETFs must obtain regulatory approval to list their shares on an exchange. Exchange listing approvals are governed by exchange rules and, under the 1934 Act, changes to exchange rules require approval by the SEC.

The end result of the intersection of regulations on issuance and trading is longer time to market for ETFs versus the roughly 75 days from filing to launch for open- and closed-end funds. The more complex approval and oversight process also means that active ETFs face greater regulatory scrutiny than active mutual funds, and as yet, some uncertainty as to what will or will not ultimately be permitted. Greater clarity with respect to active ETFs and a more uniform approach to exemptive relief will help with adoption and further competition in the industry.

Bond ETFs represent another area where regulatory changes can help extend the benefits of diversification and lower costs to broader investor segments. The specific issue is what is sometimes referred to as regulatory "look-through" meaning that ETFs are regulated with a focus on the wrapper versus the exposure offered. This approach can create challenges for buyers of bond ETFs which are regulated as equities, not portfolios of bonds. For example, a broker-dealer that holds a highly liquid short-term treasury bond ETF (basically near cash) has to treat this position as an equity position rather than a cash equivalent, which necessitates greater capital. An insurance company that, say, sells 30 different illiquid bonds and uses the proceeds to buy an investment grade ETF with 1,100 constituents may be tripped up by diversification rules, as it has gone from 30 positions to a single (portfolio) position. Analytics can help here, providing estimates of future cash flows of bond ETFs and mapping these to terms used in fixed income such as yield-to-maturity, yield-to-worst, spreads, and duration.

2.5. INDUSTRIAL ORGANIZATION

Asset managers provide investment management services, acting as fiduciaries to their clients. Business models and structures range widely from specialized boutiques (e.g., biotech equity, municipal bonds) to large firms with a multiplicity of products/strategies across regions and asset classes serving a diverse set of clients. The ETF industry is dominated by three large asset managers, who account for 82% of global AUM as shown in figure 2.5. Outside of the three largest managers, there are several different kinds of managers often with one or two hit products.

The oligopolistic structure of the industry reflects the significant economies of scale in asset management and fund administration. Yet, although concentration is high compared to the mutual fund industry as a whole (see, e.g., Office of Financial Research [2013], which finds that the top 25 mutual fund complexes managed 74% of US mutual fund assets), the industry is extremely competitive, with relentless pressure on fees and continual product innovation. This is in part because investors do not always differentiate between the various ETFs on broad indexes, viewing funds as interchangeable. There has also been a continued surge of new entrants to the industry over time (e.g., Vanguard in 2004, by creating a separate share class of its mutual funds, and Charles Schwab & Co. in 2009, focusing on retail investors) also enhancing competition.

By contrast, traditional active mutual funds based on star managers have a greater pricing leeway and do not necessarily benefit from scale. Indeed, larger funds may incur higher transaction costs because they trade in larger sizes, creating market impact. Unlike ETFs, as discussed later, inflows and outflows to the

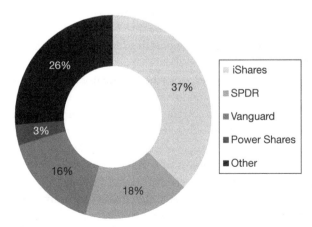

Figure 2.5 Global market share of ETF assets, January 2015.
SOURCE: http://www.etfgi.com as of January 2015.

fund that result in trading costs are not externalized to the existing fund share-holders. Capacity constraints and scarcity of alpha means limits to the economies of scale. As noted above, these traditional managers are subject to the impact of a disruptive financial innovation in the form of the ETF wrapper.

Some of the largest gains for the ETF industry in the future are likely to come at the expense of closed-end funds and more traditional active mutual funds. Indeed, it is likely to be surprising to many readers that there are many mutual funds whose holdings in ETFs comprise at least 80% of their assets. Typically, these types of mutual funds hold ETFs for asset allocation purposes. Many other mutual funds use ETFs for specific investment goals such as to gain exposure to certain asset classes (e.g., gold), for cash management purposes, or to make tactical bets. Huang and Guedj (2009) show in theory that ETFs could be preferred to mutual funds for investors in more volatile, less liquid, or more concentrated indexes. See also Agapova (2011) who documents evidence of a substitution effect between index mutual funds and ETFs that she attributes to tax clientele effects. Empirical evidence from the United States and other countries generally finds little difference in the performance of index mutual funds and ETFs, but there are many subtleties regarding these comparisons including taxation, holding period, and, most important, benchmark.

2.6. CHAPTER SUMMARY

The elegant structure of ETFs represents a hybrid between open- and closed-end mutual funds. This chapter covers the basic structure of ETFs and delves into the details of the unique creation/redemption mechanism, the key to both efficient pricing of the fund as well as tax efficiency. In contrast to open-ended mutual funds, but like closed-end funds, ETFs trade during the day in the secondary market at prices that can deviate from NAV. Unlike open-ended mutual funds and closed-end funds, ETFs issue and redeem shares only in a minimum size (creation unit) and only with market-making firms.

The arbitrage based creation/redemption mechanism of ETFs allows the number of shares outstanding in an ETF to expand or contract depending on investor demand. The creation-redemption mechanism essentially links the primary market (i.e., the underlying assets) and the secondary market for the ETF shares. This additional element of liquidity means that ETF liquidity is at least as large as the liquidity of the underlying shares. Finally, an understanding of the regulatory and legal framework is essential. Indeed, as hybrid structures, ETFs operate at the intersection of laws that complicate the approval and oversight process. This turns out to be quite important when we consider the future of ETFs, particularly around active structures, and the barriers to the adoption of bond ETFs.

PART II

Valuation, Pricing, and Trading

Price Dynamics and Arbitrage

3.1. INTRODUCTION

In this chapter, I develop a model of ETF price dynamics based on the arbitrage mechanism unique to ETFs based on Madhavan and Sobczyk (2016). The intuition is that deviations of price from intrinsic value are corrected over time through the arbitrage mechanism of creation and redemption. The fund's unobserved intrinsic value is typically not observed, but NAV and the market-determined price of the ETF both provide information on this value. By explicitly modeling the temporal dynamics of price and NAV, we can statistically decompose the ETF's price premium to its NAV into components corresponding to price discovery and transitory liquidity. In the subsequent chapter, I show how the model (which has eight parameters) can be estimated from a time series of prices and NAVs to yield empirical statements about the efficiency of arbitrage, staleness in NAV, and price discovery at the individual fund level.

The theoretical model developed in this chapter contains interesting special cases. One such case, given concerns about ETF pricing, is where NAV is an accurate representation of intrinsic value while the ETF price reflects noise shocks that may persist for long periods. An alternative case is one where NAV may exhibit staleness while the ETF price is statistically close to intrinsic value. We can use the general framework to analyze questions concerning price discovery, the dynamics of premiums and discounts, return autocorrelations, performance and tracking relative to benchmark, transaction costs, and liquidity sourcing in underlying and secondary markets.

3.2. CONCEPTUAL FRAMEWORK

3.2.1. Definitions

This section develops a model that builds on the arbitrage mechanism of ETFs, extending the model introduced by Madhavan (2014). Time is measured in fixed calendar intervals Δt (such as seconds, minutes, or days) and the time index is denoted by $t = 0, 1, 2, \ldots$. The individual asset in the ETF basket is denoted by $i = 1, \ldots, N$. Table 3.1 lists the variables and parameters used throughout.

Table 3.1 VARIABLES AND PARAMETER DEFINITIONS

Variable	Definition
p_t	Execution price of the ETF at the end of period t
n_t	NAV of the ETF in period t
m_t	Mid-quote price of the ETF in period t
v_t	Expected value of the ETF in period t conditional on public information
r_t	Innovation in expected value from period $t-1$ to t
π_t	ETF premium in period t
q_t	Signed volume in ETF in period t
S_t	Index value in period t
o_t	Shares outstanding of ETF in period t
u_t	Deviation of price from expected value in period t
h_t	Security holding weights of the ETF at time t, a $N \times 1$ vector with element $h_{i,t}$
h_b	Benchmark security holding weights of the underlying index, a $N \times 1$ vector
a	Forecast alpha (excess return), a $N \times 1$ vector
θ	Volatility or standard deviation of returns
V	Covariance matrix, a $N \times N$ vector
φ	Staleness parameter $(0 \leq \varphi \leq 1)$

I will interpret the price variables as inclusive of corporate actions and dividends. Further, if they are represented in natural logs so that first differences are continuously compounded returns. The change (or innovation) in expected values conditional upon public information over the interval from $t-1$ to t is denoted by $r_t = v_t - v_{t-1}$. The return over longer periods is just the sum of interval returns: From period 0 to T, the total return is $r_{0,T} = \sum_{t=1}^{T} r_t = v_T - v_0$.

3.2.2. Pricing and Liquidity

To understand ETF price and premium dynamics, I need to model three distinct values: (1) the ETF secondary market price, (2) NAV, and (3) the (unobserved) expected value of the ETF. I can interpret the price/value variables as represented in natural logs, so that first differences are continuously compounded returns. The expected value of the asset at a point in time t is denoted by v_t. As discussed earlier, I do not observe expected value. Changes in conditional expectations are innovations, meaning that given information today, any change in beliefs about value over the following day should come as a surprise. I model v_t as a random walk with drift:

$$v_t = v_{t-1} + r_t, \tag{3.1}$$

where $r_t \sim (\mu_r, \sigma_r^2)$ is a stochastic return with mean μ_r and variance σ_r^2.

The ETF price is expected value, v_t, plus a transitory shock u_t that can take on positive or negative values depending on liquidity demands:

$$p_t = v_t + u_t. \tag{3.2}$$

Here, u_t is the "true premium" that arises from transitory liquidity pressure. For an arbitrager who trades the ETF and the underlying basket, the gross profit (excluding transaction costs and fees) from trading by buying the cheaper asset and selling the more expensive asset is $|u_t|$ per share traded. The profit of a market maker is not the ETF's premium to NAV (unless true value aligns with NAV) but the deviation of price from expected value, u_t. While creations and redemptions are at NAV, this is really an end-of-day accounting or book entry transaction. When price is above expected value (plus a premium for transaction costs, taxes, commissions and fees, etc.), the market maker can sell the ETF while simultaneously purchasing the basket of securities (or obtaining that exposure through some other mechanism such as a swap) to make an expected profit. Of course, the market maker or other investor may choose not to hedge their position but simply sell the ETF and carry some inventory risk from an unhedged position.

To see this, suppose the ETF is overvalued so that $p_t > v_t$. The arbitrager sells short the ETF and buys the underlying basket locking in a gross profit of u_t per share. In the reverse case, when the ETF is undervalued relative to fair or intrinsic value, $u_t < 0$, and the arbitrager buys the ETF and sells the underlying basket for a profit of $-u_t$ per share traded. Note that $|u_t|$ may be larger or smaller than the quoted half bid-ask spread. Large trades may trade outside the quotes while others can negotiate inside the quotes. The gross profits of an arbitrager who trades x_t (signed positive for the case where the arbitrager buys the basket and sells the ETF and negative in the reverse case) is $u_t x_t$.

How much does an arbitrager trade? The arbitrager may incur a price impact in both markets, plus conversion fees, denoted by F. We can model this conveniently by first assuming that (as in reality) fees are negligible. In many models, impact is linear in the amount traded, so that total transaction costs are λx_t^2. With linear impacts, the profit of the arbitrager who trades x_t net of impact costs is $u_t x_t - \lambda x_t^2$, which implies that the optimal trade is $x_t = u_t/2\lambda$ It follows that the gross profit of the arbitrager is $u_t^2/2\lambda$ Arbitrager actions do not take prices fully to fundamental value, and hence I model the true premium as:

$$u_t = \psi u_{t-1} + \varepsilon_t, \tag{3.3}$$

where $\varepsilon_t \sim (\mu_\varepsilon, \sigma_\varepsilon^2)$ is a liquidity shock and ψ is the autocorrelation coefficient. This representation (see also Poterba and Summers 1988) is intuitive—true pricing errors are serially correlated but are corrected over time.

3.2.3. Speed of Arbitrage

Lower values of ψ imply faster error correction, with the extreme case of $\psi = 0$ implying that errors are corrected immediately. Equation (3.3) can be also motivated by a model where investors respond similarly—but not simultaneously—to news and macroeconomic shocks. Arbitragers who trade in the opposite direction to capture the true premium offset the impact of flows on prices. In the earlier description, the expected price impact in both the ETF and underlying markets causes arbitragers to scale back their trades so prices do not immediately adjust to value. It is worth noting that in addition, inventory constraints, redemption costs, and risk aversion, can also be incorporated into the model to explain why pricing errors are not instantly eliminated by arbitrage. So, ψ is positively related to dealer inventory costs, risk aversion, price impact, and uncertainty over fundamentals, and is positively related to the autocorrelation in exogenous flows.

I can compute speed of mean reversion in terms of the half-life, that is, the time horizon needed on average to halve any given pricing error. For example, the half-life is 1.5 days if this is the average time for a pricing error of, say, 0.8% to fall to 0.4%. Since the "true" premium is a stationary process, the expected premium h periods ahead from period t is $E[u_{t+h}] = \psi^h u_t$. So, if the half-life is h, then $E[u_{t+h}] = 0.5u_t$ and the half-life is thus:

$$ h = \left(\frac{\ln(0.5)}{\ln(|\psi|)} \right). \tag{3.4} $$

Intuitively, arbitragers act to correct pricing errors so their trading causes a convergence of price to expected value. Lower values of ψ imply fast arbitrage and less serial dependence in pricing errors. As market makers are risk-averse and face market impact costs, price does not instantly revert back to expected value (net transaction costs), but rather corrects over time. This is also the case if dealer capital is limited. Note that ψ also reflects the correlation in flow from period to period. If flows are strongly temporally correlated and investors crowd on the same side of the market, the ETF will trade at prices above or below fundamental value for multiple periods.

CASE STUDY: LIMITS OF ARBITRAGE

The VelocityShares Daily 2× VIX Short-Term ETN (TVIX) provides a good example of how arbitrage is essential to keeping prices in line with fundamental value. This is a leveraged fund designed to track two times the daily return of the S&P 500 VIX short-term futures index. To manage the exposure, the fund issuer will trade futures, swaps, or other positions. On February 22, 2012, Credit Suisse, the sponsor of TVIX temporarily suspended creations of shares citing rapid asset growth that exceeded what the company termed "internal limits." Indeed, in the two weeks prior to the halt, assets in TVIX had grown from $500 million to $692 million. The announcement caused an immediate and dramatic spike in the ETF's premium to NAV, from essentially zero just before the suspension to 16% on February 23, 2012, eventually getting as high as 89.4% by March 20, 2012. The next day, TVIX fell 29.3% and a further 29.8% on March 22, 2012, when Credit Suisse resumed creations. The collapse of the premium entirely explained the two-day return, as VIX futures had actually appreciated. A similar case occurred in 2009 with the United States Natural Gas Fund (UNG) when share issuance was suspended. Again, the excess premium (about 50%) only collapsed when creations resumed. In both cases, buyers who bought at abnormally large premiums would have incurred significant negative returns even in the absence of changes in the underlying markets.

3.2.4. Premiums and Discounts

The observed premium (or discount) is defined as the deviation of the ETF price from the NAV of the fund:

$$\pi_t = p_t - n_t, \tag{3.5}$$

where n_t is the NAV at time t. (In our subsequent empirical work, I will use the published end-of-day NAV for n_t.) I model NAV as a weighted average of current value (possibly with pricing noise) and past NAV:

$$n_t = (1 - \varphi)v_t + \varphi n_{t-1} + w_t. \tag{3.6}$$

Here $0 \leq \varphi \leq 1$ captures possible staleness and $w_t \sim (\mu_w, \sigma_w^2)$ is an error term that reflects microstructure effects.[1] Any pricing noise will be reflected in w_t. For example, for bond ETFs, NAV is based (by regulation) on a bid pricing convention so that w_t has mean (denoted by μ_w) equal to negative half the average bid-ask spread of the underlying bonds. Dispersion in w_t thus reflects variation in the bid-ask spread due to changes in volatility or liquidity. It also reflects the point above that different investors may execute at different prices.

3.2.5. Special Cases of the Model

This general formulation captures a range of special cases that are of interest from a practical viewpoint:

CASE 1: NAV IS A TRUE MARKER OF VALUE
When there is no staleness in NAV (i.e., pricing providers are accurately reflecting current valuations) and pricing errors are minimal, $\varphi = 0$ and $w_t \sim 0$. Then

---

1. An equivalent and intuitive representation of NAV is as exponentially weighted average of noisy estimates of current and past values where the weight on the j-lagged price is $(1 - \varphi)\varphi^j$ so that $n_t = (1 - \varphi)\sum_{j=0}^{\infty}\varphi^j(v_{t-j} + \breve{w}_{t-j})$ where $\breve{w}_t = w_t / (1 - \varphi)$ is the rescaled noise term.

equation (3.5) implies that on average NAV equals expected value and consequently, from equation (3.2), any ETF premiums and discounts purely reflect transitory liquidity shocks. We might expect this to be the case in a domestic equity fund where the constituent stocks are traded very actively and the provider uses current quotations for valuation. Arbitrage profits are given by the deviation of price from NAV.

Case 2: NAV is Stale

The opposite case is when $\varphi > 0$, so that NAV exhibits staleness. For example, illiquid fixed income assets are often traded in dealer markets, where current quotations may not be available on a timely basis or may not be representative of current market conditions. Pricing providers using last trades for NAV will not capture current valuations. Of course, providers may use proprietary methods such as matrix pricing to adjust stale stock or bond quotes, but it is not clear if these adjustments can capture all the relevant changes in spreads or rates for a given bond or beta adjustments for a stock. Alternatively, $\varphi < 0$ would correspond to overreaction where the pricing provider places too much weight on new information.

Case 3: ETF Prices are Noisy

When the speed of arbitrage adjustment is low (i.e., $\psi \gg 0$) and the variance of liquidity shocks ε_t is large, the ETF price is subject to large shocks that are relatively persistent, that is take several periods to dissipate, irrespective of whether NAV is accurate or not. The economic implication is that noise traders cause prices to deviate from value, but that limits to arbitrage (e.g., trading costs) keep the market from efficiently pricing the fund. An example might be the events of August 24, 2015, when prices of many stocks and ETFs deviated substantially from underlying value. For example, the iShares Select Dividend ETF (DVY) traded down over 35% although the underlying assets were down at most 7%. Why did arbitrage not work? In many cases, potential arbitragers were wary of trading on potentially suspect data feeds or had concerns their transactions may be cancelled under exchange "erroneous trades" rules.

3.2.6. Practical Illustration

A motivating example is provided by the iShares iBoxx High-Yield Corporate Bond ETF (HYG). For the period January 2, 2014, to July 15, 2014, I plot in figure 3.1 the NAV returns on day t against the previous day's NAV return. A positive relation between the current and previous day's return is evident. The autocorrelation in returns is 0.33, which is both economically and statistically significant. Over the entire sample of HYG returns, the coefficient of today's NAV return on the previous day's return is positive (0.54) and statistically significant; R^2 is high for a return regression at 30%.

However, the returns of the ETF on day t against the previous day's return looks very much like an efficient market example. There is no predictability (R^2 is

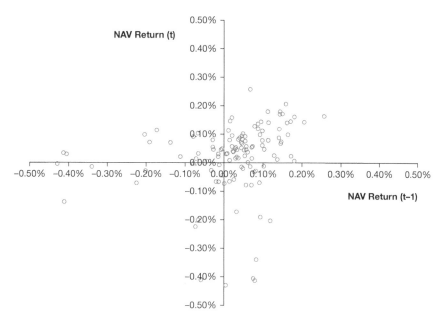

Figure 3.1 Plot of HYG daily NAV returns against previous day's NAV return, January 2, 2014, to July 15, 2014.

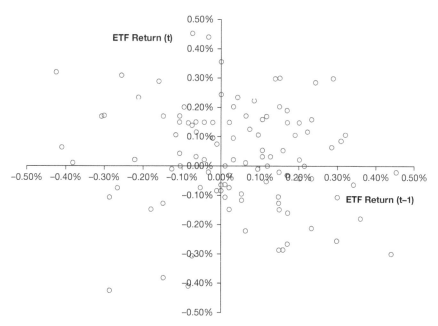

Figure 3.2 Plot of HYG daily returns against previous day's return, January 2, 2014, to July 15, 2014.

zero) and indeed the correlation of ETF daily returns to past returns is essentially zero. For this fund at least, there is staleness in NAV pricing, even in 2014. Past dependence, particularly in the crisis period, is high.

However, the returns of the ETF on day t against the previous day's return shown in figure 3.2 looks very much like the classic efficient market example with zero correlation between subsequent daily returns.

3.3. THEORETICAL RESULTS

3.3.1. Decomposition of Premiums

Using the definition of the premium $\pi_t = (p_t - n_t)$ I get by substituting the expression for price:

$$\pi_t = (v_t + u_t) - n_t, \tag{3.7}$$

I can solve[2] equation (3.6) to express the premium as:

$$\pi_t = \varphi(r_t + \varphi r_{t-1} + \cdots) + (1 - \varphi)(w_t + \varphi w_{t-1} + \cdots) + \varepsilon_t + \psi \varepsilon_{t-1} + \psi^2 \varepsilon_{t-1} \cdots \tag{3.8}$$

This expression shows the composition of the ETF's premium into three terms: (1) *price discovery*, the product of the staleness factor and a weighted average of past fundamental returns; (2) a weighted average of past NAV *pricing noise*; and (3) *transitory liquidity*, captured by a weighted average of past liquidity innovations. When NAV is current and pricing noise is minimal, $\varphi = 0$ and the premium is $\pi_t = \varepsilon_t + \psi \varepsilon_{t-1} + \psi^2 \varepsilon_{t-1} + \cdots$ or a weighted average of all past flow shocks. Higher values of $\psi_{,,}$ which correspond to greater autocorrelation in flows and less efficient arbitrage, imply that past shocks have a greater effect on premiums.

EXAMPLES OF PRICE DISCOVERY

On July 8, 2015, the Athens Stock Exchange was closed in line with the closure of the country's banks in the midst of crisis. Also on that day, almost half of all listed companies in China voluntarily suspended trading and a further 800 stocks had their share trading automatically halted after reaching a daily limit down movement of 10%. Yet in both cases, ETFs continued to trade normally and in several cases were used as the basis for fair valuation of mutual funds.

---

2. From the autoregressive formulation of liquidity shocks I have $u_t = \varepsilon_t + \psi \varepsilon_{t-1} + \psi^2 \varepsilon_{t-1} + \cdots$ so the premium is $\pi_t = [1 - (1 - \varphi)(1 - \varphi L)^{-1}](v_t + w_t) + u_t$. As the return $r_t = (1 - L)v_t = v_t - v_{t-1}$ the expression follows.

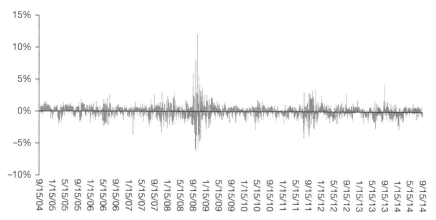

Figure 3.3 iShares MSCI Emerging Markets ETF premiums (in percent), September 2004 to September 2014.
SOURCE: Based on data from Morningstar Direct.

3.3.2. Economic Significance

As a practical example, consider the iShares MSCI Emerging Markets ETF (EEM) in the period from September 2004 through September 2014. The average premium on a daily basis for this fund is just 0.05%, and the average absolute premium is 0.64%, based on data from Morningstar Direct. However, there is considerable variation over time as shown in figure 3.3 with a minimum daily premium of −6.20% and a maximum of 12.07%. We see similarly large premiums and discounts in many other funds, including bond funds.

Should an investor be concerned about buying at a large premium or selling at a large discount? Is there a profitable trading strategy to capture the mean reversion in the premiums? While these premiums and discounts appear large in economic terms, the results previously discussed suggest that they may be attributable to staleness in the NAV of the fund. The great majority of the fund's constituents trade outside of US hours, so the last trade price for an Asian stock may be 16 or more hours old. In the following chapter we will demonstrate how to figure out what is a true premium of discount.

As the return and liquidity shocks have zero mean, the average premium mean reverts over time. For fixed income funds, the convention of using bid prices to compute NAV implies a positive mean for the premium but for equity funds, the average premium should be zero. From an investor perspective, a deviation of price from NAV need not imply that the ETF is mispriced, an important point as some investors may avoid buying at a premium or selling at a discount.

3.3.3. Volatility

Some commentators have emphasized cases where ETF return volatility is greater than that of NAV returns. However, it is straightforward to explain this with the model. Ignoring for simplicity any NAV pricing noise w_t, I can express NAV returns as:

$$n_t - n_{t-1} = (1 - \varphi)r_t + \varphi(n_{t-1} - n_{t-2}).$$ (3.9)

The variance of NAV returns is:

$$\sigma^2(n_t - n_{t-1}) = \sigma_r^2 \frac{(1 - \varphi)^2}{1 - \varphi^2}.$$ (3.10)

So, NAV return variance is a fraction of fundamental variance σ_r^2. This fraction $\frac{(1 - \varphi)^2}{1 - \varphi^2} < 1$ when $\varphi > 0$ and decreases with staleness. If there is no staleness, $\varphi = 0$ and $\sigma^2(n_t - n_{t-1}) = \sigma_r^2$. Note that microstructure noise can imply that NAV returns have greater volatility than fundamental returns, but I do not expect this effect to be economically significant.

The return on the ETF is $(p_t - p_{t-1}) = (v_t - v_{t-1}) + (u_t - u_{t-1})$. As the first term is the return innovation, the variance of ETF price returns can be shown[3] to be:

$$\sigma^2(p_t - p_{t-1}) = \sigma_r^2 + 2\sigma_\varepsilon^2(1 + \psi)^{-1}.$$ (3.11)

The first term is fundamental return variance and the second reflects variance from liquidity shocks. So, if there is staleness in NAV, ETF return volatility will exceed that of NAV returns. The differences are greater the higher the degree of staleness and the larger the variance of liquidity and other random shocks. Over longer intervals, the return variance will scale with time, so for an interval T I have $\sigma^2(r_{0,T}) = \sigma_r^2 T$. The variance of the microstructure shock difference component of ETF returns, $\sigma^2(u_t - u_{t-1}) = 2\sigma_\varepsilon^2(1 + \psi)^{-1}$ and does not scale with time, so tracking difference narrows over longer intervals.

A related issue concerns whether ETF trading propagates volatility into the underlying securities, increasing transitory volatility and having other detrimental effects.[4] Ben-David, Franzoni, and Moussawi (2014) argue that ETF liquidity shocks are propagated via arbitrage trades to underlying markets, creating nonfundamental volatility. Their metric of ETF "mispricing" is the volatility of the

3. Let L denote the lag operator, i.e., $Lu_t = u_{t-1}$. Then, $u_t = (1 - \psi L)^{-1}\varepsilon_t = \varepsilon_t + \psi\varepsilon_{t-1} + \psi^2\varepsilon_{t-2} + \cdots$

The shock change $(u_t - u_{t-1}) = \varepsilon_t + (\psi - 1)(1 - \psi L)^{-1}L\varepsilon_t$, so $\sigma^2(u_t - u_{t-1}) = \sigma_\varepsilon^2\left(1 + \frac{(1 - \psi)^2}{1 - \psi^2}\right)$

which can be simplified to $2\sigma_\varepsilon^2(1 + \psi)^{-1}$. Note also that $p_t - p_{t-1}$ follows an ARMA(1,1) process.

4. See also Da and Shive (2013) who note that "at least some ETF-driven return co-movement is excessive." Similarly, Broman (2013) argues "ETF mispricing" is only partially mean-reverting. The fact that ETFs were disproportionately affected in the Flash Crash of May 6, 2010 (ETFs accounted for 70% of trades ultimately cancelled by exchanges) has fueled discussion regarding ETF flows, return volatility, and systemic risk. See, e.g., Wurgler (2010) and Ramaswamy (2010).

daily premium or $\sigma(\pi_t)$ in our notation. Using our model, the premium can be written as (I ignore the impact of microstructure noise in NAV for simplicity):

$$\pi_t = \frac{\varphi}{1-\varphi}(n_t - n_{t-1}) + u_t, \tag{3.12}$$

where the error term u_t follows a first-order autoregressive process. This expression makes it clear that "mispricing" is contemporaneously correlated with return volatility, so a regression of broader market volatility on "mispricing" will necessarily show statistical significance. In other words, an alternative explanation to shock propagation is that after an innovation in fundamentals, ETFs lead price discovery, NAV "catches up" over time, with no evidence of causality.

3.3.4. Autocorrelation

The autocorrelation of ETF and NAV returns is also quite different. Using the definition of NAV, I have $n_t - n_{t-1} = (1-\varphi)r_t + \varphi(n_{t-1} - n_{t-2})$, so that the covariance of successive NAV returns is

$$E[(n_t - n_{t-1})(n_{t-1} - n_{t-2})] = \varphi E[(n_{t-1} - n_{t-2})^2] = \varphi\sigma_r^2 \frac{(1-\varphi)^2}{1-\varphi^2} \tag{3.13}$$

At lag k the autocorrelation in NAV returns is φ^k. Formally, $\Delta n_t = (1-\varphi)$ $(1-\varphi L)^{-1} r_t$, so that the variance of NAV returns is $\sigma_r^2 \frac{(1-\varphi)^2}{1-\varphi^2}$. Since φ is non-negative, the autocorrelation in NAV returns is non-negative too and increases with staleness. To the extent there is stale pricing, NAV returns trend and are predictable. Similarly, the covariance of successive ETF price returns is

$$E\left[(p_t - p_{t-1})(p_{t-1} - p_{t-2})\right] = E[(u_t - u_{t-1})(u_{t-1} - u_{t-2})] < 0. \tag{3.14}$$

(This follows because $\Delta p_t = r_t + \varepsilon_t + (\psi - 1)(1 - \psi L)^{-1} L\varepsilon_t$. As the first two terms are innovations and the last term is negative, the cross-product with the lagged price change is negative too.) So, in contrast to NAV returns, the autocorrelation of ETF price returns is negative, reflecting the effect of transitory liquidity shocks that reverse over time.

3.4. CHAPTER SUMMARY

Premiums and discounts in ETFs are a persistent source of questions from policymakers and practitioners largely because there is no such analogue for an open-ended mutual fund. Specifically, why do ETFs trade at premiums or discounts, and how does this affect tracking error? Why are ETF returns sometimes much more volatile than the volatility of returns of their underlying indexes? How does

ETF pricing and liquidity work in times of market stress? Do large premiums/ discounts at these times reflect pricing errors? Are these persistent and if so, is this an arbitrage opportunity? How should investors incorporate deviations from NAV into their investment decisions? Should they avoid buying funds trading at steep premiums or selling funds at a significant discount? And for policymakers, do ETFs on less liquid asset classes such as high-yield bonds pose systemic risks? Is there any evidence from the crisis on how these investment vehicles performed?

The key idea of this chapter is that observed fund premium or discounts can be decomposed into price discovery and transitory liquidity components. Staleness arises because NAV does not fully capture current valuations, and the lag in adjustment can give rise to economically significant premiums or discounts, especially in times of market stress. ETF return volatility will be greater than that of the underlying NAV returns if NAV is stale. The framework established here can be extended in several directions. We can include ETF flows by explicitly modeling their dependence on past flows and return innovations and linking flow innovations to transitory price pressure, and we can make the model more realistic by incorporating cross-correlations in the shocks terms and time-dependence in the parameters. These, however, are subjects for future research. In conclusion, ETF pricing dynamics are driven by arbitrage, and a deeper understanding of this key mechanism can help practitioners better utilize these powerful tools for gaining a wide range of diversified exposures at low cost.

Valuation

4.1. INTRODUCTION

As shown in the preceding chapter, the prices of an ETF can depart from NAV because of liquidity pressures or because NAV itself does not reflect the most recent valuations of the constituent securities. What matters for arbitrage pricing is the intrinsic value of the fund. Intrinsic value need not equal either the market-determined price or the NAV reported by a pricing vendor. Nor does intrinsic value necessarily have to lie between price and NAV; it is possible for it to be higher or lower than both observed values. But intrinsic value is not readily observable. For a domestic fund with actively traded and quoted constituents, intrinsic value should align closely with NAV (i.e., there should be no staleness). Similarly, as pricing vendors improve their valuation algorithms, reported NAVs should be better indicators of value. The challenge comes from less active funds, especially international and fixed income funds, where quotes or trades may not be timely. It is especially evident for intraday indicative values, where reported figures for fixed income or international funds may be based on transactions hours or even days before.

This chapter explores two approaches to value an ETF, focusing on international and fixed income funds. The most intuitive valuation is a "bottoms up" or line-by-line valuation that is aggregated up to fund value. A more complex statistical or "top down" approach is to value the fund using the past history of noisy prices and NAVs, extracting the intrinsic value embedded in both time series. This type of filtering approach has seen considerable use in engineering and science to extract signal from noise. As we shall see, both approaches are useful to traders and investors.

4.2. INDIVIDUAL SECURITY BASED VALUATION

4.2.1. Fundamental Value

The fundamental value of an ETF is in theory straightforward to compute. At any time t, the estimated intrinsic value of an ETF is given by a weighted average of the estimated values of each of the N component securities plus the estimated value of current assets (CA) such as cash in excess of liabilities per share:

$$E[v_t]=\sum_{i=1}^{N} w_i m_{i,t} +(CA/o_t),\qquad(4.1)$$

where w_i is the share of stock i in the creation unit and $m_{i,t}$ is the estimated value of the security, say the prevailing midquote. The inputs to the valuation equation are in theory readily available except for the estimated values of the individual securities. As an aside, the estimated cash position may not be immediately obvious as it includes items such as accrued interest.

This formula is already different from the NAV formula which replaces $m_{i,t}$ by the last recorded price, possibly adjusted for currency movements in international securities. If the component securities are actively traded domestic stocks, the "bottoms up" estimated value should be accurate, barring any errors from stale quotes, bid-ask bounce, or items such as accrued interest, and so on. But in the case of international funds or less liquid securities, such as high-yield bonds, the estimated value is harder to compute because mid-quotes are either not available or are stale.

4.2.2. Valuing Bond ETFs

A bottoms-up approach is to create an estimated value from a model for each security we want to value. Consider first a bond fund comprised of N bonds. If a bond is currently quoted, then I can use the bid price and $m_{i,t}-(s_t/2)$ as the basis of expected value where $(s_t/2)$ is half the current bid-ask spread. Recall that for bonds, the reference price is the bid price, which is also how NAV is determined. What if no quotes were available? Matrix pricing is common for bonds. This involves:

- **Grouping**—Bonds with similar characteristics such as maturity, credit rating, issuer, industry/sector, and so on are grouped in matrix format, assuming they share a common yield curve relative to benchmark.
- **Interpolation**—The price of a bond is then approximated using linear interpolation. Implicit in this estimation is that the trading size is a round-lot or an institutional-sized trade, because as shown by Hendershott and Madhavan (2015), odd- and micro-lot prices can be quite different.
- **Intrinsic Valuation**—Matrix prices are typically indicative prices/valuations using the implicit yield curve. They do not constitute firm offers to trade. Matrix pricing is most reasonable for bonds where there is an active, liquid market for "similar" securities.

Matrix Pricing Example

As a simple example, suppose I want to value a three-year duration corporate bond (in yield space) from an energy company that has not traded today. Two "similar" energy bonds (ratings, issuer type, and maturity) have traded today, a bond with two-year duration with yield 5% and a four-year duration bond with yield 7%. Then the matrix price of the bond is roughly 6%, with additional refinements on the weighting of cash flows and so on.

The intuitive matrix pricing procedure can be generalized in a straightforward way. The basic idea is to adjust the last recorded price for interest rate and spread movements. The last recorded price at time $t - \tau$ might be a trade (recorded in TRACE with an intraday stamp) or a quote, and denote this by $p_{i,t-\tau}$. Then, the estimated value at time t is

$$m_{i,t} = (1 + \Delta_i(t,\tau))p_{i,t-\tau}, \tag{4.2}$$

where $\Delta_i(t,\tau)$ is the adjustment factor based on relevant events since the last reference price. One might, for example, model $\Delta_i(t,\tau)$ as a linear function of changes along the appropriate benchmark yield curve multiplied by the (negative) bond's key rate durations plus a spread adjustment for changes in credit risk over the period.

Example of Bond Intraday Valuation

To illustrate, consider a corporate bond with duration $D = 1.5$ years that trades at a constant spread over the benchmark yield curve of treasuries. Say the bond last traded at noon at a price of $98 when treasury yields were at, say, 2.5%, and assume further the yield curve is flat. Since the last reference price, yields have risen to 2.6% (up 0.10% in yield space) and credit spreads (measured by CDX) have remained constant, implying the adjustment factor $\Delta_i(t,\tau) = -0.10\% \times 1.5 = -0.15\%$, so estimated value is $98(1 - 0.15\%) = \$97.853$.

In general, there could be multiple adjustments for movements along the benchmark yield curve as well as other factors such as credit spread movements. The reference price for a bond could be a recent trade or quote. We would also make adjustments for the size/side of the trade/quote, using only those prices that are reasonable.

4.2.3. Valuation of International Funds

The present calculations of NAV for international funds simply take the last recorded price (perhaps 15 hours old for some markets) and adjust by exchange rate movements since the close. That procedure has many flaws. International mutual funds offered investors liquidity on a daily basis allowing them to purchase or sell fund shares to the mutual fund company at the end of the day. In the past, some short-term speculators have exploited this fact to profit at the expense of long-term shareholders (see Goetzmann, Ivković, and Rouwenhorst 2001), trading on the high correlation between daily US market returns and the subsequent day's return in international markets. A simple strategy of buying international mutual funds when the US market is up and selling when it is down was very profitable. Such "market timing" activity was often concentrated in retirement accounts where it was easy to move money in and out of domestic and international funds without tax consequences, imposing a return drag on "buy and hold" investors.

GREEK STOCK MARKET SHUTDOWN

During the financial crisis in Greece in 2015, the local equity market was closed from June 29, 2015, to August 3, 2015. During this time the US-registered Global X FTSE Greece 20 ETF (GREK) continued to trade, gapping down almost 20% when the Greek Stock Exchange was shut. Prior to this event, GREK traded closely with its underlying index, the FTSE/ATHEX Custom Capped Index. Upon reopening in August, the price of GREK was relatively stable while the underlying benchmark index moved down to the ETF's level. This is suggestive that ETFs are important contributors to price discovery.

Funds often use short-term trading fees and other restrictions, such as minimum holding periods, to limit trading profit opportunities, but these may not be sufficient to eliminate speculative trading entirely and are unpopular with fund investors. Consequently, mutual funds have increasingly implemented fair value pricing to adjust their fund's NAVs based on recent market movements based on adjustments to the prices of international stocks given the information observed between the close of the foreign market and 4:00 p.m. EST when US markets close. Only the largest fund complexes can reliably compute adjustments for a universe of (often) 40,000 global stocks within a short time window, so commercial solutions are popular.

Since the price of ETFs is market determined, there is no economic need to fair value the ETF itself, unlike a mutual fund where transactions occur at NAV. However, traders wishing to estimate intrinsic value for an international fund during market hours need to estimate the underlying value of a foreign security that is not traded. Since there is no direct observation on the fair value price of a foreign stock at 4:00 p.m. EST, the next day's opening price is commonly used as a proxy. Of course, events occurring between 4:00 p.m. EST and the opening of a foreign market might change stock valuations, but are unlikely to introduce a systematic bias.

The logical starting point for a fair value model is a multifactor equation:

$$\Delta_i(t, \tau) = F_1\beta_{1,i} + \cdots F_k\beta_{k,i} + \varepsilon_i, \tag{4.3}$$

where $\Delta_i(t, \tau)$ is the return from the close of the stock in the foreign market to its open the next day, F_k is the return of a factor k that is observed after the foreign close to the domestic close (in the United States at 4:00 p.m. EST), $\beta_{k,i}$ is the loading of stock i on factor k, and ε_i is the error term to reflect the fact that the model is statistical in nature. The factors are chosen to best capture the unobserved change in value, including intraday market, industry or sector movements during our trading hours, and so on.

Implementation of fair value pricing is described in Madhavan (2004). A hierarchical or waterfall approach is suggested where the fair value adjustment is based on the best available proxy for each component stock's return. So, if a foreign stock has an actively traded ADR, one can use the ADR's return net of foreign exchange movements to proxy for the local stock movement while the foreign market is closed. If the ADR is thinly traded or there is no ADR, one can use a beta to the foreign stock's industry or sector return (e.g., for a foreign airline, one might use a beta to US airlines, again adjusting for foreign exchange). If such proxies are difficult to find, one can always simply estimate the foreign stock's beta to the US futures market and use that as a proxy.

The key point to note about the multifactor model is that the loadings are stock-specific, so that each security has an individual adjustment. Note that the choice of factors might also vary from stock to stock. The multifactor approach can also be generalized to a hierarchical or nested model, where the choice of model depends on whether the coefficients are estimated with statistical reliability. For example, for a thinly traded stock, the factors might be the intraday US market return (using futures from the close of the foreign market to the US close at 4:00 p.m. EST) and the corresponding returns to the stock's sector or industry. But for a larger capitalization stock, such as Vodafone Group PLC, an actively traded American Depository Receipt (ADR) may exist, which might form an additional factor that replaces the market factor. It is clear that different approaches will lead to different estimates of fundamental intrinsic value.

4.3. STATISTICAL ESTIMATION

4.3.1. Top Down Approaches

An alternative to the bottoms up or fundamental valuation is a "top down" statistical approach. The intuition is that the past time series of ETF prices and NAVs can provide us with information on the embedded intrinsic value that can be extracted statistically without having to value the underlying components. This type of filtering approach has seen considerable use in engineering and science to extract signal from noise, but has also been applied in economics and finance for random walk decompositions. Most relevant is Hasbrouck (2003), who uses a vector error correction model to examine the information share of ETFs relative to floor-traded and electronically traded futures (E-minis) contracts for major US equity indexes. He finds that for the S&P 500 and Nasdaq 100 indexes, most price discovery occurs in the E-mini contracts. Our focus here is not on the relative contributions of different exposure vehicles, but a fund-specific analysis of the speed of price discovery, broken down by asset classes and exposures.

A related strand of the literature focuses on ETF premiums and discounts. Petajisto (2013a) examines the deviation of midquote prices of ETFs from their NAVs showing they are larger in funds holding international or illiquid securities. Chacko, Das, and Fan (2014) use ETF premiums as a metric for bond market illiquidity. See also Engle and Sarkar (2006) who examine intraday premiums and Tucker and Laipply (2013) who examine the time-series properties of select bond ETFs. Our analysis looks across asset classes and exposures, and provides a decomposition of the premium and speed of error correction.

4.3.2. State-Space Representation

Empirical estimates of the model developed in the previous chapter at the individual fund level are of economic interest because they provide insights regarding the efficiency of the arbitrage mechanism measured by the estimated "true" deviations between price and (unobserved) value through ψ. We are interested, for example, in learning why some funds exhibit greater price efficiency than others, and the length of time it takes for pricing errors to be corrected. The degree to which a fund's NAV is stale (as captured by a positive value φ) is also interesting as staleness implies predictability in NAV returns, and as shown here, is related to the difference in volatility in ETF price-based returns versus NAV returns. Further, the model estimates let us decompose the premium to estimate the portion of the average premium attributable to liquidity versus price discovery. While market makers and others in the ecosystem with proprietary models, data, and views on flow may have accurate views of the true premium and trade on this, many other investors do not have such data and may sometimes postpone a purchase or sale based on observed premiums or discounts. As noted earlier, the existence of a premium or discount need not imply any mispricing, as illustrated later.

There are several possible approaches one can take to estimate the model given time-series data on prices and NAV for a given fund. As shown earlier, price and NAV returns depend on the parameters, so armed with expressions for return volatility and autocorrelations, I have enough moment conditions to estimate the model's parameters. Alternatively, one can estimate the model using a multivariate state-space (Kalman filter) representation. I adopt the state-space representation because it aligns with the model directly and lets us explicitly estimate the unobserved true premium, u_t. The Kalman filter is the best possible (optimal) estimator for a large class of problems where I want to make inferences based on observations of noisy signals, and is used in a variety of real-world applications where estimates are based on mechanical, optical, acoustic, or magnetic sensor data (see, e.g., Hamilton [1994] for further details).

The state-space representation consists of two elements: (1) the measurement (or observation) equation with price and NAV, expressed as a function of the unobserved state vector (expected value), and (2) the transition (or state) equation that expresses the dynamics of the state vector. The Kalman filter works by using the measurement equation to create dynamic forecasts of the state vector, much like a conventional regression. In our case, the measurement equation is:

$$\begin{bmatrix} p_t \\ n_t \end{bmatrix} = \begin{bmatrix} \psi p_{t-1} \\ \varphi n_{t-1} \end{bmatrix} + \begin{bmatrix} 1 & -\psi \\ 1-\varphi & 0 \end{bmatrix} \begin{bmatrix} v_t \\ v_{t-1} \end{bmatrix} + \begin{bmatrix} \varepsilon_t \\ w_t \end{bmatrix}. \tag{4.4}$$

The transition equation describes the random-walk process for unobserved expected value:

$$\begin{bmatrix} v_t \\ v_{t-1} \end{bmatrix} = \begin{bmatrix} 1 & 0 \\ 1 & 0 \end{bmatrix} \begin{bmatrix} v_{t-1} \\ v_{t-2} \end{bmatrix} + \begin{bmatrix} r_t \\ 0 \end{bmatrix}. \tag{4.5}$$

There are eight parameters to be estimated for each fund: The coefficients φ and ψ (staleness and efficiency) and the means and variances of the shocks ε_t, w_t, and r_t. It is worth noting that the framework in equations (4.4)–(4.5) can be extended to explicitly include ETF flows, data that are publicly available. Specifically, I can model flows as serially correlated and related to past return innovations. I expect flows to be positively related to the liquidity shock ε_t reflecting market impact. This augmented model has three additional parameters of economic interest: flow autocorrelation, return sensitivity, and the market impact coefficient.

4.4. ESTIMATION

Madhavan and Sobczyk (2016) estimate the state-space model using maximum likelihood for the universe of all US-domiciled ETFs from January 1, 2005, to January 31, 2014. They restrict attention to physically backed ETFs on equities and fixed income, excluding exchange-traded notes (which are really debt instruments), leveraged and inverse products, and other synthetic funds. Estimation uses daily closing prices and NAVs, log-transformed to be consistent with the model, and they require that funds have at least 252 consecutive trading days of history.

Summary statistics for the sample in terms of assets under management and trading characteristics are provided in table 4.1, broken down by asset class and

Table 4.1 DESCRIPTIVE STATISTICS FOR US-DOMICILED ETFS

	Equity		Fixed Income	
	Domestic	International	Domestic	International
Number of funds	387	403	113	44
Total AUM ($MM)	892,804	382,021	191,240	21,998
Average Bid/Ask Spread (bps)	16.6	52.4	28.6	54.8
Average Premium (bps)	−1.8	18.3	18.3	16.7
Average Absolute Premium (bps)	23.8	73.4	37.6	69.8

SOURCE: Madhavan and Sobczyk (2016), based on data for January 1, 2005, to January 31, 2014.

Table 4.2 STATE-SPACE MODEL ESTIMATES

		Equity		Fixed Income	
		Domestic	International	Domestic	International
NAV staleness coefficient (φ)	Mean	−0.08	0.15	0.40	0.41
	Frac. significant > 0	0.03	0.74	0.83	0.95
Arbitrage speed parameter (ψ)	Mean	0.24	0.43	0.61	0.79
	Frac. significant > 0	0.80	0.77	0.96	1.00

SOURCE: Based on statistics in Madhavan and Sobczyk (2016) using Bloomberg and BlackRock data, January 1, 2005, to January 31, 2014. Significance is the fraction of the estimate that is greater than zero, based on a one-tail t-test at the 5% level.

exposure. For the sample, total assets under management (AUM) represent almost $1.5 trillion in 947 funds, which is comprehensive in the sense that total AUM in US ETPs was $1.86 trillion as of June 2014.[1] Most of the funds and assets in the sample are in domestic equity ETFs, followed by international equity. Domestic equity funds are the most liquid by conventional measures such as the spread, trading frequency, or dollar value traded. Consistent with Petajisto (2013a), international equity funds have the largest absolute premium of 73.4 basis points, versus 48.7 for all funds. Note that there is considerable variation in absolute premiums over time at the individual fund level.

The economic model has eight parameters per fund (or 7,576 total), but the focus is on the two parameters of greatest interest namely the staleness coefficient and the speed of arbitrage. In table 4.2 the mean estimates across all funds of the staleness and arbitrage speed parameters are reported, broken down by asset class and exposure category, as well as the fraction of the estimated coefficients that are significantly greater than zero. Also estimated, but not reported here, are the standard deviations of the three innovation terms (to NAV, price, and value) and their respective means.

Observe that the staleness parameter estimates increase moving from the most liquid asset classes (domestic equity) to the less liquid asset classes (fixed income), consistent with our prior beliefs. For domestic equity, staleness is, in general, both economically and statistically insignificant, in line with intuition. The speed of arbitrage (which is measured *inversely* by ψ) increases with liquidity, ranging from 0.24 in domestic equity to 0.79 in international fixed income. The corresponding half-life for correcting a given unobserved pricing error is less than half a day for the average equity fund to almost three days for an international

---

1. Madhavan and Sobczyk (2016). ETF assets are sourced using shares outstanding and net asset values from Bloomberg. Asset classifications are assigned based on product definitions from provider websites and product prospectuses.

bond fund. Again, these estimates are consistent with our intuition that domestic equity exhibits relatively low staleness compared to international fixed income.

A multivariate analysis allows us to examine how arbitrage speed, staleness, and pricing errors vary across funds while jointly accounting for fund size, trading activity, and exposure characteristics. Madhavan and Sobcyzk (2016) regress fund-level estimates of arbitrage speed, staleness, and the standard deviation of noise shocks on log AUM, log of dollar average daily volume (ADV), and indicator variables taking the value 1 if the fund has a fixed income or international focus (i.e., non-US geography), respectively, and 0 otherwise. Fixed income and international funds exhibit significant NAV staleness and slower error correction, as expected.

4.5. ANALYSIS OF PREMIUMS, ARBITRAGE, AND PRICE EFFICIENCY

4.5.1. True Premiums

A case application of the model to a particular fund yields valuable insights. Consider the iShares iBoxx High-Yield Corporate Bond ETF (HYG) during the 2008–2009 Financial Crisis. High-yield funds like this one are often central to regulators' concerns about illiquid markets and how funds may react under stress. This case can nicely illustrate how the model can be used to understand reported premiums or discounts. Using the estimated model, the implicit state vector (i.e., the time series of $\hat{v}_t$) can be recovered. This is plotted in figure 4.1 along with the daily closing price and NAV.[2] Both price and NAV move closely together until the start of the crisis, and the estimated state variable lies between these values. In September 2008, price moves down sharply relative to NAV, increasing the discount, and the staleness in NAV is apparent. In March 2009, when the market recovers, price leads NAV upward. In this period, the recovered state variable tracks price quite closely, similar to the results reported by Tucker and Laipply (2013).

Consistent with these observations, a regression of HYG's daily NAV returns in the crisis period on the previous day's return yields a coefficient of 0.551 (t-value of 10.82) while the corresponding coefficient for ETF daily returns was slightly negative and statistically insignificant.[3] Recall further that the model shows that ETF returns will exhibit greater volatility than NAV returns if there is staleness, and indeed, the volatility of HYG daily returns from April 2007 to end-December 2013 is approximately twice that of NAV returns, 93 versus 41 basis points.

2. The model is estimated (consistent with our framework) with log values, but for illustrative purposes I plot the dollar values in figure 4.1.

3. This is not just a result of the crisis period. I obtain similar results using a sample from April 13, 2007, to December 31, 2013. The autocorrelation in total NAV daily returns in this period is 0.544 (t-value of 26.65) versus −0.009 (t-value of −0.37) for ETF daily returns.

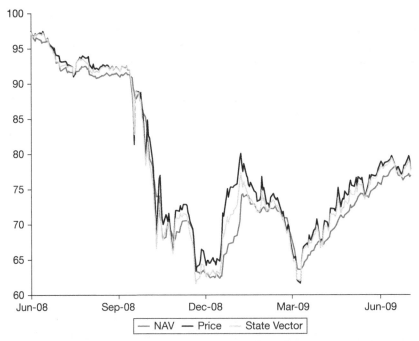

Figure 4.1 iShares High-Yield Corporate Bond ETF (HYG) Prices, NAV, and State Vector, June 2008 to June 2009.
SOURCE: Madhavan and Sobczyk (2016).

4.5.2. True versus Reported Premiums

Why are premiums and discounts relevant? Many investors in ETFs including financial advisors, retail clients, hedge funds, and so on are concerned that buying (selling) at large premium (discount) is unfavorable. While market makers typically have the tools to form a good estimate of intrinsic value, their data/models are proprietary. The estimated residuals $\{\hat{u}_t\}$ yield a time-series estimate of the "true" premium for a given fund at any point in time. This approach can be used to produce a step-ahead estimate of the true premium and the speed with which it is corrected for a given fund on a daily basis.

EXAMPLE: MUNICIPAL BOND DISCOUNTS IN JUNE 2013

As a recent example, consider the iShares S&P National AMT-Free Municipal Bond Fund (MUB) in June 2013, following significant outflows over concerns about rising interest rates, defaults, and risk. On June 21, 2013, the observed premium was −2.86% based on Bloomberg data, but our estimate of true premium that day using the state-space model was −1.32%, roughly half that amount.

In figure 4.2 I plot the estimated true premium $\{\hat{u}_t\}$ against the observed premium $\{\pi_t\}$ for HYG in the period April 13, 2007, to December 31, 2013, where consistent with the model, both variables are log transformed. A regression of the true

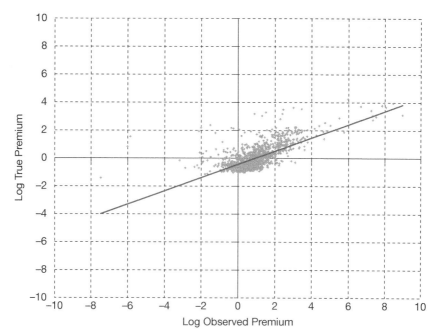

Figure 4.2 Observed versus true premiums for iShares High-Yield Corporate Bond ETF (HYG).
SOURCE: Bloomberg and BlackRock data, April 13, 2007 to December 31, 2013.

premium on the observed premium yields a slope coefficient of 0.47 (t-value 38 and adjusted R-square of 0.461), indicating that roughly half the observed premium on average is due to price discovery. In recent years this fraction has been higher (up to 0.8 in 2014) because NAV is more precise and closer to intrinsic value.

4.5.3. Price Discovery

Recall that the premium at any point in time can be expressed as $\pi_t = p_t - n_t = (p_t - v_t) + (v_t - n_t) = u_t + (v_t - n_t)$. In the extreme case where the ETF price always reflects true value, the first term u_t will be zero and the entire premium reflects staleness or pricing errors in NAV. Alternatively, if there is no NAV staleness and/or noise, then $n_t = v_t$ and the premium entirely reflects the shock u_t to the ETF price through the secondary market. The standard error of u_t is

$$\sigma_u = \frac{\sigma_\varepsilon}{\sqrt{1 - \psi^2}}.$$ This term is positively related to the volatility of transitory liquid-

ity shocks σ_ε and is also increasing in ψ, meaning that more efficient arbitrage means smaller residuals. I define the price discovery component of the premium as the portion of total variance that is not attributable to transitory noise shocks, that is:

$$D = 1 - \left(\frac{\sigma_u}{\sigma_\pi}\right)^2, \tag{4.6}$$

where σ_π is the standard deviation of the observed premium.

CHINESE NEW YEAR AND PRICE DISCOVERY

During Chinese New Year in latter part of January, some Asian markets (e.g., Korea, Taiwan, China, and Malaysia) are closed for extended periods depending on where the holiday falls in the lunar cycle. The Taiwan Stock Exchange, for example, is typically closed for seven consecutive working days. Yet, even though the underlying instruments are not traded, ETFs on these countries (and emerging market funds) continue to trade with tight spreads and large volumes. Interestingly, upon the reopening of these countries' stock exchanges, there is generally little price deviation from the implied value from the US-domiciled country funds, suggesting efficient price discovery.

Over all funds, the average value of D is about 0.46, meaning that roughly half the premium is attributable to price discovery. The price discovery component D declines with fund size. In other words, transitory liquidity shocks constitute a larger fraction of the premium for smaller, less actively traded funds. The estimates make intuitive sense in that roughly 74% of the variation in premiums for large international funds is due to price discovery. That figure is lowest for small international fixed income funds. From a practical perspective, the results confirm our intuition that for the most active funds, where AUM is the largest, apparent premiums or discounts reflect staleness (or pricing errors) in NAV as opposed to transitory liquidity pressures in the ETF market.

4.5.4. ETFs in the Financial Crisis

Anecdotal evidence suggests that ETFs played an especially important role in the financial crisis when liquidity in underlying securities, particularly in fixed income, was scarce. To examine this issue, Madhavan and Sobczyk (2016) estimated the model during the financial crisis (see table 4.3, Panel A, from January 1, 2008, and to December 31, 2009) and post-financial crisis (table 4.3, Panel B) using funds with at least a full year of trading history (252 trading days) in each subperiod.

Observe that the NAV staleness coefficients are higher in the crisis period for fixed income funds, perhaps reflecting the decline in trading activity, particularly in individual corporate bonds. Interestingly, the arbitrage speed parameters are consistently smaller during financial crisis (Panel A) than in the post-crisis period (Panel B), supporting the view that ETFs serve as price discovery vehicles during times of market stress.

4.6. CHAPTER SUMMARY

There are three distinct relevant valuations for an ETF: the market-determined equilibrium price of the fund, the NAV, and what I term intrinsic value. The key to arbitrage is the difference between intrinsic value and price, since NAV may

Table 4.3 STATE-SPACE MODEL ESTIMATES DURING AND
AFTER FINANCIAL CRISIS

		Equity		Fixed income	
		Domestic	International	Domestic	International
Panel A: Crisis (January 1, 2008, to December 31, 2009)					
NAV stale-ness coefficient (φ)	Mean	−0.08	0.17	0.35	0.51
	Frac. signifi-cant > 0	0.02	0.73	0.88	1.00
Arbitrage speed parameter (ψ)	Mean	0.22	0.23	0.57	0.74
	Frac. signifi-cant > 0	0.66	0.60	1.00	1.00
Panel B: Post-Crisis (January 1, 2010 to December 31, 2014)					
NAV staleness coefficient (φ)	Mean	−0.04	0.19	0.29	0.43
	Frac. signifi-cant > 0	0.04	0.74	0.84	0.95
Arbitrage speed parameter (ψ)	Mean	0.27	0.29	0.58	0.86
	Frac. signifi-cant > 0	0.83	0.77	0.96	1.00

SOURCE: Madhavan and Sobczyk (2016), based on data for January 1, 2005, to January 31, 2014. Significance is the fraction of the estimate that is greater than zero, based on a one-tail t-test at the 5% level.

be stale. A bottoms-up valuation of an ETF proceeds security by security. For domestic equity funds, with accurate and timely quotes, valuation presents little difficulty other than adjustments for cash or for other terms that might affect overall valuation. For bonds or international funds, values need to be adjusted for possible staleness in quotes or reported last prices. The general approach adopted here is straightforward—to adjust previous prices/quotes based on market factor movements from the last recorded valuation.

An alternative is a "top down" model-based approach that is in contrast to the bottoms-up security specific valuation. The advantage of using a model to esti-mate the intrinsic value is that we can estimate other parameters of interest such as the speed with which arbitrage works to correct pricing errors. This chapter tests an eight-parameter model to better understand price dynamics. I estimate the model individually for all 947 US-domiciled equity and fixed income ETFs from 2005 to 2014 using a state-space model. The major findings are as follows:

- The observed fund premium or discounts can be decomposed into price discovery and transitory liquidity components. These components vary systematically across asset class, exposure, and fund size.

- The NAV of international equity funds and bond ETFs, particularly smaller funds, can exhibit staleness, but this is largely insignificant for domestic equity funds. Staleness arises because NAV does not fully capture current valuations, and the lag in adjustment can give rise to economically significant premiums or discounts, especially in times of market stress.
- I estimate the speed with which unobserved pricing errors in a given fund are corrected through the arbitrage mechanism. Arbitrage acts quickly to correct pricing errors for domestic equity funds, with a half-life of 0.43 days versus 6.56 days for international fixed income funds.
- Apparently large discounts to NAV in periods of bond market stress such as the financial crisis reflects efficient pricing, not illiquidity. This result should mitigate concerns that ETFs are the source of additional volatility or of systemic risk.
- The cross-sectional findings provide strong evidence that observed premiums largely reflect price discovery, particularly for ETFs with constituents trading outside of US market trading hours.

It is interesting to compare the "top down" state-space estimates with a "bottoms up" security-by-security valuation to gain a deeper understanding of the limits of arbitrage. This, however, is a subject for future research.

Performance and Benchmark Tracking

5.1. INTRODUCTION

The objective of an ETF portfolio manager is to closely track the underlying or benchmark index. Unlike an active manager whose goal is alpha generation, a passive manager gets no credit for performance in excess of the benchmark. Passive asset managers actually scrutinize any return deviation, positive or negative, from the benchmark return to understand why the fund is not exactly giving investors their desired exposure. Large deviations are considered poor performance, even if they work in the favor of the long investor.

Of course, indexes themselves are not investable and there are many factors that can cause deviations of return from benchmark, some that are quite complex. As it is such a key issue, I will cover this in detail, beginning with common misunderstandings on terminology and then moving to performance measurement. Specific examples taken from actual funds will help explain the nature of tracking error. I also highlight the role the asset manager can play in mitigating tracking error through fund design, an element not well understood even by experienced practitioners. The focus is on equities and bonds; derivative-based funds that use futures/forwards to gain exposures have a completely different set of issues and are discussed in Part III when we consider commodities, foreign exchange, and alternatives.

A closely related subject concerns the cost of ownership of the fund. Too often this is simply equated with the total expense ratio of the ETF, but I will show here that this is not correct. In many cases, the true cost of ownership is lower, but it is important for an investor to understand the drivers of these costs and revenue streams that can offset them, significantly at times.

5.2. COMMON MISUNDERSTANDINGS

5.2.1. Tracking Error versus Tracking Difference

The disparity in ETF and benchmark performance is termed the "tracking difference." For example, if a fund returned 8.5% in a year when the benchmark returned 9%, the tracking difference is −0.5%. So, tracking difference measures the actual or *ex post* under- or outperformance of a benchmark over a stated period of time. In terms of our model above, where prices and index values are in logarithms and are adjusted for any distributions, the tracking difference of any period is:

$$TD_t = (p_t - p_{t-1}) - (I_t - I_{t-1}),   \tag{5.1}$$

where I_t is the (log) index value (dividend adjusted) at time t. The index return may or may not equal the NAV return, but the two should be very close. Tracking difference captures all income and costs that cause a performance deviation from the index, most importantly the total expense ratio.

The terms "tracking error" and "tracking difference" are often erroneously used interchangeably, but refer to different economic concepts. Tracking error measures the consistency with which an ETF follows its benchmark while tracking difference is just performance. While tracking difference is purely an *ex post* measure, tracking error has both *ex post* and *ex ante* dimensions. In an *ex post* or *realized sense* it is the standard deviation of the return difference between the ETF and benchmark portfolios, or the volatility of *TD*. Tracking error is typically computed using daily returns as computed in equation (5.1). (Confusingly, some use the absolute value of the return difference between the ETF and the benchmark, but the generally accepted measure is the volatility or standard deviation of return differences.) By contrast, the *predicted* tracking error is an *ex ante* concept based on the covariance matrix *V* from a risk model. It is defined as the volatility or standard deviation of *ex ante* risk given the difference between ETF and benchmark weights:

$$\sigma(h) = \sqrt{(h - h_b)' V (h - h_b)}.   \tag{5.2}$$

Both *ex ante* and *ex post* tracking error metrics matter to investors using ETFs for hedging purposes, but do not provide an indication of how closely the longer term performance of the ETF has matched its benchmark.

A physically based ETF may have high daily tracking error for institutional reasons (e.g., different valuation sources or timing versus those used to calculate the benchmark), but still have very low long-term tracking difference because the daily valuation differences net out over longer periods. In addition, standard calculations of tracking error ignore significant contributors to ETF performance, such as securities lending income.

5.2.2. NAV versus Index Returns

Most index ETFs do not fully replicate their benchmarks in the sense that their holdings match completely with the components of the index. Instead, they will hold a basket of securities designed to closely correlate with the return characteristics of the benchmark. They also may include a small percentage of "off-benchmark" holdings, such as cash, new issues, and futures contracts. This is because many benchmark indices comprise thousands of securities, including many that have small weightings and may be expensive or impossible to buy or sell. As a result, the performance of an ETF may not match that of its benchmark exactly, but will effectively match the return of the specified market exposure.

Some benchmark indices are harder to match with correlated physical securities than others, based largely on the number of investment factors that need to be correlated and the availability of index components that can be assembled to match those investment factors. Open-ended funds and other index-tracking investment vehicles face similar issues, but ETFs are more commonly offered on some of the harder-to-match benchmark indices.

In some cases, legal and regulatory constraints may prohibit an ETF from literally replicating its index. For example, there are cases in which one stock may represent 40% of an index's weight, although US ETFs are subject to a tax diversification rule that prohibits the largest holding from exceeding 25% of assets and requires that those holdings that are each greater than 5% of assets be limited to a collective sum below 50%. European ETFs are subject to a UCITS rule that prevents an ETF from investing more than 5% of its assets in securities issued by a single issuer. ETFs are sometimes managed against "capped" indices (where available), which limit the maximum weights of the largest holdings.

PRACTICAL CHALLENGES TO PURE INDEX REPLICATION

Country funds are often subject to caps, meaning limitations on holdings. The Belgium IMI Uncapped Index has a large concentrated position that exceeds regulatory rules, so an ETF designed to track Belgium cannot simply buy all the index stocks in proportion to their market capitalization weights. The MSCI Belgium IMI 25/50 Index was created to reduce concentration risk to comply with these rules. Indeed, the capped index has lower active risk of 1.79% compared to 7.16% for the uncapped index.

SOURCE: Golub et al. (2013) based on three-year annualized volatility for the period ending March 31, 2013.

Finally, some ETFs may exhibit significant tracking difference because the ETF manager makes choices that allow for greater tracking error to achieve other goals, such as enhanced liquidity of the ETF's shares. There are times when illiquid securities included in a benchmark index but excluded from an ETF's portfolio do not perform in tandem with other components of the index. If the ETF is systematically underweighted to the differently performing illiquid securities, the ETF's performance will reflect its liquidity bias. Factors causing tracking difference include tax efficiency and securities lending revenue, which enhance returns and transaction costs and fund expenses that reduce the returns to an ETF investor relative to the index. Some factors such as the treatment of index adds/deletes, corporate actions, or the drag induced by cash positions may work both ways, but are also the source of tracking difference.

The adjustment for corporate actions (such as mergers or splits) and dividends is quite important: There are more than a few press articles that simply use price-based returns that ignore dividends or corporate actions to measure ETF performance. By omitting the distribution component of returns for the ETF, these reports overstate tracking error to the benchmark index because price changes around dividend *ex dates* show as volatility. This error also understates tracking difference, making performance seem worse than in reality.

5.3. OPTIMAL DESIGN

It is not well understood that the asset manager has several elements of choice over the design of an ETF, all of which can have a material impact on performance. The asset manager can exercise control over key variables including fund structure, creation fees, the choice of index, and the use of replication or optimization for tracking and liquidity. The fund structure selected by the manager is especially important. Modern fund structures allow dividends to be continuously reinvested unlike older structures where dividends accumulate, leading to cash drag. Multi-class structures (where mutual fund shareholders interact with the same pool of investments as the underlying ETF share class) offer another source for design to affect performance because they have the potential for conflict among multiple interests. For example, redemptions by mutual fund shareholders could trigger capital gains distributions for ETF shareholders who are part of the same class. Further, transaction costs incurred by other share class investors (e.g., triggered by a large sell-off) may be shared with ETF shareholders.

A key choice variable for an ETF provider is the size of the creation unit or basket, typically $5 to $10 million. Creation unit size can have a dramatic impact on the cost of providing liquidity, especially for new funds.

CHINA AND TAIWAN FUNDS

For example, some markets (China and Taiwan) have high round lot minimums or have high-priced stocks (Samsung Electronics traded at year-end 2014 at Korean Won 1,266,000 the equivalent of over $1,164 per share) that do not divide into tradable increments at small creation unit sizes. With a small creation unit, these portfolios would take on more tracking risk or require larger cash components for creation/redemption.

Larger creation units are associated with lower liquidity because dealers must carry inventory before they can either create or redeem shares in the ETF. Longer durations increase their inventory carrying costs and hence widen bid-offer spreads. While dealers like smaller creation units, smaller creation unit sizes also make it more difficult to replicate indices with stocks that do not trade in small increments and hence higher tracking error. The balance of these two elements yields the optimal creation unit size.

CASE STUDY: OPTIMAL CREATION UNIT SIZE

Consider an emerging market ETF whose creation unit size is $5 million. A customer places a buy order of $2 million ETF that is facilitated by a market maker who goes short this amount. To hedge risk, the market maker covers the $2 million short position by creating one unit of the ETF, and finances the remaining $3 million of inventory at a 5% annual cost of capital. The market maker will try to sell the $3 million excess inventory in the secondary market over time without significant price movement. Assume the market maker will sell up to 20% of average daily volume (ADV) in the market. The 20% figure is heuristic and is commonly used by many market participants to approximate a trading intensity that has minimal market impact. If ADV in the ETF is, say, $5 million a day, the dealer will sell on average $1 million ($=\$5 \times 20\%$) per day. So, liquidating the inventory will take the market maker three days. The average inventory position over the liquidation period is $2 million ($=(\$3 + \$2 + \$1)/3$ days) so inventory cost is then $2 \times 5\%(3/365) = 0.082\%$. If the creation unit is $10 million, the same exercise implies a holding period of eight days, average inventory of $4.5 million, and hence substantially higher dealer costs of 0.49%. While this computation makes an argument for the lower unit size, there is also the tracking error to be considered. For example, at the $5 million creation unit size, the effect of round-lot minimums and high priced stocks could result in a cash component of up to 10%. At a $10 million creation unit size level, these frictions are reduced so the cash component would typically be below 5%, implying much tighter tracking.

As ADV increases, the discrepancy in costs at the two possible creation unit sizes narrows in absolute terms, so the optimal unit size will likely change over the life-cycle of the ETF. When an ETF is first launched, liquidity is critical and the optimal size is low; later, as volume and assets grow, so does liquidity and tracking error considerations typically lead to larger optimal sizes.

5.4. TOTAL COST OF OWNERSHIP

As noted, ETF investors often struggle to compare the cost of ownership of different ETFs. Expense ratios are quite low (e.g., the SPDR S&P ETF has an expense ratio of 0.09% or 9 basis points) for large domestic ETFs but are higher for niche markets or less liquid assets. Many investors focus only on the Total Expense

Ratio (TER), which represents the *explicit* fee charged by the asset manager to run the fund, but ignore many other costs and revenues that can have an impact on returns. Much like auto ownership, the explicit costs, which also include the commission costs to execute the trade, are only one part of the costs over the period of ownership. With a car, owners must also recognize that their costs over time will include maintenance, insurance, fuel costs, and so on. Similarly, with ETFs, the total cost of ownership needs to include the implicit costs and revenues. These include trading costs (e.g., bid-offer spreads and market impact), the tracking difference, and potential taxes on distributions.

CASE STUDY: HIGH-YIELD FUNDS AND TRACKING DIFFERENCE

Both the iShares iBoxx $ High-Yield Corporate Bond ETF (HYG) and SPDR Barclays High Yield Bond ETF (JNK) are popular funds offering exposure to broad high-yield bond indexes. As of November 2014, the expense ratios of the two funds were 0.50% and 0.40%, respectively. A cost-sensitive investor might thus prefer JNK with its lower expense ratio. However, based on two years of daily rolling 12-month data (ETF.com) the median tracking differences were −0.12% and −0.58%, respectively. Since bid-offer spreads are very low for both, roughly 1 basis point, the total costs are larger for the lower expense ratio fund. Selecting purely on the basis of expense ratio would, for this period of time, been the wrong choice.

A major factor is securities lending, which I consider in a separate section on risk later on in the book. Both the ETF itself and the underlying securities can be lent, generating income that offsets the other expenses involved in ETF investing. The total cost of ownership is given by:

$$TCO = TER + Trading\ Costs + Taxes\ /\ Fees - ETF\ Lending\ Revenue \\ - Securities\ Lending\ Revenue, \tag{5.3}$$

where *TER* is the total expense ratio. Using the definition of tracking difference, for a fully replicating fund, with no other revenues or costs, $TD = -TER$ meaning the only reason for a difference from NAV return is because of costs. In reality, lending revenue can make quite a difference as in the following example. Tracking difference will correctly capture these elements, but will also reflect changes in the premium/discount over the interval of interest.

CASE STUDY: FTSE 250 UCITS ETF

Consider a UK equity ETF where the total expense ratio is 0.50%, trading costs are 0.23%, and other factors including cash drag, withholding tax differences, rebalancing costs (all captured in tracking difference) amount to 0.18%, for a total of 0.91%. Offsetting this cost is the securities lending revenue of the underlying securities of 0.08% and the ETF lending revenue of 0.78%, so that the total cost of ownership (TCO) is just 0.05% (see figure 5.1).

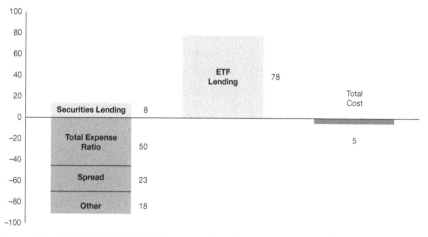

Figure 5.1 FTSE 250 UCITS ETF cost and lending components in basis points.
SOURCE: Author's estimates based on representative data (Net Unit Lending revenues
are for the year ending August 19, 2013).

5.5. CHAPTER SUMMARY

One of the most misunderstood elements of ETF investing is measuring performance and cost. Many investors are puzzled and concerned about seemingly
large tracking errors relative to the benchmark index. There is also confusion
about tracking error versus tracking difference (i.e., the slippage over time from
the benchmark's return). Indexes are not investable, and some tracking error is
inevitable. In other cases, tracking error really reflects the fact that the index is
stale because the pricing of its constituents is not current, as with an international
stock fund.

A little understood element is how ETF managers can affect liquidity, tracking
error, and costs in their funds through optimal design. The choice of the creation
unit size is a key variable, and asset managers will tinker with design through the
life-cycle of the fund to ensure the best balance in these elements.

These concepts also apply when considering the total cost of ownership of an
ETF. As shown here, investors should consider all costs and benefits. The challenge is that some elements are visible while others are harder to discern. Investors
should offset visible expense ratios and transaction costs against less visible securities lending revenues. This can make a material difference in the estimated costs
of investing and hence in the choice of investment vehicle.

Liquidity and Transaction Costs

6.1. INTRODUCTION

To be an ETF investor requires you to make a trade. Unlike open-ended mutual funds, but like closed-end mutual funds, transactions can occur on the exchange throughout the trading day so that purchases/sales of ETFs do not necessarily require investors to interact directly with the fund. So to understand ETF investing, one needs to understand how ETFs are traded and how liquidity is accessed.

This chapter provides an overview of these issues. The key point to take away is that investors can access ETFs in two markets: the primary market via creations and redemptions through APs, and the secondary market on exchanges that list ETFs (e.g., NYSE Arca), dark pools, and alternative trading venues. The practical implication of this is that ETF investors always have an additional layer of liquidity beyond just buying the underlying basket directly.

6.2. PRIMARY AND SECONDARY MARKETS

6.2.1. Defining Liquidity

A source of persistent confusion is the size of primary and secondary market liquidity, which in turn feeds into concerns about run risk or the inability of funds to meet redemptions. Unlike a mutual fund, ETF investors can access the secondary market where liquidity is provided by market makers and other investors. ETF practitioners use terms like primary market or underlying/basket market quite interchangeably, but distinguish these markets from the so-called secondary markets. There are two liquidity concepts that need to be considered:

- **Secondary market liquidity**—This refers to organized exchanges and electronic markets where investors can buy or sell ETFs and other securities, interacting with other investors or professional market makers. Secondary market has two layers: So called *displayed* or "on screen" liquidity is refers to the visible liquidity (market depth) at the prevailing quotes. Beyond visible liquidity is a hidden layer of *non-displayed* or *reserve* liquidity that lies in limit orders and reserve ("iceberg") orders away from the quoted bid or offer prices.

- **Primary market liquidity**—This is the market where an ETF's underlying basket of securities like stocks or bonds can be exchanged for ETF shares, or vice versa through AP creations and redemptions. The primary market is always equivalent to the liquidity of the underlying basket. For this reason, even if there is little additional secondary market liquidity, ETFs liquidity is *at least as great* as that of the underlying assets.

While ETFs trade intraday on organized exchanges as equities, the unique creation-redemption arbitrage mechanism links liquidity in the primary and secondary markets. The arbitrage mechanism allows the market to adjust the supply of available shares through primary market transactions in the underlying assets beyond the visible secondary market. This additional element of liquidity means that trading costs of ETFs are determined by the *lower bound* of execution costs in either the secondary or primary markets. Should APs or market makers back away, the ETF wrapper can always be "unzipped" to give the investor the underlying securities. No investor is worse off than holding the underlying basket.

6.2.2. Relative Size

A common misunderstanding is the size of creation/redemption activity relative to the total. Based on industry-wide data, Antoniewicz and Heinrichs (2014) show that secondary market liquidity is typically a multiple of primary market liquidity. In other words, most ETF investors, in contrast to open-ended mutual fund investors, do not interact with the ETF manager directly because their investments (or divestments) do not create transactions in the underlying securities. Rather, ETF investors, on average, trade with other investors on the exchange or via the temporal intermediation of market makers.

Antoniewicz and Heinrichs (2014) compute the total daily ratio of primary market activity to total (primary and secondary market) trading and relative to previous month-end total net assets. Their study examines daily creations and redemptions for all ETFs from January 3, 2013, to June 30, 2014. Daily creations and redemptions are estimated for each ETF by multiplying the daily change in the shares outstanding by the daily NAV. Aggregate daily creations and redemptions are computed by adding creations and the absolute value of redemptions across all ETFs for each day.

Grouping ETFs by broad asset classes (equity, bond, domestic, international) and by narrower asset classes (such as large-cap equity, small-cap equity, emerging markets equity, domestic high-yield bond, and emerging markets bond), they find that average daily aggregate creations and redemptions for all ETFs are a

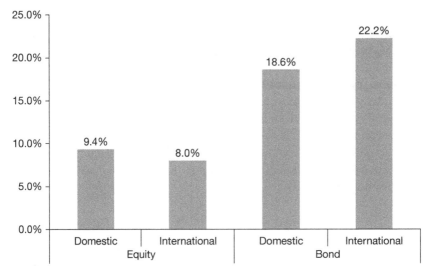

Figure 6.1 Ratio of primary to total trading volume.
SOURCE: Based on Antoniewicz and Heinrichs (2014), ICI, Washington, DC.

fraction (9%) of their total primary and secondary market trading and involve less than 0.5% of aggregate ETF total net assets (figure 6.1).

Of course, there is variation from day to day, with aggregate daily creations and redemptions relative to their total trading ranging from 4% to 25%; relative to total net assets, this activity ranges from 0.16% to 1.40%. Interestingly, the great majority of ETFs have zero primary market activity on any one day. Further, ETF creations and redemptions in aggregate are substantially less than total primary and secondary market trading across the various asset classes on a daily basis, about one-tenth of the average daily value of trading in the secondary market. Daily aggregate creations and redemptions of equity ETFs constitute only 0.36% of their total net assets, on average. For small-cap equity ETFs, aggregate daily creations and redemptions were 9% of their total trading and 0.62% of their total net assets. For emerging markets equity, aggregate daily creations and redemptions were 6% and 0.25%, respectively. These statistics confirm our idea that most ETF transactions do not "spill over" into transactions in the underlying assets.

The life cycle of funds also sheds light on how the ratio of primary to total grows. At the start of the fund, if there is no liquidity in the secondary market, all the liquidity is primary and the ratio is closer to 1. As time goes on and investors trade the fund on an organized exchange without accessing primary market liquidity, either among themselves or through the temporal intervention of a market maker, the ratio falls. In figure 6.2 I plot the ratio of primary to total volume for two iShares bond ETFs, LQD (investment grade credits) and HYG (high-yield bonds) from inception through the present. The life cycle is evident in the reduction of the ratio as secondary market activity builds over time, reducing the ratio. Secondary market activity for LQD was still a multiple (two to four times) of primary market activity even in the midst of the worst of the crisis period when bond liquidity was completely dried up.

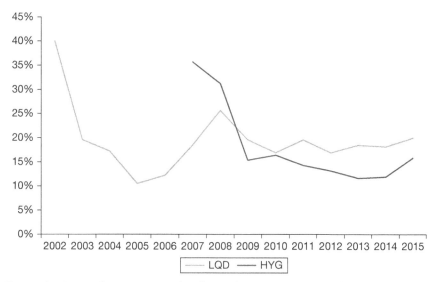

Figure 6.2 Ratio of primary to total trading volume since inception for iShares Investment Grade and High-Yield Bond ETFs (LQD and HYG).
SOURCE: Bloomberg.

6.3. WHY TRADING COSTS ARE LOWER FOR ETFS THAN THEIR UNDERLYING SECURITIES

The popular press often refers to the "financial alchemy" of ETFs in terms of liquidity creation. The premise is often that ETFs offer an illusion of being more liquid than their underlying assets.[1] Indeed, ETFs can source liquidity in both primary and secondary markets. If we focus just on secondary market, it is true that the bid-ask spreads of ETFs are frequently well below the corresponding costs of trading the underlying basket securities for both equities and bonds. Why is this the case? Is this additional liquidity illusory?

One explanation may be that broad portfolios are easier for dealers to hedge, lowering their inventory carrying costs. Even in the absence of inventory costs, information asymmetry provides a compelling explanation for why the ETF spreads would be much lower than in the underlying basket securities. The actual transaction price of the ETF is the midquote m_t plus or minus half the (effective) bid-ask spread at the time, denoted c_t, depending on whether flow is buyer- or seller-imitated:

$$p_t = m_t + \left(\frac{c_t}{2}\right)q_t. \tag{6.1}$$

Since quotations are two-sided, it is reasonable in most cases to posit that the midquote reflects expected value, so that $v_t = m_t$. The microstructure error term

---

1. See, e.g., Stephen Foley, "The Alchemy of ETF Liquidity Is an Illusory Promise," *Financial Times*, April 5, 2015.

is then interpreted as $u_t = (\frac{1}{2})q_t$. An exception would be if market makers could anticipate one-sided flow (e.g., during a sell off) and position their quotes accordingly, in which case the shock captures this premium too. The market maker's profit comes from simultaneously buying (selling) the ETF while offsetting or hedging the risk.

For an individual security, in the absence of other costs, the spread arises because order flow is informative and market makers protect themselves against adverse selection. The execution price is the conditional expectation given a purchase or sale: $E\left[v_t \,|\, q_t > 0\right] = m_t - (\frac{c_t}{2})q$. In a portfolio context, the conditional expectation given a broad index portfolio is being traded would weight only the common factor information component of flow, and hence much lower spreads. It is for this reason—access to the underlying exposure at substantially reduced cost to acquiring that exposure directly—that ETFs holding relatively less liquid portfolio securities often offer a compelling benefit to shareholders. Figure 6.3 shows that the average time-weighted bid-ask spread (in basis points) for five equity ETFs with quite different exposures. Spreads at the fund level are significantly lower than the average spreads of the underlying securities, illustrating how ETFs can provide low-cost access to less liquid markets. This differential is especially evident for international funds where domestic market liquidity remains a significant challenge and for fixed income funds.

For bond funds, where the opaque and over-the-counter nature of the underlying market (see, e.g., Hendershott and Madhavan 2015) can result in wide spreads, the differences in spreads between the underlying bonds and the fund are even more dramatic. As an aside, large spreads in the underlying bonds often mean that the convention of pricing NAV for bond funds using the bid price results in a positive premium.

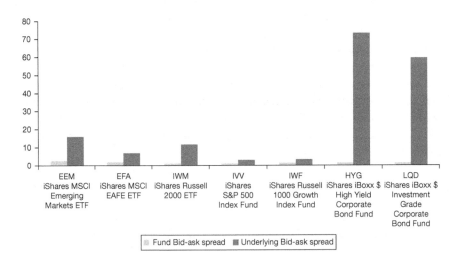

Figure 6.3 Bid-ask spreads of select ETFs and underlying baskets, in basis points.
SOURCE: Bloomberg and TRACE data, for 20 trading days ending May 18, 2015.

6.3.1. Role of Market Transparency

Transparency is an important attribute of market quality with both pre- and post-trade dimensions. Post-trade transparency (that is details of trade prices/times/sizes soon after they occur) matters because reported volumes are used to gauge liquidity. Further, only with actual transaction prices can traders assess correctly whether they are trading at fair prices from dealers. Think of buying a used car if details of purchases in similar models were not available. In Europe, for example, ETP transactions are reported voluntarily, so transacted volume is greatly understated. Lack of transparency is compounded by the proliferation of different tickers for the same security (e.g., the iShares FTSE 100 fund has 16 tickers) and multiple currencies, making the aggregation of trading data even more complex. By contrast, in the United States, all ETP trades are required to be reported so volume is accurately represented, at least on an *ex post* basis.

Pre-trade transparency, in terms of visible liquidity (so-called "on screen" depth at the prevailing bid or ask prices) can also be misleading. In general, ETP liquidity is multilayered, and so-called "on screen" liquidity or depth is just one element of secondary market liquidity, the tip of the iceberg. Indeed, market makers publicly display only a fraction of their true willingness to provide liquidity. Bid-ask spreads can overstate costs because dealers in thinly traded securities quote wide markets to prevent adverse selection. In over-the-counter markets, like those for corporate or municipal bonds, dealers will negotiate bilaterally versus competing on screen for flow, meaning quoted spreads over state costs.

6.3.2. Modeling Costs

The expected costs of trading an ETF are based on tapping both primary and secondary market liquidity. Suppose, as above, the price of the ETF depends on trade size in the secondary market. Define the price impact cost as the deviation of the average execution price from the prevailing price at the time of the order (intrinsic value or midquote if available), and model this as a linear function. Then, the expected price impact cost in the secondary market is:

$$E[p_t] - m_t = \lambda_s q_t. \tag{6.2}$$

If market makers offer limited liquidity in the secondary market, a large order will exhaust the limit order book, resulting in substantial price impact.

The alternative is to have the AP buy the basket of securities in the primary market and deliver them (for a fee F) to the asset manager in exchange for the ETF. The costs of doing this trade for a single stock is, assuming trade size is greater than a creation unit:

$$E[p_{i,t}] - m_{i,t} = \lambda_i w_i q_t. \tag{6.3}$$

Since the investor will choose the cheapest method, the actual ETF cost is the minimum of the two functions.

$$E[C_t] = \min\left[\lambda_s q_t, F + \sum_i \lambda_i w q_t\right].\qquad(6.4)$$

ETFs typically trade within a no arbitrage zone between the underlying bid and ask prices plus the explicit costs of creation and exchange fees.

Consider a real-world example. An institution such as a pension fund or university endowment seeking to trade in a high-yield bond fund will typically call the capital markets team at the asset manager. These teams can use their analytical tools (essentially the cost functions described above) to recommend a venue (primary or secondary), provide guidance as to execution costs, and recommend a trading strategy. Very often extremely large trades (relative to displayed liquidity) can be executed close to the prevailing quotations by appropriately sourcing liquidity. As noted earlier, explicit costs are economically trivial for the most part (e.g., $500 for a creation with a minimum unit size of 100,000 shares or about $9 million) so the bounds are largely determined by the spread and market impact in the underlying markets. If the investor were trading $150 million in the secondary market, a typical estimate would be about 17 basis points (0.17%) of implicit trading costs (spread and impact). Compare this with half the typical spreads of the underlying bonds or 37 basis points (Hendershott and Madhavan 2015) plus the *de minimus* creation fees in the primary market.

An illustration of the upper arbitrage bound (the lower bound is symmetric) is provided in figure 6.4. Normally, the ETF will trade in the zone (Region A) between the bid and ask prices in the secondary market. If liquidity pressures result in the ETF trading in Region B, above the intrinsic ask price but below the upper arbitrage bound, it is still cheaper to buy the ETF than the underlying basket so no arbitrage opportunity exists. But if the ETF bid price is above the upper arbitrage bound (Region C) at any point during the day, a market maker can: (1) sell the ETF shares and buy the underlying basket, incurring transaction costs in the primary market; and (2) at 4:00 p.m. the same day, deliver the basket of securities (paying applicable creation costs) in return for the ETF shares, keeping the difference.

Region C: *Arbitrage Opportunity Exists if ETF Trades Above Upper Bound*	
Upper Arbitrage Bound	*+ Exchange Fees*
	+ Creation Costs
	+ Market Impact of Purchasing underlying assets
Region B: *Execution Outsides ETF Quote but Cheaper than Underlying Basket*	*+ Half bid-ask spread of underlying assets*
Region A: *Intrinsic Value + half bid-ask spread of ETF*	

Figure 6.4 Illustration of arbitrage bounds.

EXAMPLE: DETERMINING THE ARBITRAGE BOUND FOR RUSSIAN ETFs

Consider an ETF holding Russian stocks in mid-2015. Creation/redemption costs are approximately 0.15%, and the average bid-ask of the underlying basket of Global Depository Rights trading on the London Stock Exchange is about 0.50%. So the arbitrage bound for dealers around a fund's intrinsic value (based on the bid-ask of the underlying assets plus creation/redemption fees) is 0.80%. In reality, funds like this trade at bid-ask spreads well inside the arbitrage bound.

An alternative to buying the underlying basket is to buy a derivative or correlated asset, and possibly trade that instrument the next day for the basket, and capture the profit. Either way, arbitragers will act upon any price variance above the arbitrage upper or lower bounds, by thereby keeping the ETF price closely in line with intrinsic value. The bottom line: ETF investors typically will transact at a better price than they could otherwise by buying or selling the underlying basket.

The additional buffer of liquidity offered by the secondary market is shown in table 6.1 for the top 10 bond funds as of June 30, 2015. The data (sourced from

Table 6.1 SECONDARY MARKET VOLUME RELATIVE TO PRIMARY MARKET VOLUMES FOR TOP 10 BOND FUNDS

Fund Name	Ticker	AUM ($ billion)	Secondary Volume ($ millions)	Secondary/ Primary ratio
Vanguard Total Bond Market	BND	26.9	224.4	3.2
iShares Core US Aggregate	AGG	24.9	226.5	6.1
iShares iBoxx Investment Grade Corporate Bond	LQD	21.1	331.3	3.9
Vanguard Short-Term Bond ETF	BSV	16.3	95.3	6.0
iShares TIPs Bond ETF	TIP	13.8	75.4	4.6
iShares iBoxx High Yield Corporate Bond ETF	HYG	13.4	594.1	4.8
iShares 1–3 Year Credit Bond Fund	CSJ	11.0	49.0	2.1
Vanguard Short-Term Corporate Bond ETF	VCSH	10.3	60.2	4.8
SPDR Barclays High Yield Bond Fund	JNK	9.7	292.8	3.3
iShares 1-3 year Treasury Bond Fund	SHY	9.0	98.4	2.8

SOURCE: Bloomberg, January 1, 2015, to June 30, 2015.

Bloomberg) covers January 1, 2015, to June 30, 2015, and shows the AUM of the fund in dollars billion, secondary market volume in millions of dollars, and the ratio of secondary to primary volumes.

6.4. CHAPTER SUMMARY

ETF investors need to understand the sources of liquidity in both primary and secondary markets. Since investors always have the option of buying (or selling) the underlying assets in the primary markets and then either creating or redeeming the ETF, the fund itself cannot be less liquid than its underlying assets. This chapter also explains why ETF transaction costs are usually small relative to the trading costs of the constituent securities. This phenomenon has been termed "financial alchemy" and likened to the repackaging of risk in collateralized debt obligations that managed to lower the perception of volatility. Is there a similar, inherent problem if the liquidity of a fund is much greater than that of its constituents? I argue here that the analogy is flawed: Liquidity is indeed higher at the fund level than at the average security level. Why? Both asymmetric information and inventory risk factors explain the dramatic differences in the costs of ETFs versus the individual basket securities. The portfolio is easier to hedge, bringing down market maker costs and hence spreads. Further, it is quite unlikely that any informed trader with private information will trade a portfolio versus the actual security or option on that asset.

Transaction costs are most important to institutional traders who are trading large blocks. Unlike a typical retail trader whose trades are likely to execute at or within the national best bid or offer quotes, these investors need to determine an optimal trading strategy to minimize their transaction costs. Optimal selection of venue is the key to predicting trading costs. Fortunately, many institutions now have access to capital market desks that have at their disposal a variety of tools to help in venue selection, trading strategy, pre-trade transaction cost forecasting, and *ex post* cost analysis.

PART III

Applications

Uses of ETFs

7.1. INTRODUCTION

Investors of various types—traders, retail investors, and institutions—use ETFs for a variety of purposes. The use of ETFs has gone from simple index tracking to more complex investment strategies, including those aimed at achieving specific outcomes targeting a particular strategy or exposure. Growing diversity in ETFs has increased adoption across the board. Entirely new categories of investors such as insurance companies and pension funds that previously would not consider an ETF (often for regulatory reasons, e.g., like an insurance company that was precluded from holding a bond ETF because it was classified as an equity instrument) are now active users. To best understand the popularity of ETFs, it is useful to consider some specific examples. These are amplified later on in the book.

7.2. CORE AND FACTOR EXPOSURES

7.2.1. Individual Investors

For individual investors, ETFs provide the versatility to build a core long-term portfolio with broad asset class exposures including equity, fixed income, and commodities. Many commentators focus on the feature of intraday trading as the primary distinguishing feature of ETFs against alternative vehicles such as mutual funds, so it is natural that many buy and hold investors do not think about ETFs as a core position. But ETFs offer significant tax advantages and are generally much cheaper than active mutual funds. The ability for intraday trading, while useful, is actually one of the less important advantages of ETFs for individual investors.

Individuals can also use ETFs to implement specific goals or outcomes. For example, a client may seek a particular yield or income using bond ETFs and dividend yield funds. Clients may target exposures to reflect tactical opinions (e.g., investing in currency hedged international equity funds to protect against rises in the US dollar against the foreign currency) or express views based on sectors, regions, countries, and so on (such as over-weighting Chile for exposure to copper).

More recently, individual investors may easily access ETFs through model portfolios where portfolio composition and rebalancing is automated through the selection of a single ticker. Retail investors may also use ETFs for portfolio completion. For example, an investor who moves from New York to California may buy a California Municipal Bond fund to add exposure to this asset class quickly and in a diversified manner.

7.2.2. Factor Exposures

Core portfolios are traditionally expressed as a mix of asset classes, as shown in the upper panel of figure 7.1. An equivalent way to represent the same portfolio is as a collection of factor exposures, as shown in the lower panel of the schematic. These factors (e.g., to value, momentum, etc.) typically span asset classes. While individual investors are only now beginning to appreciate a factor-based view of the world, institutions are actively embracing this approach as documented in Ang (2014). Institutions are also leading the way in the use of ETFs for diverse purposes, as discussed in the following section.

Figure 7.1 Core exposures and factor views of a portfolio.

7.3. INSTITUTIONAL USES

Institutions are increasingly using ETF to accomplish a variety of sophisticated objectives that go well beyond core investing. These include, among others:

- **Cash management**—Excess cash may be invested in short-term, highly rated bond ETFs that provide a yield above that of demand deposits, while offering intraday liquidity.
- **Portfolio completion strategies**—Fundamental managers who build "bottoms up" positions may use ETFs to correct unintended over- or under-weight positions in certain sectors/geographies. Similarly, bond funds may be used for credit/duration matching.
- **Transitions**—Portfolio transition management refers to the process by which institutional portfolios are reallocated efficiently to control risk and cost. For example, suppose a pension fund terminates an underperforming emerging markets manager and elects to move assets to another active manager in the same space. To control cost and risk, the pension fund hires a professional transition manager to handle this reallocation from the legacy to the target portfolio. Since that process may take time, the transition manager may gain short-term exposure to emerging markets using ETFs.
- **Efficient, low-cost shorting**—A long-short hedge fund, for example, may hedge its long positions in energy companies by shorting an ETF on that sector, mitigating the risk of a sudden jump in the price of any shorted stock due to, say, a takeover.
- **Hedging and tactical trading**—Cheap, diversified trades that can be quickly implemented are ideal for hedging positions, market timing, or placing tactical bets. For example, a manager who seeks an over-weight on Korea but does not have a currency view on the Korean Won may buy a currency hedged Korea ETF.

Transition Management Case

Let's consider a portfolio transition management example, based on an actual case. A client, a large US retirement system, had positions in approximately 2,000 individual corporate bonds representing $1.6 billion in value. The client wanted to reallocate between equities and fixed income, but faced significant challenges in selling the individual bond positions. The client approached a transition manager to help facilitate the switch between asset classes. The manager using an optimization engine and a fixed income risk model found the optimal combination of bonds that could be added to the manager's ETFs that would reduce tracking error and maximize the amount in-kinded at NAV. The result was a win-win situation: About $1.1 billion of the client's individual bond positions were in-kinded into liquid ETFs with no transaction costs, improving the client's liquidity and diversification at the same time. The asset manager's funds also benefited: Only those bonds that reduced *ex ante* tracking error were added to portfolios. Given the complexity of the solution, which involved permutations of all possible combinations of the 2,000 positions, it could not have been done without the needed analytics, in this case the optimizer and risk model.

7.4. FUTURES, SWAPS, AND ETFS

One of the more interesting recent developments is the growth in ETFs relative to derivative-based exposure vehicles. Futures, swaps, and ETFs are all vehicles for index exposure, but offer different trade-offs. Index futures and ETFs are used for a variety of investment purposes including to:

- Invest excess cash;
- Hedge exposures;
- Shift synthetic exposure rapidly; and
- Implement long-term strategic risk allocation.

ETFs resemble financial futures contracts in that they allow investors to obtain long or short exposure to market indices quickly, but are not derivatives as noted earlier. There are also important economic and operational differences though between various exposure vehicles. These include:

- Futures are unfunded instruments, which only require posting of a fraction of the investment notional (the so-called *margin*) with a clearing broker; whereas, ETFs are typically not leveraged. The futures margin can generate returns, as does the non-margin portion.
- Futures have a fixed term, usually one month (e.g., emerging markets) or three months. This means that long buy-and-hold investors that want to hold the position beyond such time horizons will have to liquidate any futures contracts approaching expiry and purchase new contracts with the cash proceeds (the so-called *roll of futures*). Unlike futures, ETFs do not expire and therefore can be held for long periods at significantly lower cost than futures.
- There are liquid markets in a variety of ETFs for which there is no equivalent liquid futures contract such as investment grade corporate bonds. Futures markets are highly liquid though with very tight spreads.
- ETFs can be bought and sold through a securities account at a broker, and do not require the establishment of a futures trading account. Futures in foreign markets require foreign exchange (FX) management to ensure that the investor handles any differences between his/her base currency and that of the futures' exposure.

In summary, the benefits of futures include, among others: an efficient usage of capital, liquidity, and transparency. Swaps are another popular alternative (as well as index funds, segregated mandates, certificates, or basket trades) to gain index exposure. Swaps are designed to pay the total return on specified indices (e.g., Markit iBoxx) and are especially popular ways to gain synthetic fixed income exposure.[1] Unlike futures and ETFs, swaps typically negotiated with a broker-dealer and their pricing is opaque. Most swaps are subject to counterparty risk.

In contrast to futures, ETFs are fully funded instruments meaning that they are not used for leverage and investors have invested the full amount of the desired exposure. Typically, ETFs do not have a maturity date (some new bond ETFs that repay principal at a specified date are an exception) and they can thus be held indefinitely. They are traded intraday like a common stock and can be lent out to generate additional fees. The benefits of ETF include: (a) a significantly larger opportunity set than futures with over 5,100 products[2] globally, (b) operational simplicity linked to the absence of rolling and with no need to manage the foreign exchange component, (c) the absence of counterparty risk,[3] and (d) full transparency of the holdings within the ETF.[4]

The increased adoption of ETFs by institutional investors, tighter trading spreads, increased liquidity, a greater diversity of exposures, and lower fees mean they are increasingly seen as a viable alternative to fully funded (meaning the portion of the investment notional that is not used for future margin is invested in money market instruments as opposed to using the contracts to gain leverage) futures positions. At the same time, the costs of maintaining market exposure using derivatives such as futures and swaps have increased for institutional investors, driven by long-run factors such as higher bank funding costs, reduced dealer balance sheets, and regulation that increased capital requirements. For fully funded investors seeking to gain an unleveraged exposure to an equity benchmark, these ETF tailwinds and futures headwinds have profound consequences.

IMPACT OF REGULATORY INITIATIVES

The impacts of financial regulatory reform on banks' cost of capital are subtle, but will become increasingly relevant as the rules take effect. For example, Basel III requires banks to increase equity to 7% of their risk-bearing assets by 2019, with global banks required to hold an additional 2.5%. The Volcker Rule, which was enacted as part of the Dodd-Frank Act, limits proprietary trading, including provision of liquidity during futures rolls. The "Liikanen" and "Vickers" reforms in

1. Credit Default Swaps (CDS/CDX) are liquid and actively traded credit products allowing investors to access credit spread exposure. Given the derivative nature of CDS/CDX, significant differences in performance versus cash bonds can arise for sustained periods of time.

2. As of March 2014. Source: BlackRock, ETP Landscape.

3. This is the case for physically replicated ETFs that do not engage in securities lending, but not for swap-based products or debt instruments such as ETNs.

4. ETFs holdings are usually published on a daily basis by ETF providers, and fully accessible to investors via providers' websites.

the European Union and United Kingdom, respectively, have similar policy goals as Volcker. In aggregate, these measures are likely to constrain banks' ability to hold inventory on balance sheets.

A quantification of the trade-offs between the two beta solutions requires an understanding of their true costs/benefits and pricing. Trade-offs change dynamically with market conditions (e.g., securities lending revenues, dividend yields, roll costs) and investor objectives (turnover, tracking error). While ETF pricing reflects the value of the underlying basket plus a transitory premium or discount, as described in section 3.2, futures pricing is more complex.

The cost of buying and carrying a portfolio of underlying securities in the index is the "cost of carry," which measures the difference between spot S_t and futures prices over the interval $F_{t,T}$ as a function of the financing rate r less the dividend rate or yield, d. The futures price (in this case also the forward price) is:

$$F_{t,T} = S_t e^{(r-d)(T-t)}. \tag{7.1}$$

Consider a fixed income example: Say the current spot price of a treasury security is $S_t = \$100$ and its yield is $d = 3\%$ (that is continuously compounded). Say the price of a one-year futures contract on the security is $F_{t,T} = \$98.25$, where $(T-t) = 1$. The interest rate implicit in this valuation is $\ln(98.25 / 100) + 0.03 = 0.0123$. So the contract is fairly priced for an investor with a financing rate of 1.23%. But when the investor rolls the position, the cost of maintaining the exposure, as implied by futures prices, may deviate from "fair value."

Equation (7.1) provides insight into the costs of "rolling" a futures position from the near $F_{t,T}$ to the k-period far contract $F_{t+k,T+k}$ to maintain the exposure over the required time frame. Specifically, we use the futures price model above to compare the "fair value" (the true economic cost, based on the investor's own financing rate $\hat{r}$ and an estimate of yield d) of a futures contract to the trading price of a futures contract to determine roll "cheapness" or "richness."

Futures can trade "rich" or "cheap" to fair value when futures curves are in either contango or backwardation. Contango refers to a state where futures (or forward) prices exceed spot prices, while backwardation is the opposite condition. Roll costs are not solely dependent on the term structure of the futures curve but also reflect liquidity pressures or one-sided markets. In particular, there is evidence that long investors roll exposures at roughly the same time, causing departures from fair value.

CASE STUDY: E-MINI S&P 500

By way of example, consider the choice between gaining exposure to the S&P 500 index using an ETF versus E-Mini S&P 500 index futures over a one-year holding horizon for a fully funded position of US$20 million. The futures roll was at the time trading rich relative to fair value (based on three-month USD Libor) for the *sixth* consecutive quarter. With three-month Libor at 26 basis points, the implied funding rate leads to a substantial difference of costs in favor of the ETF. Assuming an annual management fee of 7 basis points in an S&P 500 ETF, the cost differentials for the ETF versus the futures is 8.1 versus 43.5 basis points. Remarkably, in this particular instance, ETFs would have also been cheaper to hold for just a week, albeit with a narrower differential in costs of 2.3 versus 3.7 basis points.

The fact that ETFs are lower cost vehicles than futures, even in a highly liquid market, may come as a surprise to many readers, but the question naturally arises as to whether this is true in other markets, and if so, what factors have been driving this shift. Madhavan, Marchioni, Li, and Du (2014) examine this question and report average annualized roll mispricing (in basis points) for a variety of

Table 7.1 AVERAGE ANNUALIZED ROLL MISPRICING (IN BPS)

Region	Contract	Last Year (2013)	Last 2 Years	Last 5 Years	Full Sample
Americas	S&P 500	41.1	22.4	8.7	5.8
	Russell 2000	−27.6	−58.1	−72.5	−61.4
	Russell 1000	46.4	26.1	12.7	1.4
	Dow Jones Ind. Avg.	54.6	36.2	13.2	−4.1
	S&P MidCap	30.7	9.7	−5.0	−8.9
	NASDAQ-100	46.6	30.0	1.8	−25.2
	S&P/TSX 60	−22.6	−32.9	−35.9	−35.2
Europe	EURO STOXX 50	61.1	34.5	−2.7	1.7
	FTSE 100	52.5	38.1	26.2	2.0
	DAX-30	34.0	14.9	−16.6	−8.6
	CAC-40	29.3	17.0	−13.7	−17.8
	IBEX-35	21.4	17.4	17.5	2.6
	S&PMIB	76.6	50.6	−2.9	5.6
	OMX	8.2	5.8	3.7	11.6
	SMI	66.5	60.6	41.9	24.1
Asia	TOPIX	67.1	29.6	−6.6	−22.1
	Nikkei 225	56.2	41.7	29.8	15.4
	KOSPI 200	43.2	13.0	−75.3	−241.3
	S&P ASX 200	20.9	6.7	23.4	−34.9
	MSCI Taiwan	−183.8	−205.9	−271.6	−200.5

(continued)

Table 7.1 (CONTINUED)

Region	Contract	Last Year (2013)	Last 2 Years	Last 5 Years	Full Sample
	Hang Seng	82.2	70.4	19.2	−69.7
	Hang Seng China Enterprise	116.7	112.6	42.5	−44.4
	MSCI Singapore	32.9	57.5	36.2	62.6
	SGX Nifty	34.0	29.9	−87.5	−414.6

SOURCE: Madhavan, Marchioni, Li, and Du (2014) based on Bank of America Merrill Lynch. For most major contracts, the data span the period from June 1996 to December 2013.

Table 7.2 KEY ELEMENTS OF RETURN DIFFERENTIALS IN BETA EXPOSURE VEHICLES

Return Sources	ETFs	Futures
Benchmark return	+ Underlying basket return	+ Index return
Dividends	+ Actual dividends	+ Forecasted dividends
Securities lending	+ Sec lending income	
Financing rate		− Forecasted financing rate
Cash yield		+ Actual cash yield
Management fees	− Management fees	
Transaction costs	− Transaction costs (round-trip)	− Transaction costs (round-trip) − Cost of futures roll − Cost of cash management
Price movements	+ Change in ETF premium	

markets. It is clear from table 7.1 that roll costs are generally higher currently than they were in the past.

The S&P 500 future, for example, has roll costs of 41.1 basis points versus a full sample estimate of 5.8 basis points. Interestingly, roll costs have increased significantly in recent times as the impact of regulation and the crisis led to a withdrawal in capital commitment by banks and hence less liquidity provision overall for long rollers.

In practice there are many different return drivers shown in table 7.2 which may lead to performance differentials between ETFs and futures including:

- **Cost of carry drivers**—Implied financing rate of equity exposure, dividends/income, return on cash invested from lack of futures capital commitment, management fees; and

- **Implementation cost**—Transaction costs from executing ETF position or rolling/maintaining continuous futures position.

Morillo et al. (2012) note that in the period June 2000 to September 2011, an ETF implementation averaged –2 basis points per quarter of slippage against the S&P 500 index versus –13 basis points with fully funded futures contracts.

7.5. CHAPTER SUMMARY

ETFs have many diverse uses for retail or institutional investors. These range from core asset allocation or more traditional "style-box" type holdings. Factor-based investing will be examined in greater detail later on in the book, but offers a different way to represent exposures to stocks, bonds, or other assets. Investors also use ETFs for more tactical bets where they seek precision exposures to certain countries, regions, sectors, industries, and so on.

Institutions are also adopting ETFs for a variety of purposes including cash management, as a liquidity sleeve, in portfolio transitions, and so on. One of the more interesting recent developments is the use of ETFs to gain "Delta One" exposure as a contrast to fully funded futures contracts. In industry slang, the term "Delta One" is used to refer to instruments that offer 1:1 exposure to the returns of the underlying. So, leveraged funds and other instruments that have embedded options (e.g., floors and ceilings) are not Delta One products.

Fixed Income

8.1. A GROWTH STORY

One of the most interesting developments in recent years is the explosive growth in fixed income ETFs and assets under management. Assets in fixed income ETFs rose 900% and the number of funds was up 326% from 2009 to 2014, crossing the $500 billion mark in October 2015.[1] Fixed income ETFs are portfolios of cash bonds increasingly used by institutional and retail investors to gain quick exposure to broad segments of the fixed income markets including high yield, credits, municipals, treasuries, mortgages, and so on. Passive investing has its roots in equities where market capitalization weighting schemes are generally widely accepted, markets are liquid, and there are organized exchanges offering accurate, contemporaneous pricing. The extension of passive investing through ETFs to fixed income, however, has been somewhat uneasy because market capitalization weighting is not widely accepted and liquidity is a challenge.

Growing acceptance of ETFs comes in part from bond market liquidity challenges since the 2008–2009 crisis. Regulations imposed post-crisis have raised the costs for dealers to make markets or carry inventory, leading to declines in trade volume and average trade size. At the same time, low interest rates have led to record issuance, with dozens or even hundreds of unique securities issued by the same entity. There are over 1.5 million different municipal bonds alone as of 2015. The result is a lower fraction of outstanding bonds that dealers can trade on a principal basis. These liquidity challenges have led to calls for the modernization of fixed income markets through standardization of issuance and a move away from dealer-based markets to automated, transparent, electronic venues.

In many ways, fixed income ETFs offer such a vision of the future. They are traded on electronic markets with firm and actionable quotations that are displayed continuously. Bond ETFs provide a way for investors to achieve diversification in a single trade at a fraction of the cost of trading the underlying bonds. On a global basis though, fixed income market penetration is still very low. Although

1. Based on estimates by the Tabb Group.

equity ETFs are about 3% of the equity market, bond ETFs are just 0.4% of the global market.[2] In some segments, such as US treasury bonds and corporate bonds, ETFs only represent 0.5% and 1.7%, respectively, of holdings today. These figures suggest plenty of room for further growth, especially as the fixed income markets evolve and automate, as did equity markets decades ago.

This chapter covers the basics of fixed income exposure, beginning with the key question of how to define the universe and a sensible index methodology. We then turn to uses of fixed income ETFs, the growth of usage being closely linked to the liquidity and market structure challenges inherent in this asset class. We explore the impact of the over-the-counter structure for trading costs and transparency, and highlight the opportunity for electronic trading to grow. An important theme is the idea that ETFs—with their low cost, transparency, and equity-like trading—can lead the way for the underlying markets.

8.2. FIXED INCOME BASICS

8.2.1. Does Market Capitalization Weighting Make Sense?

The immediate challenge for passive investment in fixed income is to develop sensible weighting schemes. Market capitalization indexes are well accepted in equities for reasons discussed earlier. Stock prices embody forward-looking views of valuation, markets are transparent and liquidity in larger market capitalization (higher weight) stocks is not a problem. In fixed income, however, market cap weighting is not a natural concept and faces skepticism. Some of the resistance derives from concerns that cap weighting implies concentrated exposure to the countries or firms that have issued the most debt. For bonds, unlike equities, the notional amount of outstanding debt reflects past issuance. That should not represent a problem if index weights use the market value of bonds. But in the absence of accurate, contemporaneous bond pricing, a reliance on notional value implies a backward looking element to index construction. Illiquidity can lead to over-weights in securities that are not directly investable.

Bond indexes can be concentrated even when they hold many different issuers. As an example, consider the Barclays Global Treasury Index which represents the sovereign debt of 43 countries. Staal, Corsi, and Woida (2015) note that as of April 2015, just two countries—the United States and Japan—account for 72% of the total *ex ante* volatility risk. Those two countries drive most of the volatility in index returns despite there being 41 other country constituents (figure 8.1).

The argument against cap weighting is not as simple as it sounds: Numerous academic studies have shown that fixed income markets are informationally efficient in that bond prices correctly reflect expectations of discounted cash

---

2. Bank for International Settlements, Strategic Insight Simfund, BlackRock, Bloomberg as of 2014.

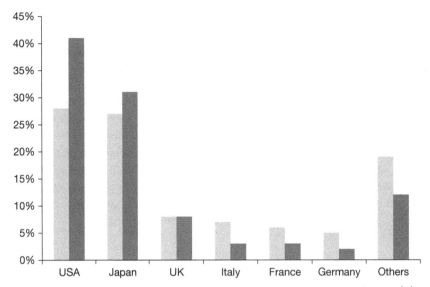

Figure 8.1 Barclays Global Treasury Index country weight and risk contribution (%).
SOURCE: Staal, Corsi, and Woida (2015), based on Barclays Bank, PLC data as of
April 2015.

flows. If this were not the case, then a simple strategy of betting against the
largest issuers would generate alpha. So a bond's price, and hence index weight,
factors in the risk of default. Capitalization weighting in bonds also makes
sense for clients concerned about liquidity because the largest bond issues are
generally the most liquid. It is certainly possible to design a custom bond index
using optimization to maximize liquidity or equivalently minimize transaction costs. As assets grow, however, more bonds must be added to the custom
index for it to remain investable, creating a challenge and reducing the value
of optimization. Hence, market capitalization weighting is still a logical choice
in bonds.

8.2.2. Active Choices in Index Construction

This is not to say that index construction is not an art. Consider the Barclays (for-
merly Lehmann) US Aggregate Index, a widely used US fixed income index that
was designed to capture the returns of the universe of US investable investment
grade bonds. When originally constructed in the 1970s, the index excluded illiquid or inaccessible sub-asset classes such as high-yield debt, preferred securities,
and domestically traded emerging market loans. These are now more liquid but
are not considered part of the benchmark.

The index's weighting scheme currently tilts toward the investable investment
grade fixed income universe, and the weight of US treasuries in the Barclays
Aggregate index has risen from 22.3% in 2004 to 35.8% by 2014, as shown (bottom area) in figure 8.2. The other components include Asset Backed Securities

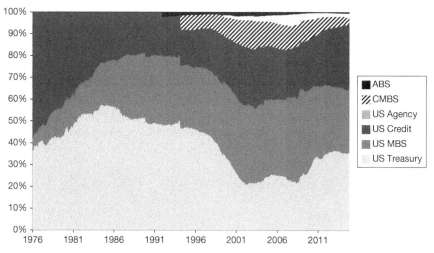

Figure 8.2 Barclays Aggregate Index components, 1976 to 2014.
SOURCE: Staal, Corsi, and Woida (2015), based on Barclays Bank, PLC data as of
April 2015.

(ABS), Commercial Mortgage-backed Securities (CMBS), US Agencies, US
Credit, and US Mortgage-Backed Securities (MBS).

However, the percentage of collateralized mortgage-backed debt (CMBS) in
the index has declined post-crisis, as the largest issuers including the Federal
National Mortgage Association (FNMA) scaled back their business. Increased
weight on treasuries has increased the duration of the index, but the Barclays
Aggregate is actually more diversified than when first incepted.

8.2.3. Defining Exposures

Can one construct a more "modern" index that is more representative of the underlying risk-return characteristics of bonds? That question is considered later on
when we discuss "Smart Beta" or factor-based approaches. Asset managers have
traditionally approached fixed income exposure like equities, with geographic or
sector exposures as their primary focus. An investor might, for example, focus on
investment grade credits, but not on high-yield, or vice versa. More sophisticated
managers are increasingly looking beyond geographies and sectors to the factor exposures implicitly embedded in their portfolios. Beyond geographies (and
therefore currency risk), the bond universe can be divided by risk factors. These
are most importantly credit quality (measured by the yield spread over treasuries) and duration.

Different types of bonds have different exposure to risk factors: For example,
call features are important for credit or asset-backed securities, but not for treasuries. Increasingly, there is interest in creating pure credit or rates exposures by
hedging out the relevant risk to create fixed income factors. For example, pure
credit exposure is obtained by betting on riskier bonds while neutralizing any

interest rate risk using treasury futures. The hedging option is binary—hedged or not hedged—as a partially hedged fund is a redundant security.

As fixed income markets mature, expect more in the way of indexes constructed to better gain diversification and exposure. For example, instead of a traditional index based on issuance, one might have an index that balances exposures to rates and credit risk. These "smart indexes" will typically have less duration than, say, the Barclays Aggregate, but may add yield (and credit risk) through exposure to other, diversifying sub-asset classes such as high-yield or international bonds.

8.3. USERS OF FIXED INCOME PASSIVE PRODUCTS

8.3.1. Bond Buyers

Bond ETFs are about 15% of total US ETP assets covering a wide range of geographical, currency, credit, maturity, and sector exposures. They vary also in assets, liquidity, and in style of management. As low-cost portfolios, they are attractive to a variety of investors. Fixed income ETFs are valuable tools for buyers of individual bonds and buyers of bond funds, as shown in the schematic in figure 8.3.

Buyers of bond ETFs fall into two categories. First, there are investors seeking diversification across fixed income who already invest using mutual funds or ETFs. For these investors, bond ETFs are very much like any other ETFs they may hold in their portfolio. Both passive and active styles of management can be accessed in ETF form. For example, it is not well known that some of the largest bond funds (e.g., MINT or BOND, the PIMCO Enhanced Short Maturity Active Fund) are active funds. Second, there are traditional bond buyers (e.g., retail investors, insurance companies, and pension funds seeking to match their liabilities) who buy individual bonds and hold them to maturity. It is difficult for

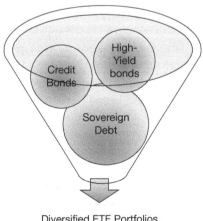

Diversified ETF Portfolios
of Cash Bonds

Figure 8.3 Schematic of ETF bond portfolios.

bond investors—even institutions like small or medium-sized pension funds—to gain portfolio diversification across different sub-asset classes of bonds, such as municipals, sovereign debt, or high-yield bonds at low cost. For traditional bond buyers, ETFs offer many attractive features including one-stop diversification at low cost. Yet, ETFs often pose operational challenges for such investors.

8.3.2. Institutional Uses

Based on a comprehensive survey, Greenwich Associates[3] finds that institutional investors are using bond ETFs for both tactical and strategic uses. Primary institutional uses include gaining passive "core" exposure to fixed income, tactical trades betting on changes in interest rates or credit spreads, and rebalancing between equities and bonds. In addition, many institutional investors use ETFs as a "liquidity sleeve" for managing temporary cash inflow/outflows, and as interim beta while shifting between managers in a portfolio transition. So, for example, an endowment fund that fires an underperforming active bond manager might retain its beta exposure to fixed income by reinvesting its funds into investment grade ETFs while seeking a new manager.

Rapid growth reflects the difficulty in trading individual bonds in any size. The strain on underlying bond market liquidity is evident in declining dealer inventories post-crisis. Reduced inventories are the consequence of higher balance sheet costs for the investment banks that traditionally supplied liquidity, in turn arising from increased regulation. Lower inventories have more of an impact on liquidity because corporations are taking advantage of the low rate environment to increased bond issuance. This is the same dynamic that has led equity ETFs to be more attractive relative to futures for fully funded investors in many situations/markets. Indeed, ETFs offer many benefits over trading individual bonds: one-stop shopping (diversification in a single trade), cheap and easy access, and most of all low trading costs and liquidity.

8.3.3. Barriers to Adoption

Challenges remain though to institutional and retail adoption. General unfamiliarity with ETFs by traditional bond investors who are used to yield conventions versus a dollar price, confused over primary/secondary trading volumes, and unaware of implicit transaction costs that are difficult to measure represent a challenge that can only be overcome over time with education. For retail traders, who are used to buying and holding bonds to maturity to generate income and save for retirement, bond ETFs—although they are simply baskets of individual bonds—are often unfamiliar. The fact that individual bonds mature on a specific date is important for individuals saving for retirement or specific goals such as

3. Greenwich Associates 2014 report "Institutional Investors Turning to Fixed-Income ETFs in Evolving Bond Market" surveyed 110 US institutional managers.

funding college education. Fortunately, the industry is moving rapidly to expand the use of bond ETFs. One recent innovation is an ETF that matures on a specific date, returning its principal to the owner. This is accomplished by buying bonds that mature within a few months of a specific maturity date. The result is a bond ETF that looks more like an ordinary bond but with much greater diversification and liquidity. These bonds are also attractive to insurance companies and pension funds that may want to match asset-liability streams.

For institutions, there are surprising barriers to adoption of bond ETFs versus buying individual bonds arising from regulatory and investment guidelines. Bond ETFs are traded as stocks with equity-like CUSIPs and settlement. Some institutions might not be able to use bond ETFs because they are classified as equities, violating their charter to hold only bonds. Or an insurance company that replaces multiple bond holdings (i.e., many CUSIPs) with a single ETF (i.e., one CUSIP but possibly holding 1,000+ bonds) may violate diversification rules intended by regulators to protect investors from concentrated bets. Internal barriers exist too. Many institutional trading desks are still segmented by asset class, and it is not at all uncommon for equity and fixed income trading desks to be separated physically with minimal interaction. This means that natural buyers of bond ETFs like the fixed income team at a pension or endowment fund might not be able to do so because this is viewed as an equity trade to be handled by the equity desk. More important, traditional tools used by fixed income investors such as yield-to-maturity, yield-to-worst, spread duration, credit rating, and so on are not readily available for ETFs.

Finally, agency considerations impede the broadening of the investor base. For example, active managers are compensated for selecting individual bonds, even if their holdings largely replicate the major characteristics of broad indexes. This means that these managers are being paid in part for providing simple index exposure beta, not for superior security selection or alpha. It is not surprising that these managers would not elect to hold ETFs with significantly lower costs. These barriers to adoption are rapidly being broken down through education, market structure reform, and regulatory changes. The general consensus among market professionals is that the fixed income ETF sector will continue to see rapid growth relative to other asset classes.

8.4. ROLE OF ANALYTICS

Analytics can help in providing needed perspectives for bond ETF buyers allowing them to translate ETFs into more familiar bond terms. For example, a bond buyer who struggles to understand the price of an ETF in dollars might gain a better understanding from seeing the individual bonds being held by the fund, their weights, and relative values. Intrinsic value—as discussed earlier in the book—is important in giving investors confidence that the price they execute at in value terms is reasonable.

Take yield-to-maturity, which is basically the internal rate of return of a bond held to maturity. A simple average of the yield-to-maturities of the individual portfolio of bonds may be misleading because the yield calculation is inherently non-linear. We can solve this problem by defining a cash flow for each year based on the $i = 1, \ldots, n$ bonds held by the fund. At time $t + k$, let $C_{t+k} = \sum_{i=1}^{n} CF_{i,t+k}$ denote the total coupons across all n bonds held by the fund, up to the longest maturity bonds at date $t + T$. Then, the bond ETF yield-to-maturity, for example, is the rate y that equates the price of the bond ETF with future cash flows:

$$ p_t = \frac{C_{t+1}}{1+y} + \frac{C_{t+2}}{(1+y)^2} + \cdots + \frac{C_{t+T}}{(1+y)^T} . \qquad (8.1) $$

This figure can change over time as new bonds are bought by the ETF and others expire or are sold or in-kinded out through the creation/redemption process.

BOND CONVENTIONS AND YIELD-TO-MATURITY

For example, consider a bond ETF that holds two zero coupon riskless bonds with principal $100: Bond A matures in one year and Bond B in two years. Suppose the current prices of the bonds are $90 and $80 each and let's assume the bond ETF is trading at NAV = $90 + $80 = $170. So, the portfolio holds 53% (= $90/ ($90 + $80) of Bond A and 43% Bond B. It is straightforward to show the yield-to-maturities of Bonds A and B are, respectively, 11.11% and 11.80%, so that the weighted average yield of the portfolio is 0.53(11.11%) + 0.47(11.80%) = 11.43%. But this is not the real yield-to-maturity of the bond ETF. With cash flows of $100 in each year, the yield-to-maturity of the fund is $y = 11.55\%$, which is higher than the average yield. Check that this is the solution to:

$$ p_t = \$170 = \frac{\$100}{1+y} + \frac{\$100}{(1+y)^2} $$

We can similarly derive fund statistics such as duration. However, for mortgage funds, these calculations require some care because pre-payment reduces expected cash flows.

So, although they exhibit negative convexity, computations may show positive convexity unless we replace the coupons with expected cash flows factoring in a reasonable pre-payment model. As such models are proprietary; there may be differences across providers in this figure.

A similar problem comes with credit quality. While in theory the default risk of the individual constituent bonds might be straightforward to assess, evaluating portfolio risk is more complex. As with the yield-to-maturity example, the average credit quality of a portfolio of bonds (be it in an index fund or ETF) can be highly misleading. The major rating agencies such as Moody's Investors Service or Standard & Poor's rate bonds individually. The change in rating from say AAA to AA (or from Aaa to Aa2), although a step away in quality, implies an order of magnitude greater risk. Thus, simple averages can be quite misleading.

Hill, Nadig, and Hougan (2015) provide an example of a hypothetical fund of 10 equally weighted bonds. Nine are top rated (AAA by Standard & Poor's or Aaa by Moody's) but one is rated BB+/Ba1. The default probability associated with the top rating is 0.10% while that with the BB+/Ba1 rating is 7.30%. The average rating of the fund corresponds to an AA+/Aa1 rating, still a 0.10% default probability. However, looking at the weighted average probability of default yields:

$$0.9 \times 0.10\% + 0.1 \times 7.3\% = 0.82\%. \tag{8.2}$$

The default probability of 0.82% implies a much worse credit quality equivalent to A-/A3.

8.5. FIXED INCOME MARKET STRUCTURE AND FUTURE OPPORTUNITIES

8.5.1. Over-the-Counter Markets

Central to understanding the challenge and opportunity for bond ETFs is the over-the-counter, dealer-centric nature of fixed income market structure. Over-the-counter (OTC) markets are characterized by off-exchange, bilateral negotiations with dealers. This traditionally telephone- and voice-based market structure dominates trading in many asset classes: foreign exchange, spot commodities, nonstandard derivatives, and corporate and municipal bonds. As shown in figure 8.4, a centralized trading paradigm like an electronic equity market (left panel) operates in contrast to an OTC market (right) where trading is typically intermediated through a small group of dealers at the center.

The $8 trillion corporate bond market is of particular interest because of its size and importance in capital formation. A majority of a firm's capital-raising occurs in OTC traded corporate bonds. Recent regulatory requirements have improved trade reporting, leading to a growing literature providing insights into the magnitude and determinants of fixed income trading costs in OTC markets dominated

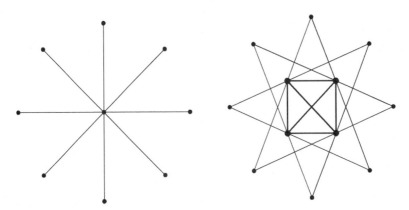

Figure 8.4 Centralized and over-the-counter trading paradigms.

by dealers. This structure makes it inherently very difficult to create portfolio exposure products such as ETFs.

The evidence to date suggests that the relatively large transactions costs facing investors stem from the OTC structure of the bond market and the proliferation of nonstandardized financial instruments. Unlike equities, where there may be only one share class of a particular stock there may be multiple bonds by the same issuer with different coupons, maturities, and call features. For example, General Electric has 905 different bond issues as of 2015 but only one US-listed common stock (GE), based on data from Bloomberg.

8.5.2. Bond Market Liquidity and Transaction Costs

Edwards, Harris, and Piwowar (2007) and Goldstein, Hotchkiss, and Sirri (2007) document large transactions costs in corporate bonds. Contrary to theories based on asymmetric information or inventory control, costs are higher for smaller trades. Harris and Piwowar (2006) find, for example, that municipal bond trades are significantly more expensive than equivalent-sized equity trades, which is surprising given that bonds are lower risk securities. One explanation may be the lack of pre-trade transparency that confers rents to dealers in bilateral trading situations. Green, Hollifield, and Schürhoff (2007) develop and estimate a structural model of bargaining between dealers and customers and conclude that dealers exercise substantial market power. Bessembinder, Maxwell, and Venkataraman (2007) argue that improvements in post-trade transparency associated with the implementation of the TRACE system provides market participants with better indications of true market value, allowing for a reduction in costs.

EXAMPLE: TRADING FREQUENCY IN CORPORATE BONDS

Most bonds trade in OTC markets, where illiquidity and the lack of transparency make NAV calculations difficult and prone to staleness. As an example, consider iShares iBoxx Investment Grade Corporate Bond ETF (LQD), which seeks to track the investment results of an index composed of US dollar-denominated, investment grade corporate bonds with approximately 1,115 constituents (individual bonds). Despite LQD's size ($16 billion) and liquidity (the bid-ask spread is typically below a basis point), less than one-third (28%) of bonds in the basket traded once or more a day during the months January and February 2014, based on FINRA TRACE data.

Liquidity in investment grade bonds declined in 2014. Based on TRACE data, the number of investment grade corporate bonds that traded every day declined from 29% to 15%, while the frequency of bonds trading less than five days per month increased from 2% to almost 5%. The number of high yield bonds that traded daily declined from 12% to 10%. Indeed, figure 8.5

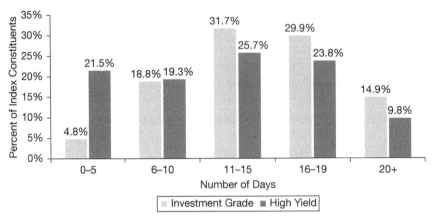

Figure 8.5 Frequency of bond trades, 2014 monthly average.

illustrates the extreme nature of illiquidity in the bond market, showing that some 21.5% of high-yield bonds in the popular iBoxx Index trade only 0–5 times a month.

8.5.3. Electronic versus Voice Trading

A number of approaches have been used to calculate transaction costs in sparsely traded fixed income markets. Unlike equity markets, intraday bid and ask quotes for corporate bond markets are not readily available. The simplest approach is to compare roughly contemporaneous buy and sell prices of the same bond to impute a spread. As the TRACE data identify whether a transaction is buyer- or seller-initiated, imputed spreads are straightforward to compute. Hong and Warga (2000) follow this approach to estimate what Harris and Piwowar (2006) refer to as a benchmark methodology by subtracting the average price for all sell transactions from the average buy price for each bond each day when there is both a buy and a sell.

Hendershott and Madhavan (2015) compute trading costs measured using the difference between average prices for all buy and sells for each bond for bond days when there is both a buy and a sell in the traditional "voice" OTC market and in an electronic bond trading venue. Their key findings are shown below in figure 8.6, which is based on data reported in their study.

The figure shows one-way trading costs in basis points for a sample of all US investment-grade corporate bond trades in the Financial Industry Regulatory Authority's (FINRA) Trade Reporting and Compliance Engine (TRACE) from January 2010 through April 2011, several million individual trades. Here Electronic refers to MarketAxess trades; Voice trades are all TRACE reported trades excluding electronic auction trades.

Several observations are in order: First, note a steep decline in trading costs with trade size within each type of market, the opposite of equity markets.

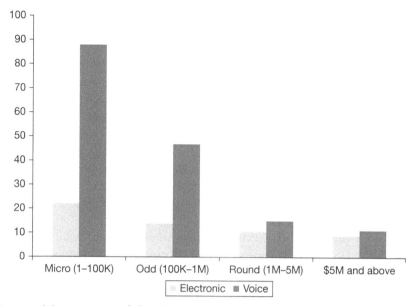

Figure 8.6 Investment grade bond trading costs in basis points by trade size.
SOURCE: Hendershott and Madhavan (2015).

Further, there are substantial cost differences between electronic and voice. For investment-grade bonds, odd-lot electronic trades average 13.8 basis points, while for voice trades the cost is substantially higher at 46.7 basis points. The costs for voice trades fall to 10.5 and 8.9 basis points in the round-lot and maximum trade size categories, respectively. Electronic costs fall with trade size as well, albeit more slowly. These costs are similar in magnitude to previous estimates of corporate bond transaction costs. While electronic costs are lower than voice, the characteristics of bonds traded via the electronic and voice mechanisms differ, with bonds likely to be more liquid (e.g., bonds with larger issue sizes) trading more electronically.

As expected, trading costs in high-yield bonds are much higher than in investment-grade. The differentials are greatest in the smaller trade sizes. Comparing across voice and electronic markets for high-yield and investment-grade bonds, the differentials are large initially for smaller sizes but narrow as size increases. It is not obvious that there are systematic differences by trade side, although for voice it appears that buys are more costly than equivalent-sized sells. That is not the case in the electronic market. In short, electronic bond trading offers the potential for lower costs and transparency. There are some specific regulatory steps that can be taken to advance down this path, which are detailed in the conclusion to this chapter, but in many respects, the future is already here: Fixed income ETFs allow investors to mitigate the costs of trading individual bonds and achieve standardization and diversification in a single step. These funds are traded on electronic venues with a high degree of pre- and post-trade transparency.

8.6. FIXED INCOME MARKETS IN STRESS

8.6.1. Liquidity Illusion

Recently, there have been several concerns raised about the bond market ETFs, particularly in times of stress. The Bank of International Settlements recently warned[4] of "liquidity illusion," meaning "liquidity seems to be ample in normal times, but vanishes quickly during market stress." Several commentators, along these lines, have focused on the fact that bond ETFs provide intraday liquidity and could be subject to redemption risks in stressed times. For example, one report[5] notes: "Investors are also looking to exchange-traded funds as sources of liquidity, even though regulators have questioned how easily the products could honor obligations during large withdrawals."

In Part V of the book, I discuss the policy implications of these concerns in more detail. Despite their being quite a lot of confusion on this point, in reality, ETF managers do not in fact have any obligations to provide secondary market liquidity. Secondary market prices are determined by the interaction of buyers and sellers: If there are no buyers, there is no trading activity. Asset managers do, however, have an obligation to handle redemptions from APs as spelled out in the prospectus of the fund. This is typically an in-kind transaction, meaning the manager will simply "unzip" the wrapper and hand back the individual bonds. So the idea that ETFs need cash reserves to handle redemptions comes from confusion with mutual funds, as we see later on.

What does the empirical evidence say? Interestingly, in several periods of bond market stress, including the financial crisis of 2008–2009 and the "Taper Tantrum" of May/June 2013, we see ETFs contributing to financial market stability. Specifically, when the underlying bond markets freeze up because dealers "step away" from making markets, investors actually gravitate to the ETF as a low-cost, transparent vehicle. Contrary to the idea that ETF liquidity is ephemeral, the ratio of secondary to underlying bond market volumes actually rises in these recent times of stress.

In figure 8.7 underlying volumes for investment grade credits (sourced from TRACE) are shown against the volumes of the iShares $ iBoxx Investment Grade Credit ETF (LQD) in the period of the financial crisis. As underlying bond market volumes fall, activity in the ETF actually experiences a large increase. Further, secondary volume remains a multiple of primary market volume, showing that there is an additional layer of liquidity around ETFs where sellers can trade directly with buyers, and without transmitting pressure to the underlying markets. Finally, the ETF also serves as a mechanism for price discovery, as illustrated in the case that follows.

---

4. Bank of International Settlements Annual Report, June 28, 2015.

5. See Katie Linsell, "BIS Warns of Increasing Risk of Liquidity Trap in Bond Markets," Bloomberg, June 28, 2015.

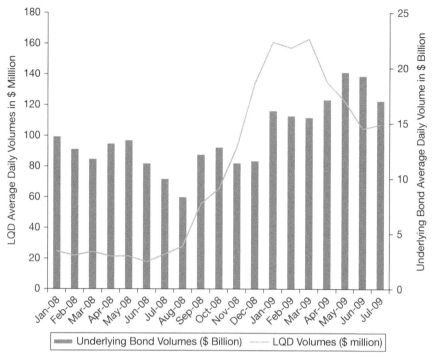

Figure 8.7 Secondary and underlying bond volumes in the financial crisis.

8.6.2. Case Study: The "Taper Tantrum" of 2013

One of the bigger concerns as ETFs extend to less liquid asset classes is their pricing in times of market stress. Once again let's focus on an illiquid asset class—high-yield bonds in a rising interest rate environment. As a case study, consider the so-called "Taper Tantrum" of the summer 2013. The episode began on May 22, 2013, when the Federal Reserve unexpectedly announced that it would begin tapering back its $70 billion a month bond and mortgage backed securities purchase program. The policy statement surprise sparked widespread fears of rising interest rates. Bond prices fell steeply in the period June 18–19, 2013, followed by a rebound on June 24–25, 2013.

The episode was associated with what looks like mispricing in large high-yield ETFs namely widening discounts in mid-June followed by economically large premiums (over 1%) later in June as the underlying bonds rebounded. While daily premiums and discounts of 1% and above might not sound large, they are a significant fraction of returns when yields are so low and hence a source of concern for buyers of ETFs. Is that evidence of dislocation in ETF pricing (akin to what some equity ETFs experienced on the morning of August 24, 2015) or is it really attributable to stale NAV pricing? The question is very important for public policy and regulation, as well as for the potential future of passive investing in bonds through ETFs. Here we consider two very different approaches to answering this question, both of which suggest that bond ETF premiums really reflected price discovery, not dislocation.

Tucker and Laipply (2013) suggest an ingenious way to isolate the effect of stale pricing. Consider a plot the premium of the iShares High-Yield Bond ETF (HYG) price relative to its NAV and the premium of the most liquid (frequently traded) bonds in the universe. The liquid bonds are traded daily so their prices are less subject to staleness. Indeed, we see in figure 8.8 that the premium of the liquid bonds is at all times below 0.5% in absolute value, within the bounds of the bid-ask spreads of the component bonds, although the fund itself exhibits much wider premiums/discounts.

A different approach uses the state-space methodology developed earlier in chapter 4 to recover the intrinsic value of the fund, and then compares the "true" premium of price to intrinsic value against the reported or "actual" premium. In figure 8.9, the reported premium (shown as dots) of price to NAV is plotted daily for all of 2013 (this includes the Taper Tantrum of June) against the true premium of price to estimated value using the Kalman filter (solid line). The dispersion in actual premium to true premium is evident, showing the impact of stale NAV. Even in the Taper Tantrum period of June 2013, when actual premiums vary widely, the true premium is relatively stable.

Practitioners usually use a rule of thumb of 0.5% for transaction cost arbitrage bounds for this fund, and it is clear that except for a few dates, the true premium is within these normal bounds despite high variation in actual premiums. Not surprisingly, the deviations from this simple arbitrage bound occur during the Taper Tantrum when one can argue that transaction costs were considerably higher.

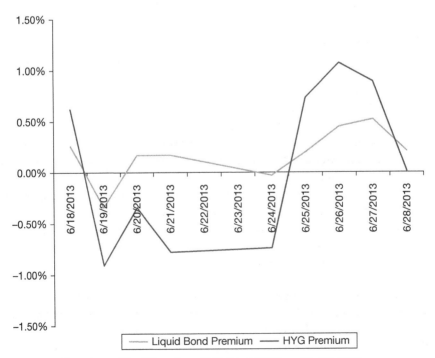

Figure 8.8 Premium of liquid bonds and HYG to NAV, June 18–28, 2013.
SOURCE: Based on figures reported by Tucker and Laipply (2013).

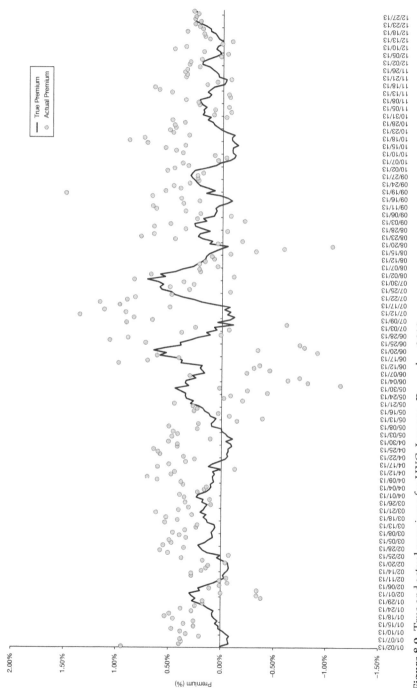

Figure 8.9 True and actual premiums for HYG, January–December 2013.
source: Author's estimates based on the approach of Madhavan and Sobczyk (2016).

The bottom line is that even in times of extreme market stress, the ETF pricing mechanism keeps price in line with value even though reported premiums/discounts might be large due to lack of current pricing in the OTC market for bonds.

In summary, bond ETFs act to reduce systemic risk. Systemic risk arises when a leveraged financial institution—typically, a bank—cannot function in its central role of intermediating capital. The ETF ameliorates this risk by giving buyers and sellers a safety valve, a way to trade when financial intermediaries cannot extend capital. In the crisis of 2008–2009, ETFs provided an added buffer of liquidity. ETFs offer many of the benefits bond market reformers have long urged including transparency, liquidity, and low transaction costs.

8.7. CHAPTER SUMMARY

One of the fastest growing segments of the ETF business is fixed income. The opaque and illiquid nature of the OTC markets for bonds leads to high transaction costs. These factors present the greatest opportunities for improvements in liquidity through standardization and equity-like electronic trading. In these dimensions, bond ETFs are leading the way: they are transparent, low-cost, diversified baskets of bonds that trade intraday on organized exchanges and automated venues.

But nonetheless, challenges and impediments to the growth of ETFs in fixed income remain. First, there is the question of how best to create an index when the notion of market capitalization weighting is not widely accepted within the asset class. There are many ongoing innovations in this space that attempt to redefine weighting schemes; fixed income "Smart Beta" has enormous opportunity. Second, premiums and discounts in bond ETFs are a persistent source of misunderstanding among investors and others, along with a general lack of understanding of how ETFs operate. I show here that seemingly economically significant premiums/discounts often reflects price discovery by the ETF combined with slower adjustment of NAV. Third, there are repeated concerns about the possibility that bond ETFs may be the source of systemic risk and that there is a "mismatch" between ETF liquidity and that of the underlying bonds. These complex issues are considered in greater depth later on in Part V of the book, but the evidence to date shows that bond ETFs perform well in stressed markets.

Regulators can play a key role to extend the benefits of ETFs more broadly to investors by removing artificial regulatory barriers to ETF investment. For example, many regulatory schemes do not consider ETFs as an investment type, typically treating ETFs as equities even if the underlying exposure is to bonds. Examples include capital rules for insurers and broker-dealers and investment eligibility and diversification rules for insurers. So, an investment in a portfolio of short-term US treasuries should be treated similarly for regulatory risk purposes whether the investment is made directly into cash (or cash equivalents) or through an ETF. In other words, regulation should "look through" the wrapper to the true underlying risk exposure. Regulation can affect market structure and help alleviate bond market liquidity issues. Bond market structure issues vary by region, but some obvious wins are: (1) in Europe, consolidated reporting of trades (currently, ETF trades are reported on a voluntary basis) will make it easier to understood true liquidity; (2) in the United States, there is a need to streamline the process for bringing ETFs with less liquid underlying securities (e.g., municipal bonds) to market.

The challenges of liquidity in OTC bond markets have led to calls for standardization of terms, issuance cycle, and maturity dates to address fragmentation. A reduction in the proliferation of CUSIPs would concentrate liquidity, reducing trading costs. Similarly, an effort to shift from opaque, OTC trading to a more transparent, electronic market with actionable quotes would greatly enhance liquidity. An influential example is the bespoke and OTC options market that was standardized in the early 1970s with the introduction of maturities on a quarterly schedule and strike prices in fixed increments. That standardization later paved the way for efficient electronic trading of options, now one of the most efficient markets for securities. In these dimensions, bond ETFs are already paving the way. In conclusion, fixed income ETFs offer the benefits of low-cost, instant diversification as well as challenges in bond markets. There are considerable opportunities to extend their benefits while at the same time focusing on those segments that pose potential risks to the financial system.

Commodities

9.1. INTRODUCTION

Commodities are homogeneous physical assets that are traded in *bulk form* using *standardized* contracts. I distinguish here between commodities like gold that are standardized and tangible real assets such as farmland or real property that are difficult to access and are heterogeneous. Some investors do not regard commodities as an asset class because, unlike stocks or bonds, they do not represent claims to cash flows over time. Commodities trading also has a speculative element that purists do not view as consistent with longer term investment objectives. Semantics aside, commodities and real assets are attractive to many investors because they are perceived as a hedge against inflation (empirical evidence suggests otherwise though, as noted in Ang [2014]) and as a diversifier to a traditional stock and bond mix.

These two factors have led to considerable interest in gaining commodities exposure through ETFs. Still, only 4% of ETF assets are held by commodity based funds, which offers considerable room for growth. This chapter provides an overview of how commodities ETFs work and some of the issues that arise in trying to track the returns of commodities. I then highlight some of the challenges in creating an index for commodities and the implications this has for investors in these funds.

9.2. HOW COMMODITY ETFS WORK

9.2.1. Types of Commodity Funds

The main categories of commodities include energy (e.g., natural gas, crude oil), metals (precious, like platinum, and industrial, like zinc), and agricultural products (e.g., wheat, cocoa). The ETFs that are focused on commodity exposures—either tracking a single commodity or a basket of commodities—fall into three categories:

(1) **Physical Commodity ETFs** that hold the actual physical assets such as precious metals like gold or silver;

(2) **Derivatives Based ETFs** that invest in futures (or other derivatives such as swaps or options) contracts; and

(3) **Commodity exposures through equities**, such as energy exposure through oil and gas companies. These groups are not necessarily mutually exclusive. Some commodity funds may use both futures and equities to gain exposure in tax-efficient ways that track closely.

Most commodity ETFs generally do not actually hold the underlying physical commodities. The reason is that it is often impractical to hold physical underlying holdings. Other than precious metals (e.g., gold and silver ETFs that hold physical bullion), storage costs are prohibitive. So, commodity ETFs (including broad commodity index or model-based ETFs) must access exposure indirectly by holding claims to future delivery of the commodity.

The regulatory environment is also different for commodity funds. In the United States, traditional ETFs and mutual funds must comply with the Investment Company Act of 1940. But commodity funds face different regulation: Funds that use futures are regulated by the Commodities and Futures Trading Commission (CFTC) while those that invest only in physical commodities are regulated by the SEC under the Securities Act of 1933. These differences matter, as we will see later on when we discuss the impact of regulation on position limits.

9.2.2. Example—Natural Gas

Consider, for example, a typical fund that tracks natural gas (in the energy group) using futures to obtain complete notional exposure to the underlying commodity. The actual holdings of the US Natural Gas Fund (UNG), for example, on January 12, 2015, based on the fund's website at the time, are shown in table 9.1.

The fund in this example owns two different natural gas futures contracts and cash and treasury bills. The value of the fund's total net assets equals $636 million,

Table 9.1 HOLDINGS OF US NATURAL GAS COMMODITIES FUND

Security	Quantity	Price	Market Value
Commodity Interests			
NYMEX Natural Gas NG FEB15	14,792	2.795	$413,436,400
ICE Natural Gas LD1 H FEB15	31,872	2.795	$222,705,600
US Treasuries and Cash			
US T BILL ZCP 02/26/15	50,000,000	99.99	$49,997,250
US T BILL ZCP 04/30/15	50,000,000	99.99	$49,996,500
US T BILL ZCP 03/26/15	150,000,000	99.98	$149,975,479
Cash (US Dollars)	582,756,003	1.00	$582,756,003

which when divided by the 44.96 million shares outstanding yields the NAV of \$14.15. The deviation between fund assets and its cash position may reflect accrued liabilities (pending settlements, fees/commissions owed). So, although the fund is notionally fully exposed to natural gas, from an accounting viewpoint its positions are entirely cash or cash equivalents.

9.2.3. Futures Based ETFs

Futures contracts present several non-trivial issues for an ETF manager. Most important is the effect of rolling contracts from the near (maturing) end to the far contract. Some funds use a simple front-month futures strategy meaning that expiring contracts are just replaced by rolling into the nearest month contracts. Investors sometimes assume a commodity ETF will track spot returns, but the shape of the futures curve can lead to a material impact on returns. In a state of contango, which is common in many commodities, futures prices exceed spot prices and the futures curve is upward sloping. Higher futures prices (contango) capture storage or carry costs as well as expectations of future prices. In this situation, the simple front-month strategy leads to negative roll yield that can act as a drag on returns.

EXAMPLE: HOW CONTANGO CAN AFFECT RETURNS

Some commodities like natural gas or crude oil, for example, tend to trade in contango with significant negative roll yield, making it difficult to track the physical spot. Suppose, for example, the current spot price in March of natural gas is \$2.50/million BTU on NYMEX. Suppose that in March the April future is trading at \$2.60/million BTU. Each futures contract represents 10,000 million BTU, so a single contract requires an outlay of \$26,000. A (hypothetical) natural gas ETF with \$26 million in net assets in March would thus need to buy 1,000 April contracts to get the required exposure. Fast forward a month later to April. Suppose the spot price is \$2.55 (up 2%) and the futures price for May is \$2.65. Further, suppose the April futures contracts that the fund bought in May are soon to expire trade now at \$2.55, close to the spot price. When the fund rolls its futures position, it sells the 1,000 contracts (at \$2.55) and reinvests the proceeds by buying 962 May futures at \$2.65. In April, the fund's NAV is down −1.9% even though spot returns were +2% from March.

More recently, commodities ETFs like the PowerShares DB Oil (DBO) have started to use "flexible-futures" trading strategies. Many active commodity funds employ flexible strategies rather than automatically rolling into the near month. Flexible strategies can include blending contracts with different maturities or model-based rules to optimally select the best upcoming contract based on liquidity characteristics. In this respect, these newer commodity ETFs add an active element to an otherwise passive strategy. This development offers an interesting blend of active and passive styles, very much in keeping with the observations made elsewhere in the book.

Position limits on the size of notional exposures pose a very different challenge for fund managers using futures. Position limits on futures or forward may be externally imposed by regulators or may reflect internal risk controls. Managers of funds who have grown large relative to their markets or that operate in illiquid, thin commodities are likely to be most affected. In some cases, position limits can have an impact on the creation/redemption process and hence on pricing.

Finally, the effect of flows into and out of commodity ETFs on the physical underlying assets is a source of considerable debate. Regulators and policymakers have expressed concerns that ETFs provide easy and cheap access to illiquid markets, thereby introducing a new element of trading that is speculative in nature. In this view, rapid changes in investor sentiment can lead to large flows that can distort underlying spot commodity markets. We will consider these arguments and their factual basis later on in Part V.

9.3. COMMODITY INDEXES

The choice of index can make a major difference in commodities where, like fixed income, notions of market capitalization weighting do not translate exactly. Consider two popular commodities benchmarks: the S&P GSCI Total Return Index (GSCI) and the Bloomberg Commodities Index (BCOM). The target sector weights (as of end-2014 based on data from the two providers) are shown in figure 9.1.

Some large differences are immediately apparent based on differences in the choices regarding:

(1) **Universe**—Both benchmarks include only the commodities with a sufficiently liquid futures market, but differ in whether they include or exclude certain commodities: The S&P GSCI Index does not include soybeans oil and meal (but Bloomberg does) while Bloomberg does not include gas oil, cocoa, feeder cattle, and lead (which is in the S&P GSCI).

(2) **Weighting scheme**—Weighting also plays a major role in return differences between the two indexes: The S&P GSCI index is production weighted, leading to high concentration in energy (including oil, gasoline, and natural gas) of 71.25% for GSCI versus 31.21% for Bloomberg. Bloomberg's weights are likewise production-based but also consider liquidity and are constrained to avoid excessive concentration in a single sector or commodity. Production weighting also means a lower weight for precious metals (2.76% for GSCI versus 16.18% for Bloomberg) including gold.

(3) **Maturity and contract choice**—Which contract schedule to use? For each commodity, the benchmark must specify which contract must be considered as the front of the curve on any given month,

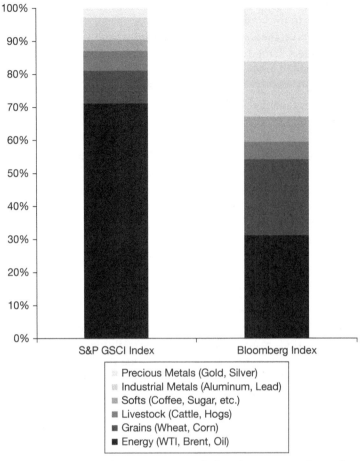

Figure 9.1 Target sector weights, S&P GSCI and Bloomberg Commodity Indexes, December 2014.
SOURCE: S&P and Bloomberg, December 2014.

based on liquidity consideration. Both the selected benchmarks invest into the front month contract, rolling the position on a monthly basis from the 5th to the 9th business day of each month. The front month was selected as the most liquid point of the curve and also the one that is closer to the spot price. The roll needs to be done over multiple days in order to minimize the market impact.

One way to quantify the differences between the two index methodologies is to use the Active Share metric of Cremers and Petajisto (2009). I estimate that the Active Share of GSCI using BCOM as the benchmark (the argument is symmetric) is 0.41, which is quite high. These differences can lead to large differences in performance.

The annual index performance for the two indexes in period 2011–2014 is shown below based on index data sourced from the providers. Although the overall

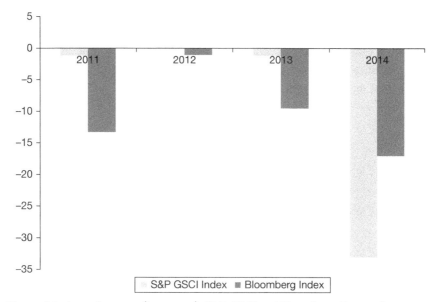

Figure 9.2 Annual returns (in percent), S&P GSCI and Bloomberg Commodity Indexes, 2011–2014.
SOURCE: Bloomberg and S&P Dow Jones Indices.

return performance of both indexes is similar (annualized returns of approximately −6.78% and −6.66%, respectively) with similar levels of risk (annualized volatility of 18.47% and 15.56%, respectively), the year-to-year performance varies quite dramatically. Without making value judgments as to which index is "better" (sensible choices underlie construction in both cases), it is clear that an investor needs to do their homework before selecting a product that matches one of these (or other) indexes.

A bullish period for energy will tend to favor GSCI over BCOM simply because of the higher weight of this sector. The reverse is true in a period of declining energy prices, as was the case in 2014. Indeed, even in a single month, the indexes can have strikingly different performance. In the month of January 2015 alone, for example, GSCI was down −7.5% and BCOM down −3.3%, based on index provider data from the two respective index providers. In April 2015, when energy prices rebounded, GSCI was up +11.1% while BCOM rose +5.7% (see figure 9.2).

9.4. CHAPTER SUMMARY

Commodities are of interest to investors who seek diversification and a possible hedge against inflation. For investors, ETFs offer in theory convenient, low-cost access to commodities. However, there are many subtleties that need to be considered. Most ETFs do not hold physical commodities because of the costs of storage but rather use futures contracts. This can induce tracking error and a possibly material return drag related to the costs of rolling a futures position when the curve is in contango. Futures position limits—either internal or external—may hinder the operation of the creation/redemption mechanism, possibly delinking price from value. Finally, the choice of index in this space is not readily apparent unlike equities where market capitalization is a natural weighting scheme. These choices can significantly affect realized returns, and a wise investor is advised to look thoroughly under the hood.

Foreign Currency

10.1. BEYOND STOCKS AND BONDS

The most exciting area of passive investing today is the extension beyond traditional portfolios of stocks and bonds to include other asset classes and strategies.
I consider first foreign exchange, one of the fastest areas of growth in ETF products, and then move on in the following chapters to volatility and more esoteric
"alternative" investments that span multiple asset classes or strategies.

The first question is why investors should be interested in foreign exchange,
indeed whether it is an investable asset class in its own right. I argue that although
currencies are relative prices for which it is difficult to form long-term views, there
are still many reasons to care about foreign exchange. New ETFs offer two ways
for investors to express their views: directly through ETFs on single/basket currencies or the increasingly popular funds that offer hedged international exposure. What should investors do? I offer a fact-based framework for thinking about
the key decision points that can guide investors.

10.2. WHY SHOULD INVESTORS CARE ABOUT FOREIGN EXCHANGE?

10.2.1. Foreign Exchange Denominates Asset Classes

By far the largest dollar volume of trading per day across asset classes is in currencies; about $5 trillion trades a day.[1] Is foreign exchange an *asset class* that investors
should seek to allocate assets to, as they do to stocks or bonds? The term "asset
class" is used loosely to describe a group of assets that are relatively homogeneous
in structure and whose risk-return characteristics cannot be replicated using other
assets. Part of the challenge in defining an asset class comes from confusion about
assets that share *trading* characteristics (e.g., currencies trade 24 hours a day in an
OTC market while equities and options trade on organized exchanges largely during market hours) versus assets that generate *returns* over time, as defined earlier.

---

1. BIS Triennial Central Bank Survey, April 2013.

A currency's value can only be expressed in terms of another currency and/or commodity, that is, as a pair. A foreign exchange rate (e.g., a currency pair such as USD/JPY) is a relative price between, say, the US dollar and the Japanese yen. So, currencies cannot produce returns the way stocks or bonds do because they are not claims to the cash flows of real assets. In other words, currencies simply *denominate* other asset classes, meaning that foreign exchange is not an asset class per se, but represents a *medium* of exchange between different asset classes.

10.2.2. Why Foreign Exchange Matters

Even if currencies are not an investable asset class, from the viewpoint of an investor there are several reasons for interest in foreign exchange as a *traded* asset class. First, and most important, as investors diversify internationally, as they should, they need to have a view on currencies. Domestic investors gain exposure to currencies from their foreign-denominated holdings in financial assets. So, investors typically get currency exposure as an accidental byproduct of their international diversification rather than a conscious investment decision. That said, currency returns have a direct impact on total return: The return to a Japanese investor from investing in, say, Switzerland depends on the local market return in Switzerland plus the appreciation in the yen relative to the Swiss franc. A further reason to trade foreign exchange is risk mitigation. Currency returns can be a significant source of volatility for a domestic investor, especially over shorter intervals.

Investors may also want to trade currencies tactically to enhance returns, as a source of alpha, if their expectation of currency returns is nonzero. Many participants in foreign exchange markets are motivated by business factors unrelated to forecasts of future changes in currencies (e.g., exporters hedging future cash flows from foreign sales), implying the potential for possible alpha or excess returns for those whose trades are purely motivated by profit. Central bank interventions and other distortions also potentially offer alpha opportunities. For such investors, it is useful to group currencies thematically as opposed to by geography, as with stocks and bonds. Specifically, investors may seek currency investments that share common factor exposure.

An exposure might be to commodities (e.g., in the cases of the Russian Ruble and Norwegian Krone for oil, the Chilean Peso for copper, etc.) or to monetary policy (e.g., higher interest rate countries or regions). So, if an investor has a tactical view on the expected currency return, they may want to invest in currencies or hedge their existing investments. If the investor has no view, there might still be reasons to hedge currency risk.

Finally, currency volatility can alter perceptions of fundamental asset values. A stronger Japanese yen, for example, has historically hurt the valuation of Japanese equities because Japan has traditionally relied on an export model. When the yen strengthens, Japanese goods become more costly abroad, reducing the earnings of exporters. Conversely, many emerging country equity markets decline when the US dollar (USD) strengthens, and vice versa, because many key imports (e.g., energy, food) are typically denominated in US dollars.

10.3. HOW TO INVEST IN FOREIGN EXCHANGE USING CURRENCY ETFS

10.3.1. Types of Currency Funds

Currency ETFs fall into two basic categories: those that track a single currency and those that track a basket of currencies. Within these two categories, there are several approaches to gain currency exposure through ETFs. I list them as follows, ordered by complexity:

(1) **ETFs backed by bank deposits in a foreign currency**—This is the simplest type of currency ETF and is not exposed to any counterparty risk. For example, a fund with assets in yen-denominated bank deposits should rise in value when the yen appreciates against the dollar. However, some currencies (e.g., China renminbi, Brazil real) are not freely tradable because of regulations intended to control inflows/outflows, which leads to the use of derivatives such as forwards or swaps.

(2) **ETFs using forwards and/or swaps**—These ETFs seek to track foreign currency returns by holding currency forward contracts and/or swap contracts issued by a third party. Swap-based ETFs have an element of counterparty risk because of default by the third-party (typically a bank). However, non-deliverable forward contracts may be the only way to gain exposure to certain foreign currencies (especially in emerging markets) where regulations may either prohibit currency exchange outright or impose prohibitively high costs. The majority of hedged funds use forward contracts, rebalanced monthly. This rebalancing interval may in theory lead to foreign currency risk during the month but this is economically insignificant. These ETFs are often implicitly "actively managed" through selection of the specific contracts/ swaps they purchase.

(3) **ETNs and Leveraged/inverse ETPs**—Many foreign exchange investors use substantial leverage and some use overlay strategies. These strategies use derivative instruments that do not require large cash outlays to manage the currency exposure arising from international investments. For such investors the attraction to leveraged ETPs is clear. These currency products are actually exchange-traded notes (i.e., uncollateralized debt instruments) and not traditional ETFs that are backed by physical securities or cash. Leveraged and inverse currency ETFs offer multiples of the day's currency return; over time though, compounding effects can reduce their return even if the investor is correct on the currency's directional movement, as shown later in the book.

As with international funds, US-domiciled ETFs are active during US market hours. However, as noted earlier, currencies trade 24 hours. So the currency volume profile over the day may look very different from the typical U-shaped equity profile, with twin peaks in activity during both US and London market hours. Investors need to be aware that ETF liquidity—and hence price volatility—may vary accordingly.

10.3.2. Hedging Currency Risk

Hedged ETFs have seen rapid growth in flows, especially with views that interest rates in the United States will rise faster than in the rest of the world, likely causing an appreciation of the US dollar. The typical domestic investor will have income and expenses in their local currency. Further, many investors are subject to home bias, over investing in their country or region. While having investments in the local currency can make sense as an offset to expenses, foreign currency exposure can help diversify the portfolio in the event the domestic currency declines.

HOME BIAS

Many investors exhibit home bias. A US investor investing in a broad basket of US stocks either through ETFs or mutual funds would (as of June 2014) have exposure to only about 42% of the world market capitalization. The remaining is in EAFE stocks (32%), Canada (3.3%), Emerging Markets (9.3%), and other regions. The failure of the typical investor to diversify outside of their home country is greater for non-US investors as their countries are a smaller fraction of the All Countries World Index. Japanese investors, in particular, would have suffered greatly from home bias in the decades following the boom in Japan of the 1980s, missing significant equity market gains in the United States.

Foreign currency hedging might also help diversify the risk from international stocks and bonds. Should an investor hedge or not hedge? There is not a single correct answer. Important considerations include:

- **Stocks or bonds?**—Hedging currency risk for foreign bond investments may make sense because the investment objective is to obtain a steady, stable stream of cash flows. But equities are increasingly in global firms with multi-currency revenues and expenses. Global multinationals, resource exporters, and other firms have little currency risk as their prices are set in world markets. Only those with purely domestic sales or expenses (e.g., Swiss luxury watch makers whose labor costs are in Swiss francs) have significant currency risk.
- **Costs**—Hedging in the short-term is simply a one-directional bet on currency movements or equivalently on interest rate surprises. Hedging can be expensive and costs cumulate over time. The cost of hedging is

proportional to the interest rate differentials between the foreign and domestic markets. Hedging is most expensive for volatile (emerging markets) currencies where it is perhaps most beneficial in terms of risk reduction. For countries like Brazil and India, domestic rates range from 7% to 8% in mid-2015 meaning costs are much higher than for developed markets.

- **Horizon**—Currency volatility is significant viewed over shorter time periods. An investor who is concerned that their local currency will increase in value relative to foreign currencies should consider hedging. For long-term passive investors, currency hedging generally does not add to returns because these are one-way bets on relative prices that are difficult to forecast.
- **Risk and leverage**—Globalization has increased significantly over the past 20 years as measured by the fraction of sales that are domestic. Consequently, basic currency hedging strategies have been less effective in reducing volatility in recent years. Even so, reducing currency volatility by hedging may be beneficial even if it detracts from returns. Specifically, if there is no performance benefit from currency volatility, then reducing that volatility should increase risk-adjusted returns and Sharpe ratios. Hedging currency risk may result in higher risk global equities portfolios as the underlying (hedged) are more correlated.
- **Leverage**—Currency hedging increases the notional exposure of the underlying stock or bond exposure, and so can also increase tail risk. Consider a 100% investment in Euro-denominated stocks that is unhedged. If the currency exposure is hedged, this position is still 100% in Euro-denominated stocks but has a 100% short Euro-long USD layer of exposure in addition.
- **Diversification**—Note that hedging need not be the most effective way to reduce currency risk. Diversification through holding assets in multiple currencies can also reduce volatility. For US investors, foreign equity investments employing minimum volatility strategies have also historically provided better risk-adjusted returns than hedged equity strategies.

Hedged strategies may produce higher risk-adjusted returns over long time periods—but not necessarily going forward (as companies are increasingly global), and not necessarily significantly. The example of the Swiss franc in January 2015 is one example of why hedging might actually *add* risk—for an unhedged US investor the abandonment of the Euro peg had little impact because appreciation in the Swiss franc was offset almost entirely by the decline in the Swiss equity market. It is an isolated case, but makes the point that hedging need not always reduce risk.

Perold and Schulman (1988) argue that hedging is a free lunch. Since the long-run expected return on a currency is zero (it is a relative price), risk reduction can only increase the Sharpe ratio. In their view, hedging should be the default policy, and maintaining an unhedged position is an active decision. Implicit in traditional unhedged positions—where a US investor holds foreign assets—is the view that the dollar will decline because the investor has long exposure to foreign currencies. Other economists argue that the optimal hedging in the long term is zero because hedging is tied to short-term factors, not the long-run drivers of currency movements.

10.4. CONCEPTUAL FRAMEWORK

10.4.1. Impact of Currency Returns on Portfolio Returns

The total return on a stock or portfolio in any given period is the return on the foreign investment in local currency terms, r_t^{LOC}, plus the return (appreciation) of the local currency relative to the domestic currency, r_t^{CUR}. Formally, I write:

$$r_t^{TOT} = r_t^{LOC} + r_t^{CUR}. \tag{10.1}$$

Over long horizons, the returns on currencies, as relative prices, may net out to zero. But there have been pronounced regimes where one currency has strengthened relative to another for several years. As an example, from May 1995 to January 2002, the US dollar strengthened significantly relative to EAFE currencies.[2] That meant that over that period, an investor that hedged their EAFE stock investment gained approximately 14% per year relative to one who was exposed to currency risk.

Hedging the foreign exposure of a portfolio can be achieved through currency futures/forward contracts. The "cost of carry," which measures the difference between spot currency price S_t and futures prices over the interval $F_{t,T}$ as a function of the interest rate differential $(i_t^{LOC} - i_t^{DOM})$ between the interest rates in local (foreign) market and the domestic market. The currency forward price is, from equation (7.1) given by:

$$F_{t,T} = S_t e^{-(i_t^{LOC} - i_t^{DOM})(T-t)}. \tag{10.2}$$

By locking in the forward rate, an investor fixes their return from hedging activity meaning they obtain the difference between the forward and the spot exchange rate at the time the hedge was initiated. This return is the component of an investor's total return attributable to hedging activity. We can express this currency hedge return over the period $(T - t)$—which is measured in fractions of a year—as $(F_{t,T}/S_t)$. As an example, consider table 10.1 which shows data for June 30, 2014, for the Australian dollar and UK pound. For the Australian dollar, the currency hedge return on an annualized basis is

$$12 \times \ln(0.94156/0.94385) = -0.029$$

So, the hedge return for the Australian dollar at the time was –2.9%. For the UK pound at this time, the cost was –0.30%, much smaller. In general, emerging

---

2. Based on Morningstar and MSCI data.

Table 10.1 Spot and One-month Forward Prices for Australian
Dollar and UK pound, June 30, 2014

	Australian Dollar	UK Pound
Spot price (in USD)	0.94385	1.70984
Forward price 1-month (in USD)	0.94156	1.70942

markets and certain other regions with high interest rate differentials will have higher hedge costs. For developed markets currently with low interest rates overall, hedging costs are quite small.

By 100% hedging returns (offered through many ETFs), an investor transforms this return relation into:

$$r_t^{TOT} = r_t^{LOC} - \theta(i_t^{LOC} - i_t^{DOM}),$$
(10.3)

where the latter term $\theta(i_t^{LOC} - i_t^{DOM})$ represents the cost of hedging which is modeled as related to the interest rate differential between the local (foreign) and domestic markets. While it seems intuitive that the volatility of a foreign investment is *increased* by currency return volatility, the reality is that this depends on the *correlation* between the currency and local asset returns. From the return equation, the variance of total returns is:

$$\sigma^2(r_t^{TOT}) = \sigma^2(r_t^{LOC}) + \sigma^2(r_t^{CUR}) + 2\sigma(r_t^{LOC})\sigma(r_t^{CUR})\rho(r_t^{LOC}, r_t^{CUR}),$$
(10.4)

where $\rho(r_t^{LOC}, r_t^{CUR})$ is the correlation between local asset returns and the currency. For a domestic investor, hedging a financial investment denominated in a foreign currency depends then on the co-movement of local returns and currency. Correlation can be negative, in which case hedging may add to risk. To see this, note that the difference in volatility between an unhedged portfolio and a fully hedged investment where $\sigma(r_t^{CUR}) = 0$ is $2\sigma(r_t^{LOC})\sigma(r_t^{CUR})\rho(r_t^{LOC}, r_t^{CUR})$. The Sharpe ratio for a 100% hedged investment (ignoring the risk-free rate) is:

$$SR^H = \frac{r_t^{LOC} - \theta(i_t^{LOC} - i_t^{DOM})}{\sigma(r_t^{LOC})}.$$
(10.5)

By contrast, the Sharpe ratio for an unhedged position is a little more complex:

$$SR^U = \frac{r_t^{LOC} + r_t^{CUR}}{\sqrt{\sigma^2(r_t^{LOC}) + \sigma^2(r_t^{CUR}) + 2\sigma(r_t^{LOC})\sigma(r_t^{CUR})\rho(r_t^{LOC}, r_t^{CUR})}}.$$
(10.6)

For a long-term investor taking a strategic view, if currency returns are expected to be zero, then the choice of hedging or not comes down to beliefs about the correlation of returns and the costs of hedging, as manifested by interest rate differentials. It is not clear whether the Sharpe ratio is higher by hedging, hedging partially, or keeping an unhedged position.

10.4.2. Optimal Hedge Ratio

Some investors blend fully hedged and unhedged exposures. The hedging option is binary a partially hedged fund is a linear combination of fully hedged or unhedged funds. What is the optimal hedge ratio? One criterion is the minimum variance hedge ratio, that is, the hedge exposure that minimizes the variance of local returns and hedged currency returns. If a fraction δ of exposure is hedged, the return from the currency hedge is $-\delta r_t^{CUR}$. Currency pairs can be confusing. In this case, an example may help. For a US investor in euro stocks, risk is an appreciation of the dollar against the euro that can erode equity returns. A hedged position for this investor means protection against a decline in the euro/dollar rate, so that a fraction h of the euro currency exposure has been sold forward. Should the euro decline, the hedge makes money; if it appreciates, the hedge loses money but that loss is offset in part by the gain on the currency.

So, the variance of a hedged portfolio is:

$$\sigma^2(r_t^{LOC}) + \delta^2\sigma^2(r_t^{CUR}) + 2\delta\sigma(r_t^{LOC})\sigma(r_t^{CUR})\rho(r_t^{LOC}, r_t^{CUR}). \qquad (10.7)$$

Minimizing total variance with respect to δ (by setting the derivative of the expression above to zero) yields the optimal hedge ratio:

$$\delta = -\frac{\rho(r_t^{LOC}, r_t^{CUR})\sigma(r_t^{LOC})}{\sigma(r_t^{CUR})}, \qquad (10.8)$$

where $\rho(r_t^{LOC}, r_t^{CUR})$ is the correlation between local asset returns and the currency.

As an example, suppose that a country's local returns have a volatility of 30% and that the currency volatility relative to the US dollar is 15%, and let's ignore transaction costs to fix ideas. If the correlation between the equity returns and currency is 45%, then the optimal delta hedge ratio (assuming stationarity) is given by the negative of the regression coefficient of local index returns on currency returns:

$$\delta = -\left(\frac{0.45 \times 0.3}{0.15}\right) = -0.9. \qquad (10.9)$$

In this example, the investor would offset 90% of the currency exposure through the hedge. Ultimately, the question of hedging (or equivalently tactical bets on a currency) comes down to views of returns, correlation, and hedging costs.

It is possible the optimal hedge ratio δ is above 1 or is negative, but practitioners typically bound the amount hedged, implicitly so as not to rely too much on historical estimates of the inputs. Correlations in particular between currency and equity returns are not stable and can vary significantly over time depending on the macroeconomic environment. Ultimately, the question of how much to hedge is an empirical question, so we turn now to the evidence to date.

10.5. EMPIRICAL EVIDENCE

10.5.1. Returns

Let's begin with whether we can predict returns to currencies over short-term periods, taking as given that longer run forecasting is likely to be unsuccessful given that relative prices are a zero-sum game. Two economic measures in particular are positively correlated with a currency's return:

- **Interest rates**—Capital will flow to countries/regions where investors perceive they can get the highest returns. Investors borrow in currencies with low interest rates and invest in currencies with higher interest rates, to earn the spread (known as "the carry trade"). Rising interest rates tends to strengthen a country's currency because more investors want to keep funds in that currency and also because rising interest rates signal stronger macroeconomic conditions.
- **Current account**—A current account surplus means a country is a net exporter, meaning foreign capital is flowing into the country to pay for the exports. Generally, a country with a current account surplus will have a strengthening currency, because buyers of the country's goods and services need to sell other currencies to buy the country's currency.

The empirical evidence suggests that most developed countries in the last three decades have experienced positive correlation. Hedging resembles making a one-way bet on the direction of that currency relative to the investor's own currency. Some analysts argue that hedging actually layers in an additional source of volatility (if the covariance term is negative) and possibly tail risk because of unexpected devaluations or deviations from pegs.

SWISS NATIONAL BANK (SNB) AND CURRENCY RISK

On January 15, 2015, the SNB stunned world markets by removing the 1.20 Swiss Franc floor against the euro and introduced a −0.75% penalty on bank deposits. The SNB took these exceptional steps as the three-year old floor was considered unsustainable given the anticipated quantitative easing by the European Central Bank. Indeed, the SNB had spent about €1bn every day in the previous six weeks to maintain the 1.20 level, actions that brought the SNB's balance sheet to almost 100% of Swiss GDP, significantly higher than other developed markets. The effects on global equity, bond, and FX markets were dramatic. The Swiss franc broke through 0.80 against the euro, ending up about 20%. Swiss equities lost 13% over the week, with exporters and banks hit hardest. Yet, on the announcement day, many US-domiciled ETFs on Swiss equities actually experienced gains of 3% to 4%. Why? The appreciation of the Swiss franc outweighed the loss in local market terms, highlighting the importance of considering currency movements as part of the overall investment decision.

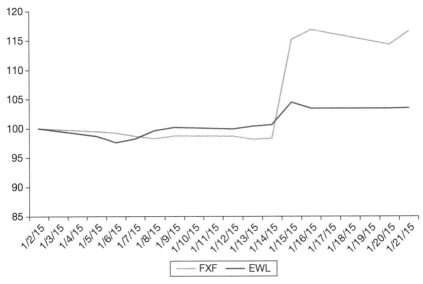

Figure 10.1 Cumulative returns to FXF and EWL in the period January 2–21, 2015 (January 2, 2015 = 100).

Figure 10.1 shows the cumulative returns (January 2, 2015 = 100) for two ETFs—CurrencyShares Swiss Franc Trust (FXF), a large Swiss franc currency ETF, and the iShares MSCI Switzerland Capped ETF (EWL) in the period January 2–21, 2015, where the data are sourced from Thompson Reuters. While the currency ETF shows a large jump, the dollar denominated ETF on the equity markets shows little variation over the period.

10.5.2. Currency Returns and Volatility

Currency volatility is significant over short to mid-term time horizons relative to local return volatility. Consider the volatility (i.e., the standard deviation of daily returns on an annualized basis, in percent) of non-US equity markets as represented by the MSCI All Countries World Index ex US) as shown in figure 10.2. At the level of a year (calendar year 2014), the volatility of currency returns and local market equity returns is roughly economically comparable. Currency volatility does not always translate into higher asset volatility for non-local investors, but over 5- and 10-year periods, hedged returns have slightly lower annual volatility than do unhedged returns.

10.5.3. Comparison of Returns

Currency volatility is not a relevant consideration over long horizons. Of course, it is actually not zero, but it is economically insignificant. Some currencies appreciate or depreciate against others for fundamental reasons over

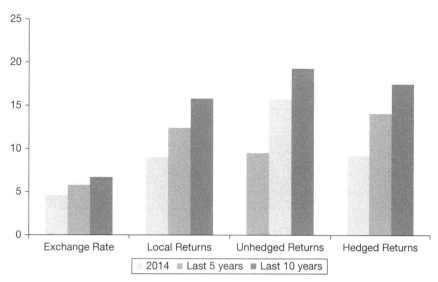

Figure 10.2 Annualized return volatility in percent MSCI ACWI x US Index.
SOURCE: MSCI, based on MSCI ACWI ex US daily returns: January 2, 2004, to
December 31, 2014.

periods of decades, but if one could forecast and trade on these movements,
they would go away. So, future currency returns, net of forecasts that are already
built into interest rate differentials, are innovations or surprises given current
beliefs. Further, the fundamental reasons that drive the currency appreciation
or depreciation (e.g., economic growth, fiscal policies, inflation) also frequently
contribute to the valuation of assets denominated in that currency. Inflows into
the UK pound may be associated with rising real estate prices in premium areas
of London.

For this reason, currency movements (when viewed from the perspective of an
investor's domestic currency) are often positively correlated to equity returns, in
which case hedging a currency for which an investor has positive expected equity
returns will frequently lower the investor's overall returns. The best case for long-
term hedging is a currency (when viewed from the perspective of an investor's
home currency) that is negatively correlated with its equity market (which is
very unusual). Japan historically has been such a case—Japanese stocks have performed best when the yen is weak.

Hedging investments denominated in a foreign currency makes sense for
investors whose home currency is likely to appreciate over time, say in the case
of a US investor investing in a country that is pursuing a weak currency policy to
boost exports. In many instances, investors in Japanese equities who hedged their
yen exposure benefited from the negative correlation between Japanese stock
returns and yen. But this strategy has not always worked. Historical relationships
between currencies, and between currencies and other assets, are not necessarily
stable. In 2014, as shown in figure 10.3, US-based investors who did not hedge
global equities suffered as the dollar strengthened. Over longer (5- and 10-year)
horizons though, the differentials were much smaller.

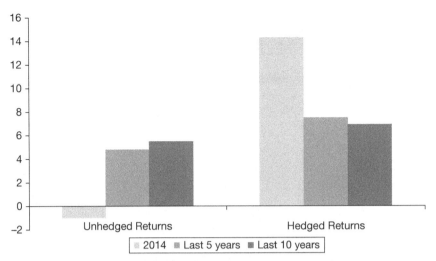

Figure 10.3 Annualized returns in percent MSCI ACWI ex US Index.
SOURCE: MSCI, based on MSCI ACWI ex US monthly returns: January 2004 to
December 2014.

10.6. CHAPTER SUMMARY

Foreign exchange is best viewed as a relative price or a medium of exchange
between asset classes rather than an income-generating asset in its own right.
Interest in foreign exchange and hence the growth of currency and hedged funds
comes from several factors. The most important consideration is the fact that foreign investments expose a domestic investor to currency risk. In the short term,
currency volatility is relatively large compared to local equity return volatility.
For bond investors seeking stable nominal cash flows, it makes complete sense to
hedge foreign bond investments. This means that investors seeking to overcome
home bias must take a view on currencies.

This chapter shows how investors can gain direct exposure to a particular currency or basket of currencies, and also why hedged funds are increasingly popular.
The framework developed here shows that for a strategic investor (one who does
not take a tactical or short-term view of the direction of currency movements),
the question of whether to hedge or not comes down to views about correlations
between local market asset returns and currencies. For the large part, these correlations have historically been positive, suggesting a risk reduction to hedging.
However, hedging comes at a cost and the most volatile investments are likely to
have the highest costs. Ultimately, the investor needs to form a view about the
currency regime that prevails and the trade-off between hedged versus unhedged
based on their investment horizon. The good news is that there are a large number
of funds available that allow full expression of an investor's views. The important
lesson for an investor is to have a view on currency returns and not "accidently"
invest in foreign exchange.

Investing in Volatility

11.1. IS VOLATILITY AN ASSET CLASS?

Interest in volatility as an asset class largely derives from the negative correlation of volatility to stock market returns. On most, but not all, days, volatility and stock prices move in opposite directions. For many investors, this suggests including volatility to further diversify an investment portfolio. Although volatility (often referred to as "vol") is often described as an asset class, it is not a traditional asset. Gastineau (2010) refers to "asset class pollution" meaning the tendency to divide investments into "more alleged asset classes than are warranted or useful." Intangible exposures (such as volatility, inflation) are commonly treated as investable asset classes although they do not generate cash flows themselves or represent a claim to a real asset. In terms of our thinking, volatility is not per se an asset class because it does not have a claim to cash flows. Rather, volatility is essentially the *second* moment of the return distribution.

But like foreign exchange, volatility products are of interest to investors because they offer the possibility of shaping the return distribution in ways that are utility-enhancing, for instance, by offsetting downside risk. That goal can also be achieved with options on ETFs, an important consideration for many investors. Again, as with foreign exchange, some investors believe there are alpha opportunities in this space driven by the irrationality of others in times of "fear versus greed" when volatility is over- or underpriced. Volatility swaps and variance swaps are also popular, but are typically the purview of institutional traders with close relationships with dealers who operate in OTC or bespoke markets.

11.2. SHAPING THE DISTRIBUTION OF RETURNS WITH VOLATILITY PRODUCTS

11.2.1. VIX Index and Volatility Futures

Volatility products related to VIX futures have been growing in popularity since the financial crisis of 2008, as they are negatively correlated with stock returns, thus offering a diversification benefit. As noted earlier, investors may want to use volatility products to shape the return distributions in ways they care about, for example, by mitigating the risk of extreme losses.

The CBOE Volatility Index® (VIX) is a popular metric for investor sentiment (sometimes referred to as the "fear" index) and equity market volatility. On most, but not all, days, the equity market and volatility move in opposite directions. The VIX Index is constructed from real-time prices of options on the S&P 500® Index (SPX) and is designed to reflect investors' consensus views of *future* 30-day expected stock market volatility.

The VIX calculation measures 30-day expected volatility of the S&P 500 Index, essentially by backing out the implied volatility in daily options prices using the Black-Scholes option pricing formula and expressing these in annualized percentages. The components of the VIX calculation are near- and next-term put and call options with more than 23 days and less than 37 days to expiration. The resulting forward-looking volatility measure is quite distinct from historical return volatility, although both expected and realized volatility are correlated. Expected volatility is generally higher than realized (trailing and concurrent) volatility, except when both are at elevated levels relative to past history, a phenomenon that likely reflects investors' demand for insurance against short-run equity market declines.

11.2.2. Futures on Volatility and Correlation Indexes

The VIX index, although watched closely by market participants, is based on a theoretical computation and hence is not directly investable. Further, the component S&P 500 options that are near maturity can have large changes in weight from day to day. There is, however, an active market in VIX futures and options. VIX futures contracts are available for all 12 months of the year, and options have expirations up to 9 months out. VIX futures are settled based on the value of the VIX index on the settlement date, either the third or fourth Wednesday of the month. This means that VIX futures will converge over time to the spot value of the index, a property that is very important in understanding the return to products based on VIX futures.

The CBOE also offers S&P 500 Implied Correlation Indexes for use in volatility dispersion (or correlation) trading. For example, a long volatility dispersion trade is a bet that index option premiums are rich relative to single-stock options. The appeal here is that correlation itself (and hence the diversification benefit) is time-varying and that there may be inefficiencies between the correlation implied at the index level versus the component stocks. Also noteworthy are active futures markets for VIX indexes using ETFs as proxies for otherwise non-investable exposures. These include the volatility of emerging markets based on the iShares Emerging Markets ETF (EEM) and gold volatility, based on the SPDR Gold Trust (GLD).

11.2.3. Options on ETFs

Most ETFs with significant volume have active options markets, although option activity is highly concentrated in the largest funds. Options are derivatives or side-bets on the value of underlying securities. As such, they are not created by the asset manager but through investor interest. Why are options on ETFs so attractive? Investors use options for both strategic and tactical uses. One example is overwriting strategies using call options to generate income. More important, options allow investors to achieve asymmetric returns, putting in floors on long positions by using puts, and possibly financing this "insurance" by selling out of the money calls. The appeal of options for investors who already access index exposures through ETFs is clear.

By far the largest open interest of all options on ETFs is in funds tracking the S&P 500 such SPY or IVV. Index options are cash-settled; whereas, ETF options resemble stock options where settlement can be in the equity. Consider a covered call strategy where a long investor (who holds say SPY or IVV) writes an out-of-the-money call on the ETF to generate income or to fund the purchase of puts for downside protection. If the market rises and the call is exercised, the investor can simply deliver the underlying ETF in contrast with having to sell the position to generate cash as with an index option.

Options on ETFs are also useful to market makers and other liquidity providers to hedge their positions, reducing inventory costs and tightening spreads. The bottom line is that active trading in derivatives improves ETF liquidity. Asset managers can play a role by providing analytics to their clients to understand the liquid nature of the options markets on some ETFs and to facilitate simultaneous transactions. Public policy can also play a role in enhancing liquidity by ensuring standardization of products, particularly in the fixed income space.

11.2.4. Historical Volatility

An examination of historical volatility (VIX monthly values) from January 2, 1990, to May 15, 2015, shows that the average monthly VIX close was 19.89 over this period. Noticeable are the spikes in volatility in crisis periods especially the financial crisis. A plot of the historical time series of VIX (from CBOE) in figure 11.1 shows that a regression trendline is essentially flat over the period despite the spike in volatility in the financial crisis period. The time series is strongly mean reverting. The idea that volatility returns to an average suggests the possibility of profiting by shorting volatility when it is above average and buying it when it is historically low, but as discussed later, it is practically very difficult to capture the return from mean reversion.

Forward-looking volatility exhibits strong temporal variation. Stochastic volatility refers to fact that volatility itself is time-varying. So-called volatility of volatility or "vol of vol" products represent the volatility of the VIX index itself. The VIX has a volatility of around 20% over its historical average, but the corresponding volatility of volatility is much higher, around 100% and exhibits a far greater

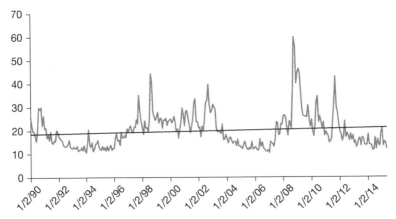

Figure 11.1 VIX monthly close, January 2, 1990, to May 15, 2015.
SOURCE: Chicago Board of Options Exchange.

range than the underlying volatility index. That offers tremendous leverage to implied volatility option traders to speculate on changes in volatility. The ability to bet on tail risk or extreme movements has driven flows toward leveraged or inverse exchange-traded products on volatility.

Attempts to capture volatility (e.g., through the popular VIX indexes) in ETF form, however, have been challenging as explained below. This is because these ETFs need to trade futures to gain exposure to volatility, as the VIX index itself is not investable directly. Investors clearly have an appetite for volatility funds, and there are also inverse and 2× leveraged versions that offer multiples of the day's return in VIX. There are also hybrid versions that offer some combination of principal or tail risk protection while giving up some upside.

11.2.5. Example: ETFs on VIX

The Barclays Bank PLC iPath S&P 500 VIX Short-Term Futures ETN (VXX)— yes, that is its full name—is designed to offer exposure to a daily rolling long position in the first and second month VIX futures contracts. The fund—which is technically an unsecured debt obligation of Barclays Bank—is extremely liquid with a penny-wide spread. Total assets under management in VXX were $1.27 billion as of May 2015, making it the largest of the VIX-related ETPs. There is also an active options market on VXX. This section will focus on this fund because of its size and liquidity, but the analysis applies to all other VIX-related ETPs. Investors often use VXX as a hedge against US equity market declines: The fund's beta to the S&P 500 Index has (since inception) averaged around −4.0.

The closing price of VXX from January 30, 2009, to May 21, 2015, is shown in figure 11.2 based on daily data. The chart also shows the daily close adjusted for corporate actions such as splits and dividends, normalized to $100 on January 30, 2009. From its inception on January 30, 2009, to May 21, 2015, VXX has had three 4:1 reverse splits to maintain a price level of at least $25. The reverse splits

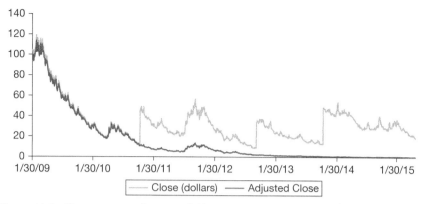

Figure 11.2 Closing prices of VXX in dollars and split adjusted close (January 30, 2009 = $100).
SOURCE: Bloomberg daily data, January 30, 2009, to May 21, 2015.

(on November 8, 2010, October 4, 2012, and November 8, 2013) are evident in the (unadjusted) close prices. Were it not for reverse splits, VXX would be trading at $0.28 in May 2015, down from $100 in January 2009. That works out to be a loss of 99.7% over the whole period or about 65% annually. Much of this decline came early on: Alexander and Korovilas (2013) note that between January 2009 and December 2011, VXX lost over 90% of its value. Compare these returns with the VIX itself in figure 11.1 over the same period.

There is also the risk dimension: Volatility is stochastic, and there are times when going long on a volatility fund is highly profitable.

11.3. RETURNS OF VOLATILITY FUNDS

11.3.1. Term Structure of Volatility

What explains the loss in VIX-related funds like VXX over this time? Recall that the VIX itself is not investable so ETFs that seek to track the index must invest in listed VIX futures. As noted earlier in the discussion of futures-based commodities funds, the expiration of futures contracts means that an ETF tracking VIX must roll its positions. The returns to the futures index on which VXX is based depends, in order of increasing importance, on: (1) interest on the futures collateral, relative negligible when rates are low; (2) changes in the VIX index (spot returns); and (3) the "roll yield," which arises because the fund rolls its futures positions by selling the near expiration contracts and buying the next-dated contracts. Historically, it has been this rolling process that has contributed the most to the return on volatility. To understand this better, consider the term structure of volatility.

Shown in figure 11.3 is the term structure of volatility, specifically the forward CBOE VIX curve as of December 19, 2014, based on data from the Chicago Board of Options Exchange, juxtaposed against a straight-line regression fit. When the term structure of volatility is in contango, as shown in figure 11.3, futures

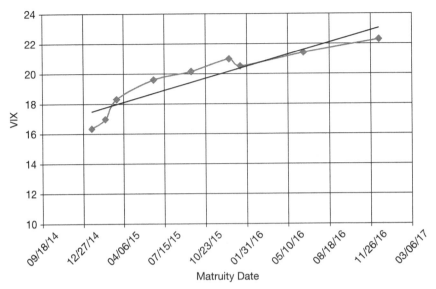

Figure 11.3 Forward VIX curve, December 19, 2014.
SOURCE: Based on data from the Chicago Board of Options Exchange, December 19, 2014.

purchases are at higher prices than spot. The contango in VIX is relatively common, as is the curvature in the middle of the curve. Why is this the case? Unlike a physical asset, there is no ability to store volatility, so the slope of the term structure reflects the nature of supply and demand.

In the case of volatility, the contango (or negative carry) is present in roughly three-quarters of the periods because investors are concerned that the future is riskier than the present, possibly having an unpredictable and disruptive ("black swan") event. Traders demand a risk premium for compensation that the markets could rapidly transition from a low-volatility regime to a high-volatility regime. In other words, the volatility regimes themselves are unstable, and there is a chance that in a crisis period, VIX can be well above its median of about 20% for an extended period of time.

Of course, the volatility term structure is not always in contango—in periods of extremely high volatility when VIX is high, investors expect mean reversion, so the term structure exhibits backwardation.

11.3.2. Roll Yield

The volatility futures price over the interval $F_{t,T}$ is related to the spot price of volatility S_t and the financing rate r_f (interest on collateral or risk-free treasury bill rate) by the futures pricing equation of chapter 7. In theory, the value of a future, setting dividend yield to zero, is:

$$F_{t,T} = S_t e^{r_f(T-t)}. \tag{11.1}$$

Here, r_f is the continuously compounded interest over the fraction of a year from date $t - 1$ to date t. So, if time is measured in months, then r_f is the monthly interest rate. Of course, as discussed in chapter 7, the actual value of a futures contract may differ from the theoretical value because of demand and supply factors. Investors in volatility, as I discuss later, typically demand a risk premium over the fair value price. However, focusing on the efficient market price lets us develop some key concepts.

Writing $f_{t,T} = \ln(F_{t,T})$ and $s_t = \ln(S_t)$, and noting that $F_{t,t} = S_t$, the return for an investor who buys a future at $t - 1$ that will expire in month T and then sells a month later at time t is the futures return plus collateral interest:

$$r_{t,t-1} = f_{t,T} - f_{t-1,T} = +r_f. \tag{11.2}$$

The roll yield is *defined* as the futures return less the spot return or:

$$y_{t,t-1} = (f_{t,T} - f_{t-1,T}) - (s_t - s_{t-1}). \tag{11.3}$$

The return to a long investor can be expressed as:

$$r_{t,t-1} = y_{t,t-1} + (s_t - s_{t-1}) + r_f. \tag{11.4}$$

Although a tautology, this expression provides a useful decomposition of the *ex post* return to a long futures position into the sum of three elements: roll yield, spot returns, and the interest earned over the period. To make this operational, we need to make some assumptions to predict the future return to an investor taking a position today.

If markets are efficient, the expected spot return $E[(s_{t+1} - s_t)]$ over the coming month is—on average—zero so the return to a long futures position taken today at time t and liquidated a month from now at $t + 1$ is:

$$E[r_{t+1,t}] = E[y_{t+1,t}] + r_f. \tag{11.5}$$

What is the expected roll yield? The approach taken in practice is to assume that the roll yield is determined by the convergence of the futures price to the spot as time passes, that is $f_{t+1,T} \to s_t$ so that (with $E[(s_{t+1} - s_t)] = 0$):

$$E[y_{t+1,t}] = E[(f_{t+1,T} - f_{t,T})] = s_t - f_{t,T}. \tag{11.6}$$

Contango—where futures are higher than spot—imply a negative roll yield. Since contango usually prevails in volatility futures, investors experience a negative roll yield on a day-to-day basis, and hence (see, e.g., Alexander and Korovilas 2013) a significant drag on the returns of volatility funds using futures over time.

Roll yield is illustrated in figure 11.4 where the solid futures curve is the current one and the future (date $t + 1$) is shown as the dashed line. The idea that the futures price rolls to the current spot is represented by the idea that the

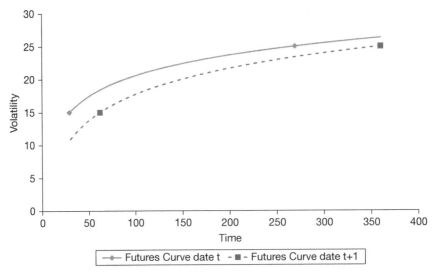

Figure 11.4 Illustration of roll yield.

one-month futures curve shifts to the right, so that the 30-day futures price stays at 15 or equivalently that the future price in 60 days converges to the current 30-day price.

EXAMPLE: COMPUTING ROLL YIELD

Consider the following data taken from CBOE following the spike in volatility after the breakdown of talks between Greece and its creditors and the steep declines in the Chinese equity market. The spot price on July 2, 2015, was 16.79 and the nearby July futures contract (VIX/U5) expiring on July 22, 2015, is priced at 16.93. If the nearby contract rolls down to the current spot and assuming spot prices stay constant, this implies a roll yield of −0.83% over 20 days, or an annualized return of roughly −15%. In periods when volatility was lower, the roll yield is even more negative. At the start of June 2015, volatility was 13.84 and the nearby contract was at 14.63, the roll yield was −5.36% over just a 16-day window.

There are, however, several practical considerations to be kept in mind. First, to the extent that there is a positive spot return, this can offset any negative roll yield, as discussed later. Second, actual futures prices can depart from the theoretical values, so the previous computation makes sense only if we expect the premium to be stationary. An increase in the premium over theoretical value would increase the return to a long futures contract, offsetting roll yield. Finally, there are periodic and dramatic spikes in VIX associated with brief periods of strong backwardation or positive roll yield. In these situations, investors who are long on a volatility fund may have substantial short-term gains.

Note that roll yield is a distinctly different concept from the notion of roll cost introduced in chapter 7 in the context of comparing fully funded futures positions to ETFs. Roll yield arises from the convergence of futures to spot, reflecting the passage of time. Roll cost refers to the difference between the funding rate implicit in a futures contract and the investor's own funding rate. Roll costs may exist whether there is backwardation or contango, but roll yield is directly related to the shape of the yield curve or term structure.

11.3.3. Speculating on Volatility

Forecasting returns to a long futures volatility position requires estimating these components. If history is a guide, roll yield is negative because the futures term structure exhibits contango. The expected spot rate over short periods is close to zero, as is the risk free rate, so roll yield is the dominant determinant. One could develop a more sophisticated return forecast by estimating a mean reverting model of spot changes where we expect on average to obtain positive spot returns if the current spot rate is below its long-run mean level as opposed to the efficient market assumptions that we employed above:

$$(s_{t+1} - s_t) = \gamma(\mu - s_t) + \varepsilon_t. \tag{11.7}$$

Here $\gamma > 0$ is a parameter that captures the speed of mean reversion, ε_t is an error term, and μ is the long-run average volatility. The model, combined with historical estimates of roll yield, can be used to forecast changes in ETPs based on futures volatility. One could also allow long-run average volatility μ to vary over time as a function of macroeconomic variables or past volatilities as do sophisticated hedge funds strategies.

In general, the negative roll yield implies gains on average to a short position in a volatility fund, but in practice it is not easy to exploit this negative return. An inverse volatility fund (like XIV) is not equivalent to a short position on a long fund like VXX, primarily because of the effect of compounding of returns discussed later in the chapter on leveraged/inverse ETPs. Short borrow costs may offset any gains from the negative roll yield. Further, as noted earlier, there are periods of backwardation and large jumps in volatility that can substantially reduce the return to a short investor.

11.4. CHAPTER SUMMARY

Interest in asset classes other than traditional stocks and bonds is increasing exponentially. Accessing these asset classes, including volatility, typically involves a deeper understanding of mechanics than with regular, physically backed ETFs on financial assets. In my view, volatility is not an asset class in the sense that it is not a financial investment that produces or lay claims to a stream of income over time. This is not to say that investors do not have legitimate reasons to seek vehicles to access volatility. Investors should have a view as to how the second (or higher) moments of returns may evolve, and depending on their risk tolerances, shape the return distribution of their portfolios accordingly.

Although volatility, on average, moves in the opposite direction of equity returns, attempts to diversify equity positions using volatility products may not always be effective because these funds need to trade futures contracts to gain exposure. The contango in the term structure of volatility can result in a negative roll yield that erodes the returns of a long investor. A better method is to use actively traded options on ETFs to manipulate the desired pattern of return outcomes directly.

Alternatives and
Multi-Asset Strategies

12.1. INTRODUCTION

Alternatives are one of the fastest growing areas within passive investing. The term "alternatives" refers to asset classes or strategies that historically were difficult or impossible for most ordinary investors to access but are now accessible through both ETFs and mutual funds. Such previously "exotic" beta is now relatively common, in many cases displacing expensive hedge funds that were the only way to gain exposure of this sort. A hedge fund is a private pool of investment capital that seeks to outperform a specified benchmark by identifying market inefficiencies. Typically, hedge funds employ leverage and often may make short as well as long bets. In 2015, global assets in exchange-traded products crossed $3 trillion (from ETFGI) exceeding for the first time ever the assets in hedge funds.

What was at one point alpha—benchmark outperformance—has now become beta. For example, in the 1980s, only the more sophisticated investors could access emerging markets and their potential for growth and diversification. Today emerging and even frontier markets, like Nigeria or Sri Lanka, are now readily accessible at relatively low cost. Alternatives are a key element of the continuing trend toward the democratization of investing, in many ways competing with hedge funds.

Alternatives raise many interesting investment questions, including how to access and value relatively illiquid assets and how best to combine them effectively. There is also the important question as to whether the ETF "wrapper" is the best one for alternative assets/strategies, or whether these are naturally delivered through hedge funds. I examine the issue of whether the allocation to alternatives is over-weighted to such strategies because of systematic biases in the estimates of return, risk, and liquidity. This chapter also lays the groundwork for Part IV of the book in which I take a closer look at active strategies, especially factor based approaches and ways to replicate hedge funds.

12.2. WHAT ARE ALTERNATIVES?

12.2.1. Alternative Assets, Alternative Strategies

Multi-asset allocation and "alternative" ETFs or mutual funds can refer to asset classes or strategies that for most investors have traditionally been costly or difficult to access, relatively illiquid, and hard to value. These funds are aimed largely at investors seeking: (1) access to "exotic" asset classes such as timber, infrastructure, or volatility; (2) low-cost access to common hedge fund strategies without some of the disadvantages such as lock-ups, gates, or minimum investments; and (3) diversification in the form of low correlation to traditional equity and fixed income returns.

Examples of alternative asset classes include real estate, private equity, infrastructure, commodities, and so on. Examples of alternative strategies include those previously accessed via hedge funds such as managed futures or spread products (table 12.1). I consider leveraged/inverse strategies in a separate chapter later on in the book.

12.2.2. Hedge Funds versus Open-Ended Funds

It is useful to differentiate alternative assets and strategies from how they are packaged up or "wrapped" for investors. For example, a long/short equity strategy or an event-driven strategy could be wrapped in a variety of ways including as a hedge fund or an open-ended fund, such as a mutual fund or ETF. Broadly speaking, alternatives in an ETF wrapper can be used to implement an alternatives strategy in three ways:

Table 12.1 ALTERNATIVE STRATEGIES

Strategy	Description
Hedge fund replicators	Use diverse assets to track a hedge fund index returns series (such as the HFRI fund weighted composite index[a]) or otherwise seek to replicate hedge fund strategies
Managed futures	Essentially momentum strategies in commodities that have low correlation with equity or fixed income returns
Real return	Multi-asset allocations that target a specific "real return" (i.e., return in excess of inflation)
Pure alpha	Specific alpha strategies such as global macro, convertible/merger arbitrage, put writing, global long/short strategies, and so on
Spread	Spread products such as those offering pure exposure to credit spreads
Smart Beta	Specific tilts toward known factors that generate historical risk premia such as value, momentum, minimum volatility, and so on

[a] HFRI is an equally weighted composite of over 2,000 constituent hedge funds.

(1) **Replication**—The fund actually owns the underlying assets, as in gold and silver funds (e.g., GLD, SLV) that own physical bullion.
(2) **Synthetics**—A derivative based approach to tracking, such as many commodities funds that use futures contracts to track the index.
(3) **Systematic Approach**—Model-based approach to creating alternative exposure that may blend replication and synthetic exposures.

The ETF wrapper may not always be appropriate for all strategies or asset classes. Some ETF asset managers do not have the exemptive relief under the 1940 Act to take short positions, as do hedge funds, and their ability to undertake leveraged strategies is constrained too.

EXAMPLE: HEDGE FUND REPLICATOR

The IQ Hedge Multi-Strategy Tracker ETF (QAI) seeks to track, before fees and expenses, the performance of the IQ Hedge Multi-Strategy Index. As of June 2015, the fund had just over $1 billion in assets, the largest in its class. The index the fund tracks attempts to replicate the risk-adjusted return characteristics of hedge funds using multiple hedge fund investment styles, including long/short equity, global macro, market neutral, event-driven, fixed income arbitrage, and emerging markets. The Fund does not invest in hedge funds and the Index does not include hedge funds as components, but rather uses other ETFs to gain exposure. As of that date, the top long holding was the Vanguard Short-Term Bond ETF at 23.59% weight. The fund also does shorts ETFs too.

The investment choices are complex and the dimensions include strategy type (e.g., rotation/timing, multi-factor), asset class (e.g., equity, commodities), region (e.g., Global, Eurozone), weighting scheme (e.g., equal weighted, risk parity, market-capitalization weighted), and style. To date, alternatives have had only modest penetration in the ETF wrapper. Hedge fund replication strategies are growing quickly, although as a fraction of total ETF assets they are still very small, under 1%. To get the risk/return characteristics of hedge funds, these ETFs may also use leveraged/inverse funds.

12.3. INVESTMENT ISSUES

12.3.1. Optimal Capital Allocation

The most critical investment question regarding alternatives is the optimal allocation of capital to these strategies. There are three key inputs into any investment decision: expected return forecasts (alpha), estimates of risk (both volatility/correlation), and transaction costs (liquidity). I argue below that all three inputs are likely to be biased in favor of a higher allocation to alternatives meaning: (a) over-optimistic return forecasts, (b) downward biased estimates of volatility, and (c) upward biased estimates of liquidity. Another set of issues deals with how best to optimally combine alternatives, which is considered in the following section, where I also will consider whether alternatives truly add more diversification to a portfolio.

Let's consider the three investment inputs in turn starting with expected return forecasts. Predicting returns is extremely difficult in the case of alternative investments because of the lack of good historical data. Alternatives are potentially subject to strong effects from survivorship bias, which leads to high return estimates based on the observed data on extant funds or strategies. Failed strategies or funds often are dropped from historical data, and it requires a lot of care to obtain a true return series. Return expectations also fail to correctly value alternative assets in a liquidation scenario when others are also likely rushing for the door, as in the Quant Crisis of 2007 or the aftermath of the financial crisis in 2008. In times of financial stress, liquidation is endogenous, and it can be very costly to sell illiquid holdings. The combination of survivorship bias and underestimation of liquidation costs leads to an upward bias in return expectations.

Now consider the second element, namely risk. Estimates of the return volatility of alternatives are quite possibly downward-biased, again causing the allocation to alternatives to be higher than if risk was correctly estimated. The reason for the bias has to do with non-trading. A smoothed daily, monthly, or quarterly index that reflects non-trading or appraisal-based pricing will result in an underestimate of volatility and correlations with other, liquid assets. To see this, suppose an alternatives portfolio (think of this as real estate or private equity) has a *reported* valuation v_t^{REP} at date t that is a weighted average of its present and past *true* value v_t^{ALT}. True value is unobserved and expressed in logs. So we can write:

$$v_t^{REP} = (1 - \varphi)v_t^{ALT} + \varphi v_{t-1}^{ALT}, \tag{12.1}$$

where $0 \le \varphi \le 1$ captures the extent of appraisal based pricing. The motivation for this model (see, e.g., Fisher, Geltner, and Webb 1994) is that many properties or private assets are actually appraised on a less frequent basis than reporting occurs. So the reported valuation of, say, a commercial property by an appraiser is a weighted average of similar buildings that sold this quarter and last quarter. Taking first differences in log values, it follows that the reported return of the alternative portfolio r_t^{REP} is a smoothed average of the past reported return r_{t-1}^{REP} and the true return r_t^{ALT}:

$$r_t^{REP} = (1 - \varphi)r_t^{ALT} + \varphi r_{t-1}^{ALT}. \tag{12.2}$$

The variance of reported returns is (assuming the volatility of return fundamentals $\sigma^2(r^{ALT})$ is constant over time) is then a fraction of fundamental return variance

$$\sigma^2(r^{REP}) = [1 - 2\varphi(1 - \varphi)]\sigma^2(r^{ALT}). \tag{12.3}$$

This fraction $1 - 2\varphi(1 - \varphi) < 1$ when $\varphi > 0$ and decreases with staleness. Similarly, although true returns r_t^{ALT} are assumed to have no autocorrelation, reported returns are positively autocorrelated. For private equity, for example, the volatility of returns correcting for smoothing is significant; volatility doubles from 11% to 22% and the estimated beta to public equity goes from 0.5 to 1.0 as shown by Pedersen, Page, and He (2014).

For the same reasons, the diversification benefit, measured inversely by the covariance of returns between alternatives and liquid, publicly traded assets such as equities, is likely understated. To see this, suppose r_t^{STK} is the return on the equity component of an investor's portfolio. Then, assuming the equity returns are serially uncorrelated, the covariance between reported alternative and stock returns, denoted by $\sigma(r_t^{REP}, r_t^{STK})$, is a fraction of the true covariance between cotemporaneous alternatives and stock returns:

$$\sigma(r_t^{REP}, r_t^{STK}) = (1 - \varphi)\sigma(r_t^{ALT}, r_t^{STK}). \tag{12.4}$$

Underestimated variance and underestimated covariances with liquid assets in turn implies an *over*-allocation (higher than warranted weight) in less liquid, alternative investments using mean-variance optimization.

Lastly, transaction costs are difficult to estimate for illiquid asset classes and strategies. Alternatives such as private equity or commercial real estate feature high entry and exit barriers. The cost of liquidating a position is unique to each investor and depends on the trading horizon, aggressiveness of order placement, and myriad other factors. In the absence of data, many use estimates from liquid public assets such as quoted bid-ask spreads that understate transaction costs and are not representative of institutional sized liquidity demands. Higher costs and less liquidity should result in a lower optimal allocation to alternatives, all things equal.

12.3.2. Impact on Portfolio Construction

Of the three factors discussed above—returns, risk, and liquidity—the underestimate of volatility is likely to be most challenging in portfolio construction. We can create, albeit with some difficulty, survivorship bias free returns by resurrecting "dead" funds. Similarly, liquidation costs can be reckoned using past experiences. But volatility is more difficult because we only observed a smoothed return series for many alternative asset classes such as real estate or private equity.

How significant is the impact of smoothing on portfolio construction? A factor based approach is one way to isolate the true variance as well as the true correlations between alternatives and public investments such as stocks and bonds. This works by first recovering the true returns of alternatives by removing the dependence on past stated returns, and then modeling the factor structure of actual returns to estimate whether alternative managers are really adding value and diversification. Pedersen, Page, and He (2014) use such an approach and find that the difference between true and reported return volatility is large. Their estimate of the true (unsmoothed) portfolio volatility for a six-asset portfolio of stocks, bonds, timber, farmland, real estate, and private equity is 8.8% versus 5.3% for the estimate based on reported index return data. Interestingly, and consistent with the model above, there is little deviation between the true and reported volatilities of publicly traded assets such as stocks and bonds. The deviation comes from the less liquid asset classes.

Pedersen, Page, and He (2014) then regress their estimate of the true return series$\{\hat{r}_t^{ALT}\}$against a set of common factors (market, size, value, leverage, credit and interest rates, etc.) to see how much real alpha and diversification is added. They conclude: "alternative assets have significant exposure to the same risk factors that drive stock and bond volatility." The implication is that investors can often replicate the payoffs to alternatives using liquid and less costly factors. In addition to higher volatility, they also find alternatives have higher expected drawdowns, greater tail risk, and higher correlations.

12.3.3. Practical Applications: Liquid Real Estate Indexes

As a practical application of the concepts above consider the creation of an ETF that tracks an illiquid alternative such as real property. Physical real estate is an alternative asset whose returns cannot practically be tracked with a fund that replicates holdings or uses synthetic instruments. Many investors want to invest in real estate directly as a hedge against inflation, a source of stable rental income, and to diversify returns. Usually, this has meant adding an allocation to publicly traded REITs (Real Estate Investment Trusts) to a conventional stock/bond portfolio. The alternative, buying assets directly through private markets requires large amounts of capital, patience to hold for long periods, and deep expertise in security selection, esoteric issues such as covenants, and continual monitoring. These attributes are typically beyond all but the most sophisticated investors.

REITs are funds focused on commercial real estate (e.g., shopping malls) and are required to pay out a substantial portion of their income in dividends. But REITs may not be the best way to achieve the original investment objective of exposure to real property: First, they typically incorporate leverage, meaning they issue bonds and carry debt. As such, their equity returns are magnified versions of the underlying asset return that an investor actually seeks to track. Second, given their focus, REIT index returns are not generally representative of unlevered property returns—they are only weakly correlated with the returns of real property indexes. An example of such an index is the IPD U.S. Quarterly Property Index which tracks the unlevered return performance of 3,913 property investments with a total value of $222 billion as of January 2015. Third, because of the nature of their investments, REIT returns are positively correlated with equity returns.

As a result, there is growing interest in investments that track real property indexes. How does one construct a liquid fund or index to track what is essentially a very illiquid asset? As shown above, property indexes exhibit serial correlation due to appraisal-based pricing. So, the first step is to remove any serial correlation in returns induced by smoothing. Statistical techniques can be used to recover the true return r_t^{ALT} behind reported returns. To see how this works, recall from equation (12.2) that $r_t^{REP} = (1 - \varphi)r_t^{ALT} + \varphi r_{t-1}^{ALT}$ so we can write:

$$r_{t-1}^{ALT} = (1 - \varphi)^{-1}(r_{t-1}^{REP} - \varphi r_{t-2}^{ALT}). \tag{12.5}$$

Substituting equation (12.5) into (12.2) and proceeding recursively, we can show that r_t^{REP} is a weighted average of past reported returns and a fraction of the present true return.

The implication of this result is that we can estimate the unobserved *true* return by purging appraisal-induced autocorrelation in stated returns. Specifically, true return is the residual from a regression of *stated* physical real estate index returns on lagged *stated* returns of the appropriate length. For example, although real estate valuations are reported quarterly, annual year-end appraisals are common implying a lag at $t - 4$. Call this estimate $\hat{r}_t^{ALT}$. Once we have identified the true return series to a non-tradable asset (such as real property), we can see how best to track this series using liquid assets.

The goal of an investable or liquid fund is to track the estimate true returns as closely as possible using a variety of traded instruments such as equities, inflation-protected bonds, corporate bonds, and so on. Formally, the investment objective is to choose optimal weights $\{h_i\}$ over the N possible liquid instruments to minimize the expected tracking error between the true return series and the liquid portfolio; that is to select h to:

$$Min_{\{h\}}E[|\hat{r}_t^{ALT} - r_t^{PORT}|], \tag{12.6}$$

where $r_t^{PORT} = \sum_{i=1}^{N} h_i r_{i,t}$ is the return on the liquid real property portfolio over the N reference assets. The expectation is taken looking forward: that is we form the optimal multi-asset liquid portfolio six months ago that minimizes tracking error looking forward to now. This approach can be used for constructing smart exposures to any other alternative asset class.

LIQUID REAL ESTATE INDEXES

The MSCI Liquid Real Estate Indexes (see MSCI Research Insight, "A Liquid Benchmark for Private Real Estate," January 2015, for details) are multi-asset class indexes that seek a risk/return profile similar to owning direct real estate but instead using liquid instruments. If individual REITs are included in the possible universe of N assets, then they are appropriately delevered (by holding their bonds as well as their equities in the correct proportions) to correctly track the returns on the real assets they hold. The procedure to construct the index is very similar to the one detailed earlier, but MSCI also includes a minimum volatility tilt in the equity component.

12.4. COMBINING ALTERNATIVES: FUNDAMENTAL LAW OF ACTIVE MANAGEMENT

Assuming we have all the risk and return inputs correct, combining hedge fund like strategies into an optimal portfolio also requires knowledge of how these are constructed to maximize performance. The fundamental law of active management (see Grinold and Kahn 2000) provides a key insight into this question by explaining the determinants of performance measured by the *Information Ratio* or IR. The IR is defined as the ratio of active returns to active risk. It is analogous to the Sharpe ratio, but distinct in that it is defined relative to a benchmark index; whereas, the Sharpe ratio is the ratio of excess return over the risk-free rate to volatility. The S&P 500, for example, has a positive Sharpe ratio (of approximately 0.39 since the 1950s based on Morningstar data) because its returns have historically exceeded the rate on treasury bills, but an S&P 500 index fund that tracks the benchmark exactly, or a closet indexer, would have zero IR as it takes no active bets.

The fundamental law states that the *IR* is the product of the information coefficient *IC* (skill) and the square root of breadth $\sqrt{N}$ (number of independent bets taken per unit of time) so that $IR = IC \times \sqrt{N}$. Skill here is measured by the correlation between actual and forecast returns. For active managers, *IC* figures like 0.05 are considered quite good. The fundamental law has been extended to allow for slippage through implementation, so *IR* is the product skill and breadth, scaled by a transfer coefficient *TC* that lies between 0 and 1:

$$IR = TC \times IC \times \sqrt{N}. \tag{12.7}$$

The fundamental law can be derived theoretically from the optimal portfolio construction of a mean-variance investor. It emphasizes the casino-like need for an active manager for odds in your favor and large numbers of bets to achieve success. An active manager who takes, say, 25 independent "bets" on a quarterly basis (100 bets a year) and has an *IC* = 0.05 and no implementation inefficiency or slippage (*TC* = 1), would have an IR of approximately 0.5. So, if this active manager had a target tracking error to benchmark of 4%, we would expect the fund manager to produce excess returns of 2% over the benchmark index. If the manager's horizon is annual so that only 25 bets are taken per annum, *IR* falls to 0.25 and the excess return from 2% to 1%.

In the case of alternatives, as argued above, *IC* estimates could be overly optimistic because of sample selection bias. Similarly, *TC* may be too high because we overstate liquidity and understate frictions. What about breadth? The challenge in the case of alternatives is to define breadth. Investing in 10 different managed futures funds is not the same as 10 different bets because the underlying strategies—and factor exposures to momentum—are likely very similar. In other words, what matters is the independent nature of the bets.

Similarly, as we will see in the following chapters, hedge funds pursuing seemingly very different strategies in diverse asset classes may have exposure to the same factor. For example, a manager buying stocks with high book/price ratios and a bond fund buying "fallen angels" are both betting on the value factor. Combining different alternatives efficiently thus requires detailed knowledge of their underlying investment strategies and correlations across different economic environments. Past experience has shown that return correlations among asset classes and strategies tend to increase in times of market stress, which may again overstate the diversification benefit when needed most.

12.5. CHAPTER SUMMARY

The fastest growing area of passive investing today is the extension beyond traditional portfolios of stocks and bonds to include other asset classes and strategies. More esoteric "alternative" investments that span multiple asset classes or strategies are now very much at center stage. Liquid alternatives are interesting because they offer diversification and potentially access to alpha (and beta) that was previously unavailable. There is considerable opportunity here for ETFs to grow by displacing active managers and hedge funds that offer commoditized strategies at relatively high cost.

That said, there are reasons to believe that the three key inputs required for an allocation to alternatives—expected return, liquidity, and risk—are likely biased in estimation toward an over-allocation to this segment. Further, an investor looking for portfolio diversification by adding multiple alternatives should be aware that merely increasing the number of different funds in their portfolio is not the same as increasing the breadth.

Active Strategies

13

Active Strategies

13.1. INTRODUCTION

In Part IV of the book, I take a closer look at active strategies that seek to generate alpha or excess returns relative to the stated benchmark. For context, refer back to table 1.1 that first introduced the notion of a continuum of strategies ranging from pure index to fully active. The key concept here is the notion that passive investing requires active choices regarding choice of assets and benchmarks. But what do we mean by active? There are different definitions, but as an operational construct, one can define any deviation from market-capitalization weighting as an active strategy. The logic follows from asset pricing theory that shows that the market portfolio is mean-variance efficient, meaning that there is no portfolio with a higher expected return for the same level of risk. So, the market portfolio—and hence a cap weighting scheme—offers a natural benchmark.

Active strategies defined this way fall into two distinct groups: (1) deviations, either heuristic or model-driven from market capitalization weights based on considerations other than alpha such as diversification risk or liquidity considerations; and (2) alpha strategies that directly attempt to outperform a benchmark, again either based on fundamental views or quantitative strategies and building on the growing interest in alternatives. In the rest of the chapter I will follow this grouping, reviewing the major strategies and their relative merits.

Finally, I review the key differences between different active investment vehicles or fund structures. The great majority of ETFs passively track an index, but an increasing number pursue active strategies of various forms, much like their active mutual fund cousins. However, the ETF wrapper is not necessarily a good fit for all strategies, especially active strategies where daily transparency into holdings may present a problem. Managers of strategies in illiquid markets or those taking concentrated positions might be concerned about "front-running," which is legally a violation of a broker's fiduciary duty to execute first for the customer ahead of their own proprietary trades. I use the term in the colloquial sense to refer to a situation market participants (not just the executing broker) anticipate the fund's intentions and trade ahead of impending purchases or sales with the intention of profiting from any temporary increase in prices from fund buying or selling pressure. As such, front-running increases the transaction costs of the fund to the detriment of fund investors. A related concern for an active manager who is engaged in costly security selection is having their investment insights/ideas compromised through the disclosure of their positions.

Actively managed portfolios are also difficult to hedge and so, unlike most index-based ETFs, market makers may struggle to keep bid-ask spreads tight and tracking error low. ETFs are also not suitable when the underlying investments do not have sufficient liquidity to accommodate daily creation and redemption activity. That said, there are many examples of successful actively managed ETFs including popular bond ETFs such as the PIMCO Enhanced Short-Maturity Active Exchange-Traded Fund (MINT). The active space is one of the more exciting areas in the ETF industry but not without significant challenges.

13.2. ALTERNATIVE WEIGHTING SCHEMES AND FUNDAMENTAL INDEXES

13.2.1. Equal-Weighting and Price-Weighting

The simplest example of non-market capitalization weights is equal-weighting, where the portfolio weight on stock $i = 1, \ldots N$ is $h_i = \frac{1}{N}$. One can call this a quantitative or model-based scheme, since it is based on a rule, but the notion of equal weighting is somewhat subjective.

EQUALLY WEIGHTED FUNDS IN THE REAL WORLD

There are many real-world examples of equally weighted funds. Consider the SPDR S&P Oil & Gas Exploration & Production fund (XOP), which equally weights component stocks. Because of this weighting scheme, the fund holds smaller stocks than market capitalization weighted funds in the sector and tends to be more sensitive to oil price movements than these funds.

Equally weighted portfolios typically tilt toward the size factor in that they emphasize smaller capitalization securities and have greater portfolio turnover than an equivalent capitalization-weighted benchmark. While the effect of size is still debated, the size factor did well until relatively recent capital market history, and such portfolios have attractive return backtests (i.e., simulated performance over past periods) in addition to simplicity in construction.

A related but more complex heuristic approach is so-called diversity weighting which is mathematically a blend of capitalization- and equal-weighting schemes.

AVOIDING DOMINANCE

Equal weighting is especially important if the securities in the fund differ radically in capitalization. An example is the iShares Exponential Technologies ETF (XT) that seeks to "track the investment results of an index composed of developed and emerging market companies that create or use exponential technologies." To avoid dominance by a few mega-cap technology stocks (e.g., Apple, Inc.) the fund equally weights the stocks it holds. Similarly, the Purefunds ISE Cyber Security ETF (HACK) also adopts a form of equal weighting, also to avoid dominance by mega-caps.

Price-weighting schemes (where $h_i = p_i / \sum_k p_k$) have a long history, including the Dow Jones Industrial Average (DJIA) and Nikkei 225, because they are straightforward to understand and compute.

APPLE JOINS THE DJIA

A committee of Wall Street Journal and S&P Dow Jones Indices representatives selects the stocks in the Dow Jones Industrial Average based on factors including a company's reputation, investor relevance, and growth history. Apple Inc., the world's highest market capitalization stock at the time, was added in March 2015 month to the DJIA following a 7:1 stock split the previous year that brought its price in-line with other constituents. Had it not been for the split, Apple would have dominated the price-weighted index. As it is, the weight of Apple in the DJIA is much less than in a market capitalization weighting scheme.

Although rule-based in theory, many indexes are in fact based on subjective criteria in addition to quantitative criteria or explicit model optimization.

13.2.2. Fundamental Indexes

Fundamental Indexes (see, e.g., Arnott, Hsu, and Moore 2005) over-weight securities with characteristics sought by investors including:

- **Firm Size**—Revenues and book value;
- **Profitability**—Profits, margins, and cash flow;
- **Risk**—Idiosyncratic and systematic; and
- **Dividends**—Yield, consistency, and sustainability.

Once the benchmark index weights have been selected (which in and of itself is an active decision), the fund replicates the holdings to the extent possible. The stated motivation for fundamental indexes is to avoid errors induced from market capitalization weighting, the idea being that a positive (negative) pricing error in a stock leads to over (under) weighting in the index. As these errors correct over time, proponents argue, a market-capitalization based weighting scheme will exhibit return drag. However, this argument implies that (see Perold 2007) that market capitalization should be a predictor of future excess returns. So, fundamental indexing is really a form of active management because it involves a tilt of some sort based on alpha drivers such as earnings and so on.

13.2.3. Diversification Strategies

Model-based approaches can reduce portfolio risk or concentration. These can resemble minimum variance portfolios, but differ in that their motivation is explicitly to reduce risk through the weighting scheme. Risk Parity and Maximum Sharpe objective functions are the most common such schemes. Risk parity achieves diversification by finding weights that equalize the contributions of each security to portfolio risk. Formally, the objective is to find portfolio weights for every security i and j such that the marginal contribution of risk weighted by holdings is equal across all assets:

$$ h_i \frac{\partial \sigma(h)}{\partial h_i} = h_j \frac{\partial \sigma(h)}{\partial h_j} . \tag{13.1} $$

As with the minimum variance portfolio, this weighting scheme depends only on the risk model through the estimated variance matrix. Max diversification is a subset of general mean-variance; it captures the correlations among securities and yields a diversification benefit. In comparison though, portfolio construction using factors gives investors the ability to tailor their own optimally diversified portfolios based on how well they can stand "bad times." So, for example, a sovereign wealth fund with a horizon of decades (and the ability to ride out long periods of underperformance of a given factor such as value) might have a very different notion of diversification than the maximum diversification portfolio.

Another objective is to maximize the portfolio's Sharpe ratio, that is, find the portfolio with the highest ratio of *ex ante* return (in excess of the risk-free rate) to volatility. Unlike the methods above, this objective requires assumptions on expected returns. One approach is to assume the expected excess return for every stock $i = 1, \dots N$ is proportional to its own volatility so that $E[r_i] - r_f = \rho \sigma_i$. In this case, the maximum Sharpe ratio portfolio requires selecting h to maximize $h' \hat{\sigma} / \sqrt{h' V h}$ subject to the constraint of full investment $h' - 1$ In the numerator, σ is the $N \times 1$ vector of stock volatilities σ_i defined as the square-root of the diagonal elements of the variance matrix V. It is clear that in this formulation the maximum Sharpe portfolio also depends only on the assumed risk structure, and hence in practical terms this closely resembles the approaches described earlier.

13.2.4. Optimized Funds

Optimized funds that balance volatility against other factors such as transaction costs/liquidity offer another example where $a = 0$, but the fund departs from market capitalization weighting. Letting $c(h_t - h_{t-1})$ denote the transaction costs associated with trading (i.e., with the *change* in holdings from time $t - 1$ to t), the objective function would be to choose h to minimize a weighted sum of variance and illiquidity:

$$Min_{\{h\}}U(h_t)=(h_t-h_b)'V(h_t-h_b)+ \gamma c(h_t-h_{t-1}),\tag{13.2}$$

where γ is the penalty on transaction cost and turnover. The transaction cost function could be simply a measure of liquidity such as bid-ask spreads in the underlying securities in which case the functional form is linear and c is simply half the bid-ask spread. In a more complex model with market or price impact, the functional form would capture the costs associated with a change in holdings, introducing a time-dependency.

13.2.5. Model-Based Transparent Active Funds

So far we have considered heuristic approaches to risk reduction or weighting including control of turnover, constraints on tracking error, or deviations from market capitalization weights based on simple schema such as equal weighting. By contrast, model-based transparent active use explicit quantitative rules govern portfolio selection. Transparent in this regard means the fund's holdings are visible on a daily basis with a one-day lag. These include minimum variance portfolios, which minimize risk subject to a fully invested constraint, and factor portfolios, which seek exposure to various economic factors and various diversification schemes.

Here, I develop a general framework to accommodate various types of active model-based strategies to select optimal holdings. The inputs are an $N \times 1$ vector of alphas $a = (a_1, \ldots, a_N)$ and an $N \times N$ covariance matrix V whose i^{th}-diagonal element is the stock's return variance σ_i^2 and whose (i,j) off-diagonal element is the covariance $\sigma_{i,j}$ in the returns of stocks i and j. In the case of the minimum variance portfolio, $a = 0$; whereas, for factor or other active portfolios, a takes on positive or negative values based on the quantitative or model-based signal.

Consider a generalized optimization problem that selects the optimal active weight h to maximize portfolio alpha $h'a$ against active risk $h'Vh$ (weighted by a risk aversion parameter ρ), subject to the constraint that the portfolio holdings add to 1 (i.e., are fully invested). Note that for simplicity the holdings here are relative to the benchmark which could be interpreted as market capitalization based weights on the desired index. Formally, I write:

$$Max\,U(h)=h'a-\rho h'Vh \tag{13.3}$$

subject to $(h'e-1)$, where $e = (1, \ldots, 1)$ is an $N \times 1$ vector.

Maximization of the objective function over h with the additional assumption that the sum of all alpha over-weights and under-weights equal zero yields the optimal portfolio (see Grinold and Kahn 2000):

$$h^*=\left(\frac{1}{2\rho}\right)V^{-1}\alpha+\left(\frac{V^{-1}e}{e'V^{-1}e}\right).\tag{13.4}$$

So, the optimal portfolio consists of two terms: The first term is the active port-folio, based on alpha forecasts, and the second term, as discussed later, is the minimum-variance portfolio.

13.2.6. Minimum Volatility Strategies

It is well known that when asset returns are jointly normally distributed, then variance is an appropriate risk measure. Moreover, given a set of expected returns, optimizing a portfolio under the assumption of normality is straightforward, since the first two moments of returns completely characterize the distribution of returns. Simplicity and elegance explains the popularity of mean-variance optimization.

Minimum-variance strategies have long been attractive (see, e.g., Black 1972) because of their high Sharpe ratios over time, low correlation with individ-ual security selection models, and consistency across markets. For investors who previously paid a large fee to hedge fund managers to duplicate minimum-variance portfolios, and a wide set of such products are now available at low cost.[1] Sensibility arguments include both behavioral explanations and economic arguments where low-risk stocks have abnormally high risk-adjusted returns. Behavioral hypoth-eses include investor attention or risk-seeking behavior where high risk, high-beta stocks are more widely followed and are overvalued. Theories based on economic fundamentals include constraint-based theories where investors are unable to fully gain their desired leverage and hence pay a premium for high-beta stocks.

Setting $a = 0$ in the expression for h^* yields the pure minimum variance port-folio. This portfolio minimizes total risk while requiring the holdings to sum to 1, that is be fully invested:

$$h^* = \left(\frac{V^{-1}e}{e'V^{-1}e} \right). \tag{13.5}$$

Clarke, de Silva, and Thorley (2006) provide empirical evidence on the perfor-mance of minimum variance portfolios relative to their market capitalization-weighted analogues.

13.2.7. Pure Long-Short Funds

The requirement to be fully invested is a key differentiator from a classic long-short fund. Without the additional constraint of full investment, unrestricted active holdings are:

$$h^* = \left(\frac{1}{2\rho} \right) V^{-1}a. \tag{13.6}$$

1. For example, various global and regional minimum-volatility portfolios are available in ETF form. Minimum-variance portfolios are obtained by carrying out mean-variance optimization with the mean returns all set to zero.

To gain intuition, note that when the variance matrix V is diagonal and assets are uncorrelated, the optimal unrestricted active weight in stock i is $h_i^* = \left(\dfrac{1}{2\rho\sigma_i^2} \right) a_i$. This is intuitive: active weights are simply proportional to the expected return in each asset scaled by that asset's return variance, i.e., $\left(\dfrac{a_i}{\sigma_i^2} \right)$. The proportionality factor $\frac{1}{2\rho}$ is inversely related to risk aversion, so more risk-averse managers take smaller bets. In practice, managers typically optimize to a specific risk target, which is more intuitive than selecting a risk aversion coefficient. Let σ_{TE}^2 denote the desired portfolio variance (the square of tracking error) where $\sigma_{TE}^2 = E[h'Vh]$. Given that a manager has optimized their portfolio, this expression implies that we can "back out" the underlying risk aversion from the target tracking error as shown in equation (13.7).

Typically, alpha is standardized because the distribution of excess return forecasts may change dynamically over time. For example, if alpha is a momentum score, the cross-sectional variance of excess return to momentum may be quite different in trending versus normal markets. Accordingly, I can take $a_i \sim N(0, 1)$. This is a reasonable assumption under the law of large numbers where each security's return forecast arises from many possible signals about fundamental value and technical factors. As alpha is standardized, and again considering the case of a diagonal V, I write $ex\ ante$ risk as:

$$\sigma_{TE}^2 = E\left[\sum_{i=1}^{N} (\sigma_i h_i^*)^2 \right] = \sum_{i=1}^{N} E\left[\left(\frac{a_i}{2\rho} \right)^2 \right] = N\left(\frac{1}{2\rho} \right)^2. \tag{13.7}$$

Equation (13.7) lets us map the tracking error to risk aversion; a higher coefficients of risk aversion implies tighter tracking error. So, $\sigma_{TE} = \frac{\sqrt{N}}{2\rho}$ so that $h_i^* = \left(\dfrac{\sigma_{TE}}{\sqrt{N}} \right)\left(\dfrac{a_i}{\sigma_i^2} \right)$. Given alpha is standardized and approximately normal, these weights are normally distributed with mean 0 and standard deviation $\left(\dfrac{\sigma_{TE}}{\sqrt{N}} \right)\left(\dfrac{1}{\sigma_i^2} \right)$.

Optimal holdings increase in the ratio of alpha to stock-specific risk (variance) and also with the manager's target tracking error, but decrease with the size of the universe. Actual holdings are just active weights plus the benchmark so that $h_i = h_i^* + h_{i,b}$. The model of positions is useful because managers may want to assess $ex\ ante$ their likelihood of taking a short position because shorting may impose additional costs or require specialized expertise such as traders who are knowledgeable about securities borrowing/lending. So, the probability that the manager takes a short position in a given stock is

$$\Pr[h_i^* + h_{i,b} < 0] = \Pr\left[\left(\frac{\sigma_{TE}}{\sqrt{N}} \right)\left(\frac{a_i}{\sigma_i^2} \right) < -h_{i,b} \right] = \Phi\left(-h_{i,b}\sqrt{N}\left(\frac{\sigma_i^2}{\sigma_{TE}} \right) \right), \tag{13.8}$$

where $\Phi(z)$ denotes the cumulative standard normal distribution evaluated at z. Since shorting costs can be significant, it is important for a fund manager to have an idea as to how likely it is to take a short position in any stock.

EVALUATING THE LIKELIHOOD OF SHORTING

Not all negative active weights are short positions, especially if benchmark holdings are non-negative, which is typically the case. For example, consider a fund that has a 3% target tracking error and a 1,000 stock universe. Using the expression above, a stock with benchmark weight of 0.5% and volatility of 30% will be shorted with probability 0.318. If benchmark weight is 0.75%, the likelihood this stock is held short falls to 0.238 and at a 3% weight it is essentially zero. Note that stocks outside the benchmark universe but within the manager's discretion (such as international stocks for a fund manager benchmarked to a domestic index but with leeway to invest abroad) have zero benchmark weight and hence are equally likely to be long or short.

13.2.8. Risk Concentration

The analysis above can shed light on risk concentration in active model-driven portfolios. This is an issue that is often a motivator for using alternative weighting schemes. Observe that the contribution of asset i to overall portfolio risk (utilizing our simplifying assumption that the covariance matrix is diagonal) is simply:

$$(\sigma_i h_i^*)^2 = \left(\frac{a_i}{2\rho}\right)^2. \tag{13.9}$$

Relative to total portfolio variance $\sum_i (\sigma_i h_i^*)^2$, the risk contribution from a single security is $(1/N)(a_i)^2$. Suppose we rank assets from highest to lowest in terms of proportional contribution to risk. The proportional contribution of the top q-th percentile of the N assets (the top qN securities) is given by $[\sum_{i=1}^{Nq} (a_i)^2] / N$. With $a_i \sim N(0, 1)$, the cumulating of squared normal alpha scores means that active portfolios will tend to be concentrated in relatively few holdings. Shown in figure 13.1 is the theoretical proportional contribution of the top q-th percentile of holdings with alpha drawn from a standard normal distribution. For example, the top 25% of active holdings represents approximately 72% of overall portfolio risk.

Real-world portfolio managers will only take positions in assets where their alpha exceeds estimated transaction costs. This typically leads to *even more* concentration than in theory. Based on my experience, for an actual active fund portfolio, the top 5% of names may account for 70% to 80% of active risk, and the top 25% for virtually all risk. So, in a fund universe of 1,000 names, performance is largely driven by the top 50 positions. That concentration risk is a driver of efforts to embed diversification formally into portfolio construction.

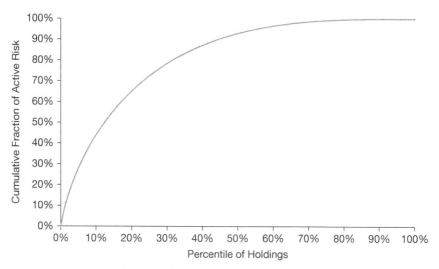

Figure 13.1 Fraction of active risk represented by percentiles of holdings.

13.2.9. Tail Risk

Recently, a growing number of financial practitioners and academics have begun to explore alternatives to variance as a measure of risk, and approaches to portfolio construction that go beyond mean-variance optimization. This interest builds on a large body of evidence suggesting that investors fear losses more than they value gains—that is, investors are "loss averse." The mean-variance approach is symmetric in its treatment of risk—the variance penalty applies to up-side risk as much as down-side risk. Further, the empirical distributions of returns of many financial assets do not appear to be consistent with the assumption of normality, exhibiting left-skew and/or fat tails, as exemplified in the financial crisis. For example, in the period January 2004 to December 2013, the S&P 500 index had skewness of −0.86 and kurtosis of 5.1, inconsistent with a normal distribution. In this situation, the mean-variance solution is not necessarily optimal.

The empirical and behavioral considerations above suggest adding a tail-risk penalty to the standard mean-variance optimization framework. One such measure is Conditional Value at Risk (CVaR), which measures the mean return, conditional on being less than the VaR threshold. (This measure is also called CoVaR in the risk literature, where it is employed to measure systemic risk.) In ordinary words, the 5% monthly CVaR for the S&P 500 in the last 10 years is the average return in the worst 6 months (120 months × 5%) in that period. Using monthly returns in the 10 years ending December 31, 2013, and conditional upon being in the lower 5% tail, the expected monthly return or CVaR is −9.75%. In other words, we would expect to lose almost 10% of the portfolio in a month, given we are in the worst 5% of the period.

Formally, I define:

$$CVaR = \frac{1}{N} \sum_{n=1}^{N} (R_n | R_n < VaR), \qquad (13.10)$$

where N is the number of observations, R_n denotes the nth return in this set, and VaR is the Value at Risk criterion. The setting of VaR defines the fraction of the left tail that goes into the CVaR calculation. Practitioners typically focus on settings delivering 5% or 1% CVaR readings.

EXAMPLE: USING CVAR TO ASSESS SYSTEMIC RISK

The International Monetary Fund (2015) uses CVaR to assess systemic risk. Their analysis of the impact of a fund's distress on systemic risk is measured by the *difference* between when the fund is *normal* state (measured by median VaR, or equivalently 50% CVaR) less in a *distressed* state (5% CVaR). Looking at about 1,500 mutual funds, they take the largest 100 funds (globally) for each of five investment focus categories: developed markets (sovereign, corporate bond, equity) and emerging markets (equity and debt). Developed market sovereign debt has the lowest systemic risk of any asset class while emerging market equity the highest. This is intuitive, but surprisingly, the study finds that a fund's contribution to systemic risk depends most on investment focus; the size of the fund's asset manager has no impact. The result should mitigate concerns about the centrality of large, global financial institutions. Rather, the focus should be on product-line and investment-focus perspectives, not size, when discussing the designation of asset managers and funds as a source of systemic risk for regulatory purposes.

The addition of tail risk as a penalty in addition to variance changes the objective-function that now becomes:

$$Max_{\{h\}} \ U(h) = h'a - \rho h'Vh - \lambda_{CVaR}CVaR(h), \quad\quad (13.11)$$

where h is the optimal active portfolio weight relative to benchmark and $\lambda_{CVaR} \geq 0$ is the penalty on tail risk. Downing et al. (2014) show that minimum-volatility constructions are competitive with minimum-CVaR in mitigating tail-risk exposure. Based on historical backtests from January 2004 to December 2013 for two different security universes (the MSCI All Countries World Index (ACWI) and the S&P 500 Index), they compare a traditional minimum volatility (MinVol) with a strategy (MinCVaR) that also penalizes tail risk.

While the Minimum CVaR portfolio will, by definition, offer the lowest *ex ante* CVaR, table 13.1 shows that, on an *ex post* basis the Minimum Volatility strategy results in lower tail risk, as measured by conditional and total value-at-risk. This is true for both universes. So, *ex post*, investors better managed tail-risk using a minimum-volatility overlay strategy than explicitly penalizing extreme losses via conditional value-at-risk (CVaR).

What is the intuition for this surprising result? By definition, a focus on tail risk means focusing on relatively rare events, putting a premium on the number of time periods over which asset returns and other data points can be measured. So, in a sample horizon of, say, 30 years the estimates of tail risk will be dominated

Table 13.1 Comparison of Optimized Portfolios

	S&P 500			MSCI ACCWI		
	Index	MinVol	MinCVaR	Index	MinVol	MinCVaR
Risk	4.2	3.1	3.6	5.6	4.5	3.7
CVaR	−9.6	−7.1	−7.9	−12.8	−7.3	−9.9
VaR	−7.3	−4.9	−5.8	−9.3	−4.8	−6.4

SOURCE: Downing et al. (2014). All numbers are expressed in monthly percent.

by a few events. By contrast, minimum-volatility approaches use factor risk models that incorporate information beyond historical returns and update estimates regularly, while CVaR calculations only update on infrequent tail events.

A practical implication of this result is that if tail-risk reduction is an investment goal, employing a minimum-volatility portfolio exposure is potentially a better way of achieving this goal. This solution can be cheap and easy to implement because it will not result in a rebalancing of the fund, and various minimum-volatility products are readily available on the market.

13.3. KEY DIFFERENCES BETWEEN ACTIVE STRUCTURES

13.3.1. Hedge Funds versus ETFs

For investors seeking alternative exposure, ETFs do have limitations. These arise in part because of the regulatory structure (in the United States, most ETFs are 1940 Act funds) that restricts what ETFs can hold and the types of strategies they can purse. Hedge funds have several advantages including:

- **Concentration**—Hedge funds can hold highly concentrated positions unlike ETFs that are subject to diversification rules;
- **Leverage**—Hedge funds can and often do use large amounts of leverage or gearing (e.g., 15:1) to amplify their returns. Leveraged and inverse ETPs have embedded gearing but at significantly lower levels than hedge funds in general;
- **Shorting**—Hedge funds can play both the positive and negative signal bets with relatively few constraints compared to ETFs;
- **Illiquidity**—Hedge funds can hold very illiquid assets (e.g., mezzanine debt), while ETFs and index mutual funds are more constrained in the nature of publicly traded assets they can hold;
- **Turnover**—As active vehicles, some hedge funds may have high turnover strategies, for example, high-frequency traders. Tax factors often preclude high turnover for passive managers; and
- **Disclosure**—ETFs are highly transparent which enables pricing via arbitrage. That level of transparency (as discussed earlier) can be detrimental in that position changes over several days might be observed

and the underlying signals reverse-engineered. By contrast, large hedge funds typically report their positions only quarterly and with a significant lag.

The flexibility hedge funds have in these dimensions allowed them to pursue strategies that ETFs cannot, allowing them to harvest risk premiums.

13.3.2. Active Mutual Funds versus ETFs

Index funds have the specific investment objective of matching the returns of a specific benchmark while active funds seek to outperform a specified benchmark. An example of an active fund is the SPDR DoubleLine Total Return Tactical ETF (TOTL), which from the prospectus is an actively managed fixed income fund that seeks to outperform its benchmark, the Barclays US Aggregate Bond Index, "in part by exploiting mispriced areas of the bond market while also including asset classes not included in the index such as high yield bonds and emerging markets debt." Index ETFs have captured a significant share of the mutual fund market, but active ETFs are still in the early part of their growth phase.

A broad range of strategies can be considered active and can be loosely grouped into (1) security screening that causes deviations from market-cap weighting (such as socially responsible investing and environmental, social, and governance [ESG], where firms are excluded based on pre-defined criteria like carbon emissions); (2) quantitative or model-based strategies (including hedge fund exposure replication and factor based approaches); and (3) fundamental strategies (such as sector rotation, etc.) where portfolio managers have discretion over security selection, timing, and so on. Active structures differ in important respects as summarized in table 13.2.

These differences most matter in respect to transparency. Active ETFs are likely to see considerable growth in future years because of their tax advantages and lower fees. It may come as a surprise to learn that many active mutual funds actually hold substantial ETF positions, either for asset allocation or tactical uses.

EXAMPLE: A MUTUAL FUND INVESTING PRIMARILY IN ETFs

The Stadion Managed Risk 100 Fund (ETFFX) is an open-ended mutual fund whose stated objective is to seek long-term capital appreciation while maintaining capital preservation. The Fund invests primarily in exchange-traded funds and in cash or cash equivalent positions. As of April 28, 2015, the fund had assets of $233 million and an expense ratio of 1.53%, and up to a 5.75% front-end load. Five ETFs account for 83.7% of holdings.

SOURCE: Morningstar and Bloomberg, as of April 28, 2015. Holdings data are as of the filing date February 28, 2015. See also Stan Luxenberg, "Why Actively Managed Mutual Funds Are Investing in ETFs," September 28, 2012, available at http://www.thestreet.com/story/ 11722087/2/why-actively-managed-mutual-funds-are-investing-in-etfs.html.

Table 13.2 COMPARISON OF ACTIVE FUND STRUCTURES

	Active Mutual Fund	**Active ETF**
Fees and loads	Can vary but are typically higher than ETFs offering static factor exposures; may charge front-end fees	Common active exposures (e.g., growth/value) are available at low cost
Subscription and redemption costs	Typically paid from fund assets	Paid by broker creating or redeeming the ETF
Transparency	Required quarterly but may be available at higher frequencies	Required daily
Liquidity	All transactions occur at the close and at the fund's NAV	Liquidity available intraday
Access	Requires set up with the mutual fund manager, although can be held in a brokerage account thereafter	Bought or sold from any brokerage account
Taxes	Redemption gains are borne by remaining shareholders in the fund	In-kind transactions do not incur capital gains

While exchange-trading is an attractive feature of ETFs for many investors such as hedge funds and others who may want to quickly put on or take off positions, it is presumably less important for investors in active strategies (including Smart Beta) who seek to capture performance in excess of the benchmark over longer horizons. But intraday liquidity and volumes in the secondary market are not necessary for active funds to gravitate toward an ETF structure. As discussed earlier, investors can access liquidity in the primary market so even if secondary market liquidity is low, an active ETF structure may still make sense from a cost and taxation perspective.

13.3.3. Active Funds and Regulation

The growing interest in active funds means that asset managers and investors will continue to seek to bring additional types of ETFs to market quickly. The next generation of ETFs will most likely be ETFs that do not track an index. While these funds may be thought of as actively managed, these products may also provide exposure to asset classes, such as short-term cash markets or alternative beta, where representative indexes are difficult to build. The United States is the region where innovation in active funds is most apparent, and this is where regulation plays a key role.

Recall that ETFs are a blend of open-end mutual fund and closed-end fund structures, and hence technically exist under the applicable US laws only through exemptive relief by the SEC. New rules such as generic exemptive relief have reduced the requirement for individual listing approval and significantly expedited the listing process for most new US ETFs. To the extent that new active products invest in securities, they would be subject to the 1940 Act and require exemptive relief. Further, the market-making aspects of these ETFs would also be subject to regulation under the 1934 Act. As described earlier, the SEC is particularly focused on the issues of how such funds would track NAV in the absence of transparency and with concerns over large spreads deriving from lack of transparency.

The SEC is currently considering a number of exemptive applications relating to actively managed ETFs that vary significantly in how they will function. In November 2014, the SEC granted exemptive relief to one such proposal from Eaton Vance to launch a series of actively managed, nontransparent products that combine attributes of ETFs and mutual funds. This structure, known as an Exchange Traded Managed Fund (ETMF), provides for NAV plus pricing much like mutual funds. That is, investors do not see intraday prices as with an ETF but rather pre-commit to a particular price premium over NAV, which is determined at the end of the day. It seems likely that more mutual fund firms will enter the ETF industry, either with an ETMF structure or some new innovation. This is an interesting area where regulation and law may have a significant impact on the future development of the industry.

13.4. CHAPTER SUMMARY

Market capitalization weights have a theoretical foundation in modern portfolio theory. On a practical basis, cap weighting provides a low turnover way to track broad indexes; they are easily implementable in liquid, investable asset classes. Departing from market capitalization weights implies some form of active investing. Active investing may make sense for many investors who are not representative of the market or care about different elements of the return distribution such as tail risk; they may also make sense in markets that are nontransparent or illiquid.

The ETF wrapper, however, is not a good fit for some types of strategies, especially active strategies where daily transparency into holdings may present a problem. There are several ways to mitigate possible information leakage, and undoubtedly many more will be proposed in the coming years. Even so, fundamental managers in illiquid markets or those taking concentrated positions might be concerned about front-running or having their investment insights/ideas compromised through the disclosure of their positions. Actively managed portfolios are also difficult to hedge. So, unlike most index-based ETFs, market makers in fundamental active ETFs may struggle to keep bid-ask spreads tight and tracking error low, a point of special focus by regulators. For this reason, there has been skepticism about active ETFs as future drivers of industry growth.

By contrast, for model- or rules-based strategies, ETFs provide an attractive way for active investing to be done in a transparent, manner that is passive in nature. Intraday tradability is not an important element for the adoption of active ETFs. Rather, the growth comes from the basic cost advantages of ETFs relative to alternatives. Such funds can be constructed either to target specific objectives (e.g., niche exposures) or alternative weighting schemes. They can also be constructed to maximize exposure to a set of model-driven alpha factors, say a value tilt. This sets the stage for a detailed drill-down into factor based investing or so-called Smart Beta in the following chapter. Finally, the regulatory environment is an important future determinant of the success of active ETFs and is covered in depth in Part V of the book.

Smart Beta and Factor Investing

14.1. INTRODUCTION

The term "Alternative Beta," "Strategic Beta," or "Smart Beta" refers to weighting schemes, either heuristic or based on formal optimization, that deviate from market-capitalization weighting. In some cases, the motivation for alternative beta is concern that market capitalization weights are too concentrated in larger cap names or, in the case of fixed income products, provide too much exposure to issuers who are most in need of borrowing. In other cases, alternative weighting schemes (e.g., those that tilt toward countries based on GDP or equally weight companies) have embedded within them an implicit factor tilt.

Factors are the fundamental long-run drivers of return. Factor based investing is more general than Smart beta, which is often a long-only delivery vehicle for a factor solution focused on relatively simple weighting schemes. By contrast, so-called factor investing is a more general approach to portfolio construction (typically a long-short implementation with leverage) that makes these bets explicit. But what are the factors? The key distinction is between compensated and uncompensated risks. Some factors, such as growth, have historically not had a premium relative to others, such as value. Over time, the market risk factor has commanded a premium over time and across regions, either because of behavioral factors (extreme loss aversion) or as compensation for risk (manifest in "bad times") that cannot be diversified away.

14.2. FACTORS

Factors are a set of commonalities among securities that drive expected returns. The number of factors, and whether they are compensated or not, is an empirical question. Academic research models expected returns in a multi-factor framework. Specifically, in a given period, the expected excess return $r_f \, E[r_i - r_f]$ over the risk-free rate of stock i (where $i = 1, \ldots, N$) is a linear function of broad macro and market conditions under which all stocks operate (the "common or systematic component") and an unsystematic return component that captures idiosyncratic, company-specific shocks. The systematic component is captured by a term that is proportional to a set of K common factor returns, F_k for $k = 1, \ldots, K$.

The proportionality term or beta on a given factor will vary from stock to stock. I write:

$$E[r_i] = r_f + F_1\beta_{1,i} + \cdots F_k\beta_{k,i} + \varepsilon_i. \qquad (14.1)$$

Here $\beta_{k,i}$ is the factor loading (or beta) on factor k, and ε_i is a mean-zero idiosyncratic component of the excess return of the stock, that is uncorrelated with the factor returns.

The linear structure is not restrictive: Potentially nonlinear effects (e.g., size squared) can still be incorporated as just an additional factor within the linear framework. Similarly, the orthogonality of the idiosyncratic shock is easy to ensure. Rather, the key to the economic content of the model is that the idiosyncratic term ε_i is uncorrelated with the idiosyncratic term for a different stock j. So the *only* source of return correlation among assets is from exposures to the factors and from the covariances among those factors.

In the Capital Asset Pricing Model, there is a single factor, so $K = 1$ and F is the return on a broad market index in excess of the risk-free rate. Recently, factor portfolios have also become popular for investors seeking exposure to particular factors such as value or momentum. Academic and industry research have identified a number of factors that, over long periods of time and across regions, have outperformed broad market indexes.

Factor investing, sometimes known as Smart Beta or Strategic Beta, seeks to capture systematic sources of return through transparent, rules based portfolio construction. I am not especially keen on the term "Smart beta" because there is an implicit comment that basic market capitalization weighting is somehow "dumb" beta.[1] Market capitalization weighting makes sense for a lot of reasons (lower turnover and costs, automatic rebalancing), but nonetheless the term "Smart Beta" has stuck. Here I use the term "factor investing" to refer to strategies that explicitly target the drivers of returns.

For investors, factor investing can reduce risks (especially unintended factor bets), reduce costs, and enhance returns. An added benefit is return clarification, meaning a better understanding of the sources of returns. As shown below in figure 14.1, the total portfolio return can be decomposed into active and benchmark returns. In many cases, as discussed later, static factor bets (that is tilts toward known premia accruing to, say, value) drive a large fraction of active returns. True alpha requires manager skill over and beyond simple exposure to factors and the market to exploit inefficiencies in individual stocks, sectors, and industries or through the timing of factor bets over and above broader market exposure. Many hedge funds simply harvest common risk premiums (e.g., those accruing to liquidity risk) at high fees, rather than offering alpha based on true stock selection or factor timing, skills that are scarce and costly.

Table 14.1 describes the most common (Smart Beta) factors, a brief description, and economic drivers or explanations, categorized by whether they are risk

---

1. The famous investor Jeremy Grantham once quipped "Smart Beta is dumb beta plus smart marketing."

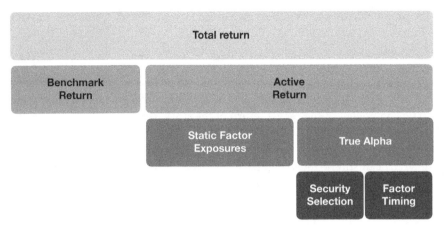

Figure 14.1 Total portfolio return decomposition.

based or rely on behavioral assumptions. The most important primary factor is the market return itself, to which most equity portfolios have substantial exposure, and needs no additional explanation. In fixed income, the primary factors are the term premium (slope of yield curve or interest rate risk) and the credit premium (spread of risky bonds over governments, or default risk).

Bonds exhibit factor exposure to value and momentum too, but term and credit premiums are analogous to the equity premium: You are exposed to these factors if you are in bonds, unless you have deliberately constructed an interest or credit hedged portfolio. Momentum and value in fixed income are somewhat different than in other asset classes (transaction costs are greater than unlevered returns), so investors need to think about how to gain exposure to these factors across different asset classes.

For example, in currencies, a carry strategy is analogous to the term structure bet in fixed income or a loading on dividend yield in equities. One might also get at fixed income factors by using bonds to capture currency carry. Systematic factors explain most active returns. For example, the Norges Bank Investment Management (Review of the Active Management of the Norwegian Government Pension Fund, January 2014) decomposed the sovereign wealth fund's active return. It found that 99.3% of active returns were explained by the choice of beta (e.g., slices like large cap), 0.4% factor over-weights such as value, and only 0.3% individual security selection.

Whether it is risk or behavior matters as behavioral premiums can be eroded as the markets become aware of the alpha opportunity. Risk based premiums, however, are presumably more robust. For example, value stocks have higher fundamental risk (such as operating leverage, uncertainty in future earnings, and cost of financial distress), less flexibility, and therefore higher returns. As with fundamental indexes, factor investing seeks to capture longer term risk premiums, by systematically tilting from cap weighting. Factor premiums should be interpreted as compensation for the risk investors bear by exposure to those factors. For example, in the CAPM, derived under assumptions of mean-variance utility and expected wealth maximization, the only relevant factor is the market portfolio. Idiosyncratic risk can be diversified away and hence is not priced.

Table 14.1 Factor Types and Economic Drivers

Factor	Asset Class and Definition	Risk Drivers	Behavioral Drivers
Size	Equities: Spread between returns of small- and large-cap stocks	High distress risk and costs require higher expected returns; lack of liquidity	Ang (2014) argues that the size effect has disappeared since it was widely reported
Value/Growth	Equities/ bonds: Measured by valuation metrics such as book/price, earnings/price, etc.	Value stocks are more sensitive to macro shocks in downturns because of higher asset bases, operating leverage, and less flexibility	Investors chase "hot" growth stocks versus "boring" value stocks; over-reaction to negative news
Momentum	All asset classes: Positive return momentum, traditionally defined using the previous 12-month returns excluding the most recent month to reflect a well-known reversal effect	High-growth firms are more risky in a macro sense and have lower asset bases	Investors exhibit over-confidence and self-attribution bias
Carry	Currencies/equities/ bonds: Strategy to capture the spread between high- and low-interest rate currencies; equity and fixed income variant is yield	So-called "peso problem" where currency crashes eliminate gains, especially when using leverage	Investors over-value yield or interest rate premiums
Profitability/ Quality	Equities: Return on equity and operating assets, stability of cash flows; consistency in dividend yield over time, lack of leverage	Higher profitability and ROE firms have outperformed	Neglected firm effects; investors undervalue stable, "boring" stocks. High leverage firms have underperformed possibly because investors do not recognize leverage risks

(continued)

Table 14.1 (CONTINUED)

Factor	Asset Class and Definition	Risk Drivers	Behavioral Drivers
Investment	Equities: Investment to assets and investment growth; net external financing and accruals	Expected investment is positively correlated with one-period-ahead expected return	
Liquidity	All assets: Securities with higher sensitivity to changes in overall market liquidity; metrics for illiquidity such as lower volume or wider spreads	Assets whose expected returns are lower (prices higher) when liquidity is scarce command a risk premium	Fear and greed; investors underestimate the value of liquidity
Volatility	Equities: Lower volatility portfolios outperform; distinctions between idiosyncratic and systematic volatility	Liquidity-constrained investors hold leveraged positions and hence overpay for high beta stocks	Glamour stocks are over-priced relative to less volatile stocks

Even in CAPM, investors may hold different portfolios, although all portfolios are just combinations of riskless bonds and the market portfolio. More risk-averse investors will place part of their portfolios in bonds; risk lovers may even borrow (i.e., short bonds) to gain leverage. The same is true for factor investors. Depending on how such investors define risk, they will hold different portfolios. For example, a longer term investor such as a sovereign wealth fund, may be willing to suffer sustained underperformance for some time and invest in value and momentum factors. A corporate pension fund, on the other hand, concerned about meeting liabilities/withdrawals in down turns, may avoid momentum and pro-cyclical factors. On average, all investors hold the market portfolio, but it should be clear that an investor may quite rationally depart from passive market weights to optimize based on their own perception of risks, tax situation, and horizon.

APPLICATION: CORRECTING UNINTENDED FACTOR BETS

For bottoms-up portfolios, the resulting basket may sometimes have an unintended factor tilt particularly if it involves security selection on a global basis. Consider a case of a fundamental global manager whose target portfolio ("client

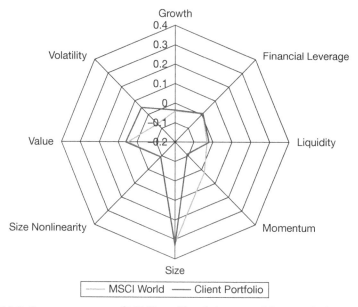

Figure 14.2 Factor exposures of MSCI world and client portfolios as of July 31, 2014.

portfolio") has an exposure to a variety of global developed market companies, with a geographical tilt toward Japan. A factor analysis using the MSCI BARRA World GEM2 risk model is shown in the radar chart in figure 4.2.

Here, the axes are the factors in the risk model and the scale can be interpreted in standard deviations. We see that the client's portfolio has an unintended bias toward stocks with higher volatility and a negative momentum factor exposure relative to the benchmark of the MSCI World Index. Using Factor ETFs allowed the client to neutralize the unintended factor tilts by trading momentum and volatility, so as to move toward exposure MSCI World.

14.3. CLOSET INDEXING

Empirical evidence suggests that many traditional active managers deliver a significant fraction of their active returns via static exposures to "smart beta" factors. One metric of active risk is $(1 - R^2)$ in a multiple regression model of fund returns on factors. For example, Kahn and Lemmon (2014) examine data for 138 global active managers in the e-vestment database from April 2011 through March 2014. They find that a large amount of variation in fraction of returns can be explained by four common factors: market, size, value, and momentum. For the average manager, simple static exposure to these factors explains about 35% of active returns, and for about a third of the manager sample, over 50% of active returns are explained by these simple factors. Investors who pay managers highly for their active bets are also getting returns that could, in theory, be partly generated by low-cost beta strategies.

Table 14.2 TOP TEN US ACTIVE OPEN-ENDED MUTUAL FUNDS BY ASSETS,
FEBRUARY 2015

Fund Name	Ticker	Fund Category	Size ($ billion)
American Funds Growth Fund of America A	AGTHX	Large Growth	147.06
PIMCO Total Return Institutional	PTTRX	Intermediate-Term Bond	134.63
American Funds Euro Pacific Growth A	AEPGX	Foreign Large Growth	126.37
Fidelity Contra Fund	FCNTX	Large Growth	106.84
American Funds Capital Income Builder A	CAIBX	World Allocation	99.20
American Funds Income Fund of America A	AMECX	Moderate Allocation	99.13
Franklin Income A	FKINX	Conservative Allocation	91.41
American Funds Capital World Growth & Income A	CWGIX	World Stock	89.43
Vanguard Wellington Investment	VWELX	Moderate Allocation	87.72
American Funds American Balanced A	ABALX	Moderate Allocation	81.61

SOURCE: Morningstar data as of February 15, 2015, for all non-index open-ended US mutual funds.

14.3.1. Mutual Fund Factors

The largest 10 US-domiciled open-ended active mutual funds collectively have about $1 trillion in assets as shown in table 14.2. This represents about 27% of the assets of the top 100 mutual funds and slightly over a third of global ETP assets.

The largest active mutual fund in the United States is the Growth Fund of America® (AGTHX), with $147 billion in assets as of mid-February 2015. The fund's stated objective, which was incepted on December 1, 1973, is to provide growth of capital through active management. From the prospectus, the fund has the flexibility to invest wherever the best growth opportunities may be, with at least 65% of its assets in common stocks. The fund has the flexibility though to invest in convertibles, preferred stocks, US government securities, bonds and cash equivalents, and in securities of issuers domiciled outside the United States. As of February 2015, the fund's A shares carry a maximum sales charge (load) imposed on purchases (other classes may offer lower loads) of 5.75%, with total annual fund expenses at 0.66%. Holders less than a year may also be subject to back-end fees. The other funds shown vary in terms of focus and style, with many emphasizing equities and either value or growth tilts.

How well do common factors explain fund returns? I form an equally weighted portfolio of five large active mutual funds focused on domestic equity and also look at five large funds (labeled A to E) individually. The academic literature has traditionally used a four factor equity model to explain a portfolio or asset's excess return in a given period, although there is an active debate over what factors actually have longevity (see, e.g., Ang 2014):

$$r_{i,t} - r_{f,t} = a + \beta_{i,MKT}\left(r_{m,t} - r_{f,t}\right) + \beta_{i,SMB}SMB_t + \beta_{i,HML}HML_t + \beta_{i,UMD}UMD_t + \varepsilon_t.$$

The factors are:

- **MKT or Market**—The monthly excess return on the CRSP overall market portfolio;
- **SMB or Size**—The performance of small stocks relative to big stocks (Small Minus Big);
- **HML or Value**—The performance of value stocks relative to growth stocks (High Minus Low); and
- **UMD or Momentum**—The performance of winners less losers over the previous 12 months excluding the most recent month (Up Minus Down).

Because fund styles vary widely (ranging from growth to income focus), I augment the original four factor Fama-French-Carhart model with two fixed income factors, term structure slope and credit spreads.[2] The term structure factor (INT) is based on the difference between long-term treasuries (10+ years) and short-dated treasury bills; Credit risk (CRD) is the difference between long-term (10+ years) corporates (B-rated) and long-term treasuries.

I estimate a linear regression for fund returns on monthly factor returns from December 1, 2009, to December 31, 2014:

$$r_{i,t} - r_{f,t} = a + \beta_{i,MKT}\left(r_{m,t} - r_{f,t}\right) + \beta_{i,SMB}SMB_t + \beta_{i,HML}HML_t + \beta_{i,UMD}UMD_t$$
$$+ \beta_{i,INT}INT_t + \beta_{i,CRD}CRD_t + \varepsilon_{i,t}. \tag{14.2}$$

The intercept a is the excess return or alpha (expressed in percent per month) to the fund over systematic factor returns. The results are shown in table 14.3. Overall, 97% of the variation in the returns of the equally weighted portfolio is explained by the six factors. That explanatory power is very high given the diversity of styles represented here. At the portfolio level, all six factors are significant at the 10% level and every factor except momentum is significant at the 5% level. At the fund level, exposure to market is statistically significant for all five funds, and there is quite a lot of variation in factor loadings across funds. Growth-oriented

---

2. See Fama and French (1993) and Carhart (1991). Recently, Fama and French (2014) propose a five factor model that adds return on equity and investment factors to their original model.

Table 14.3 Regression Based Style Analysis of Monthly Returns (%), December 1, 2009, to December 31, 2014

	Equally-Weighted Portfolio of Domestic Equity Focused Active Mutual Funds	Fund A	Fund B	Fund C	Fund D	Fund E
Alpha (α) in %	−0.08(0.001)	−0.09(0.001)	−0.03(0.001)	−0.32(0.002)	−0.05(0.001)	0.08(0.001)
Market	0.72(0.030)	0.94(0.042)	0.90(0.045)	0.69(0.060)	0.65(0.060)	0.43(0.048)
Size	−0.11(0.038)	0.01(0.054)	−0.01(0.058)	−0.31(0.077)	−0.18(0.077)	−0.04(0.062)
Value	−0.10(0.041)	−0.20(0.059)	−0.36(0.064)	−0.06(0.083)	0.02(0.083)	0.09(0.068)
Momentum	0.05(0.031)	−0.00(0.044)	0.12(0.047)	0.10(0.062)	0.05(0.062)	0.00(0.051)
Term Structure	0.15(0.032)	0.00(0.046)	0.03(0.049)	0.25(0.065)	0.20(0.065)	0.25(0.053)
Credit Risk	0.25(0.050)	0.13(0.071)	0.10(0.076)	0.24(0.100)	0.20(0.100)	0.58(0.081)
R-Squared	0.97	0.96	0.95	0.84	0.92	0.89

SOURCE: Monthly equity return data are sourced from Ken French's data library; further details on the fixed income factor construction can be found at http://www.portfoliovisualizer.com. Standard errors are in parentheses. Coefficients that are statistically significant at the 5% level of significance are shaded. Alpha (α) is reported in percent per month.

funds, for example, load negatively on the *HML* factor. Income-oriented funds load positively on the *INT* and *CRD* fixed income factors.

In other words, these funds are seeking income by moving up the treasury yield curve and also into high-yield corporate bonds. Alpha (α) is not economically or statistically insignificant at the 5% significance level for the equally weighted portfolio or for any of the individual funds, with the factors explaining the majority of the variation in returns over the period. Note that alpha is expressed in percent per month. For the overall portfolio, our estimate is −0.08% (or −0.008) which works out to be −0.96% annually; this is not significant though as the t-statistic for the portfolio alpha is −0.974 = −0.0008/0.00078. (Because of rounding, all the reported standard errors are roughly the same.) Even though the funds have an equity orientation, fixed income factors are relevant in explaining performance. This shows the importance of conditioning on basic term structure risk factors.

When I look at individual funds I can isolate the factor bets being made. Consider first Fund A, a growth fund with a long history. A regression of returns of this fund on the six factors over the same period yields an R-squared that is 0.96 (I did also estimate the four factor equity only model from February 2, 1980, to December 31, 2014, and obtained very similar results) with a strong loading on the market and a tilt to growth (negative on value).

While attractive because only return information is required, the drawback to time-series estimates is that they update only slowly over time. The time-series coefficient is the average over a particular sample used for estimation rather than the most recent period. Holdings-based methods of attribution are well-suited to capturing dynamic effects. Further, keep in mind that the Fama-French-Carhart research factors are not directly investable, although there are close proxies that are traded. That said, the fact that such a large fraction of the variation in active returns can be explained by a few simple factors is intriguing.

14.3.2. Identifying Closet Indexers

Multiple regression style models offer one way to identify so-called "closet index-ers" who charge active fees but essentially deliver index type performance or simply maintain static exposure to known risk factors such as liquidity. However, the factors must be pre-specified and a long enough time series available to reliably estimate the model. Cremers and Petajisto (2009) offer a simpler metric to quantify active portfolio management that they term "Active Share." This metric, which has gained considerable attention, summarizes how the share of portfolio holdings that differ from the benchmark index. Formally, the Active Share of a fund is:

$$AS(h) = \frac{1}{2}|h'|e = \frac{1}{2}\sum_{i=1}^{N}|h_{a,i} - h_{b,i}|, \qquad (14.3)$$

where $e = (1, \ldots, 1)$ is an $N \times 1$ vector and $h' = (h_a - h_b)'$ is a $1 \times N$ vector of active weights (i.e., portfolio weights less benchmark weights). For unleveraged

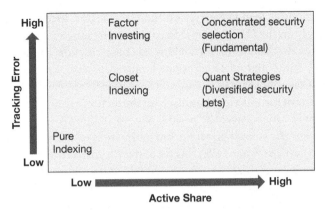

Figure 14.3 Schematic of fund strategies: active share versus tracking error.

portfolios, Active Share is a number between 0 and 100% with lower figures representing more index-like behavior.

As a hypothetical example, consider Managers 1 and 2, and their respective portfolio weights across stocks, bonds, and cash. Both have the same benchmark but their active bets lead to very different Active Shares, with Manager 2 essentially a closet index tracker.

Empirical research shows that small- and mid-cap funds have higher Active Share (75%–80%) than those of large-cap funds (60%–65%) that typically have low tracking error. Active Share is also likely to vary by the style of portfolio construction. Quant managers, for example, typically use risk models to keep their tracking error low and take many bets across a broad universe of stocks. Fundamental managers by contrast may have concentrated positions in a few "high conviction" stocks and higher tracking error. A useful visualization of where various management styles align is shown in figure 14.3.

14.3.3. Can Active Share Predict Performance?

Cremers and Petajisto (2009) compute Active Share for all-equity US mutual funds in the period 1990–2003 to characterize their extent and style of active management. See also Petajisto (2013b). They argue that active management predicts fund performance: funds with high Active Shares outperform their benchmark indexes after expenses and exhibit persistence in performance, while non-index funds with low Active Shares underperform. In figure 14.4—based on the results of Cremers and Petajisto (2009)—the average annual net excess return in percent is plotted for quintiles of Active Share. Excess performance is positively related to Active Share, especially for the most active managers (80%–100%). Their paper prompted interest in using Active Share as an element in defining an industry standard for the asset management industry, part of governance and normal market practice.[3]

---

3. See, e.g., Judith Evans, "Managers and Platforms Back 'Active Share' Disclosure," *Financial Times*, November 26, 2014.

Table 14.4 EXAMPLE OF ACTIVE SHARE COMPUTATION.

Security	Manager 1 Portfolio Weights (%)	Manager 2 Portfolio Weights (%)	Benchmark Portfolio Weights (%)	Absolute Active Weights Manager 1 (%)	Absolute Active Weights Manager 2 (%)
Stock A	25	35	34	9	1
Stock B	30	28	28	2	0
Stock C	20	18	16	4	2
Stock D	0	13	13	13	0
Stock E	0	6	9	9	3
Treasury Bonds	10			10	0
Cash	15			15	0
Total	100	100	100	62	6
Active Share				31	3

More recent evidence suggests that the fraction of truly active managers has been declining in recent years, and that much of the return differences really come from poor performance by lower Active Share funds. While Active Share is a useful metric, it should not be used in isolation because the metric is highly sensitive to the definition of the universe. Frazzini, Friedman, and Pomorski (2015) argue that the empirical basis for Active Share as a predictor of performance is weak. They conclude that Active Share correlates with benchmark returns, but does not predict actual fund returns.

14.3.4. What Does Active Share Measure?

We can gain some insight into Active Share by focusing on the key element in the Active Share metric, namely the typical (absolute) active weight of a position. Recall that when the variance matrix is diagonal, the optimal unrestricted active weight in stock i is proportional to the expected excess return scaled by the variance of the stock's returns: $h_i^* = \left(\dfrac{1}{2\rho\sigma_i^2}\right)a_i$. We also can solve out for the risk aversion parameter ρ as shown earlier given the target tracking error of the fund and write $h_i^* = \left(\dfrac{\sigma_{TE}}{\sqrt{N}}\right)\left(\dfrac{a_i}{\sigma_i^2}\right)$. So active weight is proportional to the excess return scaled by risk, where the proportionality factor increases with the manager's target portfolio tracking error and decreases with the size of the universe.

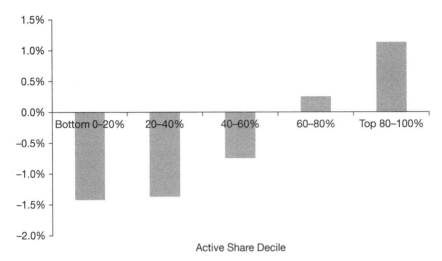

Figure 14.4 Annual excess returns for deciles of active share.

Typically, alpha is standardized so we can approximate the distribution of the manager's excess return forecasts as normally distributed with mean 0 and standard deviation 1. Using the properties of the normal distribution, the expectation of the absolute value of a_i is $E[|a_i|] = \sqrt{\frac{2}{\pi}}$ We can take expectations to get the average absolute active weight of a stock:

$$E\left|h_i^*\right| = \sqrt{\frac{1}{2\pi N}}\left(\frac{\sigma_{TE}}{\sigma_i^2}\right). \tag{14.4}$$

In other words, the expected absolute active weight increases proportionately with the fund's target tracking error (relative to the variance of an average stock) and decreases with the size of the universe.

EXAMPLE: ACTIVE SHARE

Consider a fund manager with a universe of 100 stocks whose average volatility is 30% and whose tracking error to the benchmark is 3%. The expected absolute active weight of a stock is then 0.40% and Active Share is 0.20. If the universe is extended to 500 shares, the average absolute active weight falls to 0.18% but Active Share rises 0.45.

The relation of absolute weight at the 3% and 5% tracking error target against size of universe is shown below in figure 14.5. This is a highly nonlinear relationship. As the universe expands, the manager presumably moves toward less liquid, higher volatility securities so that σ_i is higher as N increases. That effect will cause a further shrinking of the absolute positions as the universe expands, ultimately limiting the increase in Active Share. The implication of this is that Active Share is simply another way to capture portfolio concentration, or more precisely the (lack of) overlap of the fund's holdings with its benchmark. So, the measure does not necessarily have predictive power beyond other metrics such as tracking error and so on.

So, we conclude that Active Share, like other metrics such as tracking error, represents active risk relative to the benchmark.

WHAT DOES ACTIVE SHARE REALLY MEASURE?

There are some misconceptions about Active Share that are worth highlighting. First, higher Active Share does not necessarily translate into higher volatility, although it does mean higher tracking error. In the hypothetical example in table 14.4, manager 1 has an Active Share of 31% versus just 3% for manager 2. It is clear that manager 1 is taking more active risk relative to the benchmark, although doing this by putting 25% of the portfolio into cash and riskless bonds. Manager 2 is a closet indexer, but is presumably incurring higher volatility by being all in equities. Second, a large Active Share is not necessary for a manager to significantly outperform. Frazzini, Friedman, and Pomorski (2015) provide a highly stylized example of a long-only manager who is benchmarked to the S&P 500. The manager successfully avoids holding the five stocks with the lowest returns each month and holds the remaining S&P 500 stocks proportionally to their index weights. From January 1990 through October 2014, the manager's alpha is 4.51% annually but the mean Active Share is just 2.2%.

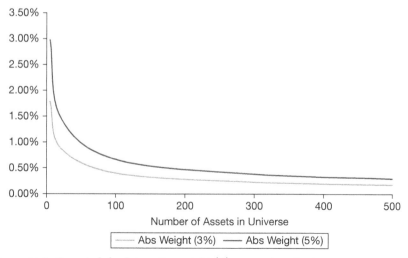

Figure 14.5 Expected absolute active weight (%) versus size of universe.

This makes Active Share useful in evaluating fees, but not necessarily predicting returns. Consequently, most practitioners recommend using Active Share in conjunction with other metrics including tracking error or regression based approaches.

14.3.5. Multi-Manager Factor Risk

The ability of factors to mimic active portfolio returns is more pronounced when an investor employs multiple managers. Even if individual managers primarily take stock-specific risk, the investor's overall "fund-of-funds" portfolio may have significant active factor risk. This is illustrated in the example based on Kahn and Lemmon (2014).

WHY ARE SMART BETA EXPOSURES HIGHER IN MULTI-MANAGER PORTFOLIOS?

Consider a pension fund that uses five fundamental value managers. Suppose each manager obtains 3% of their active risk from constant exposure to the value factor and 4% from stock-specific risk (which is orthogonal to the value bet and is uncorrelated across managers). So the total active risk (or the volatility of returns relative to the benchmark) for each manager is 5%. To see this, note that the total active return variance is the sum of the variances of the two components (which are uncorrelated) so that $\sqrt{(0.03)^2 + (0.04)^2} = 0.05$. At the single manager level, only 36% of active variance comes from the common value factor, because the ratio of variances of the common value factor to total active variance is $0.36 = \dfrac{(0.03)^2}{(0.05)^2}$. The remaining 64% $\left(\text{because } 0.64 = \dfrac{(0.04)^2}{(0.05)^2}\right)$ comes from stock-specific risks. Note that I take the ratio of variances, not volatilities, to assess risk contributions because volatiles, unlike variances, do not add. If the investor allocates an equal dollar amount to each of the five managers, the resulting aggregate portfolio will have active variance of 0.00122 consisting of a variance contribution from exposure to the value factor (risk which does not diversify across managers) of $0.009 = 0.03^2$ plus stock-specific variance (which does diversify across managers) of $0.00032 = \dfrac{(0.04)^2}{5}$. So the tracking error relative to benchmark (or active risk) of the fund-of-funds is only 3.49% $\left(0.0349 = \sqrt{\dfrac{0.03 + (0.04)^2}{5}}\right)$.

At the overall portfolio or fund-of-funds level, 73.8% $\left(= \dfrac{(0.03)^2}{(0.0349)^2}\right)$ of the active variance comes from the value factor, and only 26.2% comes from stock-specific variance. While the five individual managers are each largely making stock-specific bets, collectively they are mainly making a single factor bet, one that is usually available at low cost through ETFs or other index fund structures.

Kahn and Lemmon (2014) generate 1,000 random portfolios consisting of ten managers each drawn from a sample of 138 global investment managers. Factors explain about 43% of the multi-manager active returns, versus about 35% for the individual managers.

14.3.6. Long Only versus Long-Short Implementation

Observe that the alpha that derives from a K-factor model is not the sum of the alphas from each of the individual factors. That is, if I have a model where alpha is comprised of signals $k = 1, 2, \ldots, K$ with weights w_k the optimal holding vector for each individual factor is:

$$
h_k^* = \left(\frac{1}{2\rho} \right) V^{-1} a_k + \left(\frac{V^{-1}e}{e'V^{-1}e} \right). \tag{14.5}
$$

Then it is not in general the case that $h^* = \sum_{k=1}^{K} w_k h_k^*$ because the active portion of the portfolio is weighted by the covariance matrix. In other words, an optimal portfolio with exposure to multiple factors is not the same as a weighted average of single factor portfolios. Intuitively, the stocks in each portfolio are weighted differently and the constraint that I be fully invested does not allow offsets in weights that are possible when building a single, optimized portfolio.

14.4. FUNDAMENTAL ACTIVE ETFS

14.4.1. Reverse Engineering

Active ETFs following proprietary strategies face several hurdles. The most important issue has to do with the ability of others to infer the underlying alpha or excess return forecast. Unlike most open-end mutual funds and closed-end funds, ETFs disclose all (or substantially all) portfolio holdings on a daily basis to facilitate secondary market trading. Portfolio transparency is key to ETF pricing, but raises the possibility revealing information about changes in an ETF's portfolio that may be market-sensitive and raises the cost of executing future transactions. While this is not generally a concern for model-based strategies of the types discussed earlier, this may make it difficult to pursue certain active investment strategies (e.g., security selection in small-capitalization stocks or thinly traded bonds) through ETFs.

Since holdings are published daily (albeit with a lag of a day), one can in theory invert the reported holdings h_t to estimate alpha:

$$
\hat{a}_t = 2\rho V \left(h_t - \left(\frac{V^{-1}e}{e'V^{-1}e} \right) \right). \tag{14.6}
$$

So, a can be recovered up to a scalar, since the fund manager's risk aversion parameter ρ is not observable to an outsider. This assumes that the covariance matrix V is observed but this is a reasonable assumption given that these are usually based on well-established risk models.

With a time series of holdings, the signals underlying the alpha forecast can in theory be reverse-engineered, leading to a conundrum: If the manager can successfully forecast excess returns, then their signals can be readily copied if implemented in an ETF structure which by nature is highly transparent. Successful managers will then find their intellectual property quickly eroded. Some ETFs do indeed use published hedge fund holdings (through 13-F filings) to create portfolios of successful fund managers.

Case Study: Global X Guru Index ETF (GURU)

Hedge funds with over \$100 million in US equity investments must file 13F documents quarterly. The Solactive Guru Index uses a proprietary methodology to select high conviction ideas from a pre-selected set of hedge funds based on 13F data. High turnover hedge funds are excluded. The Global X Guru Index ETF (GURU) seeks to track this index. These funds operate on the assumption that published holdings, which are only available with a substantial delay, are representative of current positions and more important that the hedge fund managers they are mimicking are consistent in their generation of alpha. As positions may be changed quickly, there is less opportunity for this type of mimicry to erode alpha returns over time.

A closely related concern with active funds is front-running. Since alpha is based on a set of underlying signals (e.g., book/market, earnings/price, quality, etc.) that will typically decay slowly, I can write:

$$\alpha_t = \gamma\alpha_{t-1} + \xi_t, \tag{14.7}$$

where $0 < \gamma < 1$ captures the autocorrelation in alpha and ξ_t is a shock that captures new signal innovations. Thus, if holdings are publicized, future trades can in theory be forecast, especially if the manager uses a transaction cost function to scale trades to avoid market impact, leading to a dependence of trades (i.e., $h_t - h_{t-1}$) on current and past alphas. Trading ahead could increase the fund's transaction costs and erode its alpha.

14.4.2. Nontransparent Active ETFs

An alternative in theory is a more opaque or nontransparent structure where exact holdings are not public (e.g., the manager provides general portfolio characteristics) or are not reported in a timely manner. A concern for ETFs, unlike active mutual funds, is that the creation/redemption mechanism needs transparency to keep bid-ask spreads and tracking error low. However, there may be effective ways to convey the risk characteristics of the fund (much as with a principal bid) for hedging purposes without divulging exact positions or by using a blind trust mechanism. Nontransparent active funds based on fundamental (non-quantitative) styles of security selection or opportunity seeking (i.e., trading on availability, buying assets at the bid and selling at the ask) present another opportunity for investors and are difficult to mimic.

14.4.3. Inferring Holdings from Public Data

Even if holdings are not published or are not published regularly, as in a nontransparent ETF structure, holdings can be approximated from a time series of intraday NAV and security prices. For example, suppose NAV for a domestic active fund is reported at intervals of $\Delta t = 15$ seconds, as is current US practice. This means that I observe a value equal to $n_t = \sum_{i=1}^{N} m_t^i h_i$ every 15 seconds, where m_t^i is the last recorded price (or quote) of asset i at time-stamp t and h_i is the (unobserved) active holding. Market participants see pricing data in real-time. Even if the underlying holdings of the fund are not disclosed, it is not hard to back them out. Specifically, each observation of intraday NAV is a linear equation in N unknowns, the active weights h_i. To estimate the N unknown holdings vector (assuming positions are constant) requires at least N equations of this type, that is, a calendar duration of $T = \frac{N}{\Delta t}$.

As an example, suppose that we know that a particular active fund takes position in a specified universe of just four stocks. We observe the following four data points on intraday NAV and the corresponding public prices of the four stocks, A–D at four times. Let n denote the 4×1 vector of the NAVs (the values in the second column) and denote further by M the 4×4 matrix of stock prices (based on the last four rows and columns of table 14.5).

From these data, we can compute the 4×4 inverse of the price matrix M^{-1} shown in equation (14.8):

$$M^{-1} = \begin{pmatrix} -5.61 & -54.98 & 65.35 & -4.70 \\ 41.05 & -1.76 & -54.09 & 14.77 \\ -5.92 & 34.00 & -28.71 & 0.63 \\ -5.84 & -13.25 & 32.30 & -13.21 \end{pmatrix}. \tag{14.8}$$

It is straightforward to recover the weights of the stocks A, B, C, and D in the fund by multiplying $M^{-1}n$ to yield the vector $h' = (0.60, 0.10, 0.10, 0.20)$. This procedure would work too if the fund were long-short as long as the matrix M has full rank and can be inverted. If prices do not move much between reporting intervals, then the matrix M may not be of full rank and we may need to sample at longer intervals to do the inversion.

The point of this example is to show that even in realistic case with a universe much larger than a few stocks, estimation is straightforward as NAV is a linear

Table 14.5 HYPOTHETICAL EXAMPLE OF REVERSE-ENGINEERING
OF ACTIVE HOLDINGS

Time	ETF Intraday Value	Intraday Price Quotes			
		Stock A	Stock B	Stock C	Stock D
10:34:00	25.756	30.34	12.45	51.89	5.59
10:35:00	25.741	30.33	12.42	51.89	5.56
10:36:00	25.727	30.32	12.41	51.84	5.55
10:37:00	25.701	30.32	12.39	51.80	5.45

function. In the general case, let M denote the $N \times N$ matrix of observed prices (row k of this matrix contains the last prices for each of the N possible assets in the universe at period k) and n the $N \times 1$ vector of reported intraday NAVs. Then, assuming M has full rank and hence can be inverted, the estimated average holding vector of the active fund is:

$$\hat{h} = M^{-1}n.$$ (14.9)

For example, if the universe consists of 500 assets, we need a minimum of about 2 hours and 5 minutes to solve for the manager's active weights. As a technical aside, with longer durations beyond the minimum needed of $T = \frac{N}{\Delta t}$, this computation can be rolled forward over the day or it can be used to *over-identify* $\hat{h}$ and provide a statistical confidence interval using the Generalized Method of Moments (GMM) approach.

14.4.4. Practical Issues

As a practical reality, however, concerns regarding reverse engineering and front-running are unwarranted. First, managers may change holdings during the day so any reverse engineering is only an approximation to the average active weight over that interval of time. Further, intraday NAV is typically computed against *yesterday's* holdings. In the example, we are estimating on yesterday's average holding on a rolling basis. Second, portfolio managers may employ multiple implicit or explicit constraints (e.g., sector or industry caps, etc.), and the resulting portfolio becomes very difficult to reverse engineer due to the nonlinear impact of constraints. Third, even if the portfolio were reverse-engineered and replicated (presumably with less tax efficiency), the investors in the fund would not be impacted except to the extent that their alpha is eroded. Finally, note that mutual funds following active strategies are no different in this regard. There have also been many examples of successful active funds using fundamental strategies, especially in bonds, where it is difficult or impossible to front-run or copy the underlying strategy given the opaque and OTC nature of the market.

14.5. CAPACITY AND CROWDING

Will crowding reduce the benefits to factor based investing? The key is the driver of the factor return. Take for example a liquidity premium. This might be compensation for risk in the sense that investors are paid for the risk of possibly having to liquidate their position at prices below fundamental value in downturns. As investors crowd into less liquid assets, the risk premium paid falls. This diminishes the gains to a longer run investor.

Successful hedge fund managers periodically close their funds to new investments. Capacity constraints are the key to maintaining alpha generation. As an active fund grows in asset size, so does the average size of a trade. Greater liquidity demand (relative to average daily volume or market depth) increases transaction costs. The increase in cost directly erodes net alpha to the point where the manager is unable to add value.

Open-ended mutual funds and ETFs are not able to close to new investments if they are successful at generating alpha. If they do, then they will likely trade at a premium to NAV for possibly extended periods of time. While this is a limitation on the growth of active ETFs, the reality is that more money chasing the same themes means less likelihood of successful alpha generation. In other words, if active funds adopt the ETF structure and exceed their capacity, alpha will be diminished and these funds will trade more like the market in general. The same comment applies to so-called Smart Beta strategies. Crowded trades simply mean these factor strategies will look more like the market, and any risk premiums will dissipate.

14.6. CHAPTER SUMMARY

Factor investing seeks to capture systematic sources of return through transparent, rules based portfolio construction. Typically this involves a long-short implementation along with appropriate leverage. Smart Beta can be viewed as a long-only delivery vehicle for a factor solution focused on alternative weighting schemes. For investors, factor investing can reduce risks (especially unintended factor bets), reduce costs, and enhance returns.

An important benefit of thinking in factor space is return clarification, meaning a better understanding of the common drivers of returns and risks. A traditional mix of stocks and bonds blends together various diverse factors such as value and momentum. These factors cut across asset classes, the way that different foods are comprised of a common set of nutrients (see Ang 2014). Specifically, the total return of a portfolio can be decomposed into benchmark and active returns. In many cases, as discussed blow, factor risk drives a large fraction of active returns. True alpha requires manager skill over and beyond simple exposure to factors and the market to exploit inefficiencies in individual stocks, sectors, and industries or through the timing of factor bets over and above broader market. Many expensive active managers are closet indexers, whose returns can be replicated by combinations of ETFs offering various factor tilts such as value/growth.

The ETF structure offers favorable tax benefits and lower structural costs relative to traditional active managers. However, these benefits are mitigated by the daily transparency offered by ETFs. For this reason, model-based or liquidity/opportunistic strategies are likely to drive growth in active ETFs.

PART V

Public Policy, Regulation, and Systemic Risk

Flows

15.1. INTRODUCTION

In the last section of the book, I review several recent topics around ETFs and their ecosystem that have been the subject of considerable discussion by regulators and policymakers. These include the impact of passive flows on underlying securities, concerns about leveraged and inverse ETPs, the Flash Crash of May 2010, and finally whether considerations specific to ETFs such as excess shorting, settlement failures, and the withdrawal of APs may create systemic risk. Throughout, I seek to provide a fact-based analysis of the relevant issues. But often the conceptual framework also needs to be questioned too. For example, one might argue that flows into ETFs cause underlying securities to move together increasing cross-stock correlations. However, even if ETFs did not exist, there are many alternative investment vehicles such as open- or closed-end mutual funds that investors can use to gain the same exposures.

The starting point for our discussion is an empirical analysis of flows. As discussed, most secondary market volumes do not induce transactions in the underlying markets, meaning buyers and sellers exchange shares of the ETF on organized exchanges without there being any changes in shares outstanding. Here, by flows we mean primary market creations or redemptions that are associated with changes in the ETF's shares outstanding and hence assets under management. We begin by asking what is special about ETF flows, and then turn to modeling these flows, and then to possible applications of the analysis. We specifically return to consider the question posted above: What is the impact of flows on the underlying stocks?

15.2. WHY ARE FLOWS IMPORTANT?

The rapid growth of assets and diversity in ETFs has generated considerable interest in the drivers and return implications of these flows. Several factors make ETF flows interesting for analysis. First, institutional investors and hedge funds increasingly use ETFs to gain desired exposures quickly and at low cost. Consequently, ETFs flows could be informative about changes in sentiment by the most informed investors. Second, unlike mutual fund flows, ETF flows are measured *daily* for a wide range of asset classes and geographies. Third, ETF flows are less "sticky" than mutual fund flows that typically originate from retail investors. Fourth, as discussed later on, ETF flows are sometimes alleged to have detrimental impacts on their underlying basket securities, adding to volatility and impairing efficient price discovery. Finally, there are interesting regulatory issues concerning flows that tie in closely to public policy initiatives. I begin with an approach to modeling flows and then turn to the practical applications of the analysis.

15.3. MODELING FLOWS

This section provides a statistical analysis of flows of all US-domiciled ETFs from 2005 to 2014 that examines some key questions: What drives ETF flows across asset classes and regions? Are there common factors in flows? Do flows have impacts on underlying securities? Can flows predict returns at the asset class, sector, or country levels?

The dollar signed primary market flow into a particular ETF on day t is total creations less redemptions in value terms. This is equal to the change in shares outstanding times the NAV of the ETF.

$$x_t = (o_t - o_{t-1})n_t \tag{15.1}$$

It is important to distinguish between primary flows as defined in equation (15.1) and signed dollar order flow (sometimes called money flow) in the secondary market. Signed secondary market flows are the sum of signed intraday volumes where a classification algorithm is used to impute every trade as either buyer- or seller-initiated or unclassified. For example, a common procedure is to impute trades executed at the ask (bid) price as buys (sells), respectively, keeping a running total over the day. Alternatively, one could sign trades according to whether they were above or below the prevailing midquote. As noted earlier, because intraday ETF trades often net out, positive or negative order flows on a given day need not lead to a creation or a redemption. The focus here is on actual creation and redemption activity that reflects the demand for *changes* in desired exposures.

15.3.1. Universe

Daily flow data on all US-domiciled ETFs from January 2007 through July 2014 is sourced from Bloomberg. The focus is on seven broad categories of exposure including equity, fixed income, and commodity ETFs:

- US Equity ETFs;
- Developed Markets (DM) Equity ETFs (excluding US Equities);
- Emerging Markets (EM) Equity ETFs;

- US Broad Market Fixed Income ETFs;
- US Corporate Bond ETFs;
- US Treasury ETFs;
- Commodity ETFs.

Excluded are inverse and levered products and exchange-traded notes (which are essentially a debt instruments). One objective here is to understand the relation of flows (changes in desired exposure) to fundamental macro and market variables. Macro data is typically not available on a daily basis. For analysis over periods beyond a day (e.g., monthly data), define the flow for a given fund in month T as the total daily flows over all the trading days in the month, that is $\sum_{t \in T} x_t$.

Since US equity ETFs have the largest AUM by far in the sample, the raw flows into this category are also the largest across all seven groups. To compare across different exposure categories and make the time series of flows stationary, it is useful to scale flows in each exposure category by the total AUM of all funds in the same exposure bucket at the last trading day of the previous month. Specifically, define the scaled flow for all funds in exposure bucket J in month T as:

$$y_{J,T} = \sum_{j \in J}\left(\sum_{t \in T} x_{j,t}\right) \Big/ \sum_{j \in J} o_{j,T-1} n_{j,T-1}, \tag{15.2}$$

scaled by the AUM of the fund (where the AUM of fund j in month $T-1$ is $AUM_{j,T-1} = o_{j,T-1} n_{j,T-1}$) in the previous period.

15.3.2. Flow Dynamics

For each of the seven exposure buckets, I regressed monthly scaled ETF flows on the previous month's scaled ETF flows (to capture possible autocorrelation in flows) and a 6×1 vector, Z_T, that captures possible changes in desired exposures. Specifically, included in the vector Z_T is a measure of broad equity market return (proxied by the return on the Russell 3000 Index) and *changes* (or "deltas") in key macroeconomic variables: long-term interest rates (measured by 10-year treasury yields), US unemployment, headline inflation (CPI), and VIX levels. I also add a seasonality indicator variable factor set to 1 for March, June, September, and December (and zero otherwise) as flows exhibit strong seasonality. So, for each exposure bucket J (I suppress the subscript for notational simplicity) I estimate:

$$y_T = \beta_0 + \beta_1 y_{T-1} + \delta' Z_T + \epsilon_T \tag{15.3}$$

The estimates of the regression coefficients (β_0, β_1, and δ), together with standard errors of the estimates (in parentheses) are shown in table 15.1. Also shown is the adjusted R-squared for each regression. To make it easier to read this table, coefficients that are statistically significant (at 5% level) are shaded.

Table 15.1 Regression Analysis of Monthly Flows

	Global Equities			US Fixed Income			Commodity
	US	DM ex-US	EM	Broad	Corp bond	Treasury	Commodity
Constant	0.246 (0.445)	0.782 (0.273)	0.818 (0.558)	0.733 (0.312)	1.865 (0.605)	1.274 (0.626)	0.316 (0.458)
y_{T-1} (Autocorrelation)	0.073 (0.102)	0.453 (0.089)	0.191 (0.106)	0.559 (0.081)	0.585 (0.086)	-0.231 (0.113)	0.315 (0.096)
Russell 3000 Return	0.247 (0.093)	0.140 (0.054)	0.305 (0.115)	0.015 (0.053)	0.074 (0.108)	0.025 (0.141)	-0.132 (0.102)
ΔRates (10-year yield)	-0.027 (0.013)	0.008 (0.008)	-0.016 (0.017)	-0.03 (0.008)	-0.050 (0.015)	-0.038 (0.021)	-0.006 (0.015)
Δ Unemployment	-0.001 (0.015)	-0.005 (0.009)	0.057 (0.02)	0.017 (0.01)	0.032 (0.022)	0.048 (0.025)	0.062 (0.019)
Δ Inflation (CPI)	-0.008 (0.004)	-0.009 (0.003)	-0.003 (0.005)	0.005 (0.003)	-0.017 (0.005)	0.011 (0.007)	0.009 (0.005)
Δ VIX	0.036 (0.02)	0.020 (0.012)	0.021 (0.025)	0.006 (0.012)	-0.040 (0.024)	-0.003 (0.031)	-0.005 (0.022)
Quarterly seasonality	0.025 (0.006)	0.004 (0.004)	0.006 (0.008)	0.006 (0.004)	0.010 (0.007)	-0.006 (0.01)	0.007 (0.007)
Number of obs	90	90	90	90	90	90	90
Adj. R-squared	0.212	0.303	0.136	0.495	0.624	0.041	0.312

SOURCE: Author's estimates based on Bloomberg data.

The regression analysis shows that macroeconomic factors play an important role in explaining ETF flow dynamics, even after controlling for flow autocorrelation and seasonality. The adjusted R-squares for the regressions range from 0.2 for US equity ETFs to over 0.6 for corporate bond ETFs (although emerging markets and treasury ETFs have smaller values).

15.3.3. Equity Flows

Global equity ETFs are heterogeneous in their flow dynamics. The largest exposure group (by assets), US equity ETFs, shows very little autocorrelation in their flows, consistent with the view that they are used by tactical managers to quickly express their views on the US market. Unlike US equity ETFs, both developed and emerging markets ETF flows show statistically significant autocorrelation (persistence). In addition, all equity ETF flows are contemporaneously positively correlated with US equity market movements, as measured by Russell 3000 returns. As expected, US equity ETF flows are negatively correlated with long-term yields and changes in CPI inflation. There is strong seasonality of US equity ETF flows: End-of-quarter months (March, June, September, and December) receive significantly more flows compared to other months perhaps because many institutional investors and hedge funds rebalance regularly on a quarterly basis.

15.3.4. Results for Fixed Income and Commodity ETFs

Broad market and corporate bond fixed income ETFs (as well as commodity ETFs) show very strong persistence in their flows. Notable exceptions are US treasury ETFs, which show strong contrarian patter in their flows: months of inflows tend to follow months of outflows. This pattern is perhaps related to mean reversion (e.g., "fear versus greed") in sentiment. In addition, fixed income ETF flows are negatively correlated with long-term yields as one would expect: When yields rise, bond prices fell, coinciding with apparent outflows from fixed income ETFs. Broad market and treasury ETFs flows are positively correlated with unemployment and inflation. An exception is the more risky class of corporate bond ETFs, whose flows are negatively correlated with inflation. Seasonality does not seem to play much of a role for either fixed income or commodity ETF flows.

Additional variables can be easily added. For example, it is likely that investors behave asymmetrically, reacting perhaps stronger to negative or positive returns that are extreme or to volatility shocks on the downside. Such factors can be incorporated in the regression models using indicator variables in addition to those already incorporated. For example, to include an asymmetric reaction of fund flows to returns, we can add an indicator variable that takes the value 1 if returns are positive and zero otherwise. The coefficient on this variable would tell us whether flows were different for positive versus negative returns. We can repeat this for returns or volatility above a certain threshold too.

15.4. APPLICATIONS OF FLOW ANALYSIS

15.4.1. Regulatory Context

The flow analysis can be modified easily to analyze questions of interest to regulators. These include the following applications:

- **Macro-Flow Effects**—Regulators are interested in the aggregate flow–price relationship to understand whether ETF and mutual fund flows have an impact on asset prices at the macro level. For example, the International Monetary Fund (2015) estimates a vector autoregressive model of returns and flows similar to that described earlier. The model also accommodates some interesting twists such as nonlinearity in the response of flows to VIX (e.g., shocks upward might matter more), asymmetry in flow surprises, and so on.
- **Fund Flow Analysis**—Understanding how investors behave can help regulators assess the potential stress to a fund. Here the model is one of flows at the fund level (i.e., the share class level as funds with different share classes are not economically distinct) as a function of explanatory variables. These might include fund and benchmark performance, fund characteristics such as total assets, age, clientele, fees, fund types, and liquidity of underlying asset class). Again, nonlinearities in the relation of flows to returns can easily be accommodated in a standard regression model.
- **Flagship Effects**—To the extent brand name matters, a shock to a fund family's flagship product may carry over to other funds by the same asset manager. This question is mainly of interest in the context of whether large asset managers themselves pose systemic risk.
- **Stress Tests**—The residual in a fund flows regression measures the shock in flows, and the standard error can be used to gauge the potential size of withdrawals. This is again of interest to regulators who want to understand what cash/liquid reserves are needed by a fund, especially one that invests in somewhat illiquid assets or where there is a mismatch between the settlement period of the underlying assets versus the fund (e.g., bank loans). The impact of redemption fees can also be assessed, which could in theory act as a brake on withdrawals in a stressed situation.

Stress Test

As an example, suppose we have estimated a fund flow model and the innovation or surprise in flows in (say) a given week, ϵ_T, is distributed normally so that $\epsilon_T \sim N(0, \sigma_\epsilon^2)$. The probability that the fund manager experiences an *unanticipated* withdrawal (the presumption here is that the manager can plan for *expected* or anticipated withdrawals based on past returns/flows) in excess of cash reserves R in a given week is:

$$\Pr[-\epsilon_T > R] = \Pr[\epsilon_T < -R] = \Phi\left(-\frac{R}{\sigma_\epsilon^2}\right),$$

where $\Phi(z)$ denotes the cumulative standard normal distribution evaluated at z. Higher reserves and less flow volatility reduce the probability of exhausting reserves in a nonlinear manner. Reserves could be scaled relative to flow volatility to roughly equate drawdown probabilities across different funds or asset classes. We could similarly compute the CVaR of the fund using the regression model estimates.

15.4.2. Sentiment and Flows

Are flows indicators of investor sentiment? If so, can one measure sentiment on a relatively high frequency basis using flow data? Basic intuition suggests a change in sentiment will be reflected in changes in desired exposures that in turn are associated with ETF flows. But the analysis shows that flows are predictable: What really matters though is the innovation in flows that is captured by the unpredictable shocks to the flow model. The first step to capture sentiment is to calculate the flow innovations which are the exposure class residuals ϵ_T from the regression model. Then, one can look for common drivers of *flow innovations* in all seven exposures using a variety of possible statistical techniques. One of the most common such techniques is Principal Components Analysis (PCA). In our case, there will be seven components corresponding to the exposure classes examined: the first principal component is the linear combination that accounts for as much of the variability in observed flow innovations as possible. The following components in turn have the highest variance possible under the constraint that they are orthogonal to all the preceding components.

Sentiment can change quickly and the daily flow data is of greatest interest. Working with daily data, not all macroeconomic variables are available (i.e., unemployment and CPI are released monthly). To capture the daily flow of information related to macro events, three contemporaneous daily returns series are added as explanatory variables: Russell 3000 Index, Barclays Aggregated Index, and Thomson Reuters/Jefferies Commodity Index. Using the daily time series of flow innovations $\epsilon_{j,T}$ for each of seven exposure categories going back to January 2007, construct $7 \times T$ vector $\epsilon_{7,T}$ of flow innovations for each day T. Then compute daily principal component *loadings* of the flow innovations, which yields a 7×7 matrix: $\Lambda_{i=1\dots7,j=1\dots7}$.

The daily first principal component ($j=1$) loadings for each exposure series have been relatively stable at least from 2009. Although the factors are purely statistical in nature, it is natural to try to interpret loadings across "risk" dimension. Indeed, emerging markets ETF flows consistently get the highest (positive) loading;

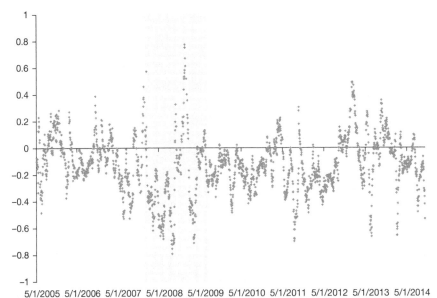

Figure 15.1 Daily flow sentiment measure, April 2005 to October 2014.

whereas, US treasuries are the most negative as the safest assets. Note that the signs in PCA are purely arbitrary in that I could reverse the signs: Nevertheless, treasuries and emerging markets are at opposite ends in this reading, consistent with the intuition just described.

Flow sentiment at time t is measured as the first principal component score (the PCA analysis is rolled forward daily in a "telescoping" manner) for the most recent flow innovation realization:

$$\text{Sentiment}_t = \Lambda_{t,1}^T \cdot \epsilon_t \tag{15.4}$$

Flow sentiment is then smoothed using 21-day (approximately one month) half-life and shown in figure 15.1 over the period April 2005 to October 2014. One can see variation in the computed sentiment, especially in the crisis period, again corresponding to our intuition. (The NBER officially recorded a recession from December 2007 to June 2009, shaded in figure 15.1.) The reduction in overall sentiment levels post-crisis is also consistent with growing economic confidence. Indicators such as this may be of potential use to investors to summarize the sentiment inherent in flow data at a more aggregate level. That is left to a future exercise.

15.5. DO PASSIVE FLOWS AFFECT CORRELATIONS?

Overall, the percentage of US equity market capitalization in index-tracking funds has increased from approximately 3% in 2000 to 10% by 2014, where that figure is roughly split between index mutual funds and ETFs.[1] There is a popular

---

1. Credit Suisse Trading Strategy, December 2014.

perception that the growth in passive index investing through exchange-traded funds has had detrimental effects on the market quality of the underlying basket securities. In particular, there is concern that ETF trading substitutes for and takes away from volume and liquidity in the underlying securities and increases the co-movement in their returns. In turn, it is argued that increased pairwise return correlation impairs price discovery and the ability of active managers to generate alpha. For instance, Wimbish (2013) notes that industry and academic experts have "long said that index-focused exchange traded funds (ETFs) cause greater stock return correlations. But a newer line of concern holds that the products may also cause additional market-wide systemic problems because of the arbitrage opportunities they produce." A closely related concern is that ETF trading substitutes for and takes away from volume and liquidity in the underlying securities.

Empirical analyses of the impact of passive flows are relatively scarce. A notable exception is Sullivan and Xiong (2012), who argue that "the rise in popularity of index investing contributes to higher systematic market risk. More indexed equity assets corresponds to increased cross-sectional trading commonality, in turn precipitating higher return correlations among stocks." Da and Shive (2013) find a strong relation between measures of ETF activity and return co-movement at both the fund and the stock levels, and this effect is stronger among small and illiquid stocks. They conclude that "at least some ETF-driven return co-movement is excessive" and that ETFs reduce the diversification benefits they were intended to promote.

Increased co-movements in the returns of ETF basket securities are in turn alleged to have had a variety of negative impacts with themes including reduced diversification benefits, greater difficulty in stock-picking during periods of high correlation, and the impairment of price discovery and reduction in liquidity in smaller capitalization stocks.[2] For example, Flood (2012) notes that "another headwind for active managers to overcome is an increase in correlations between constituents of the Russell 2000 index which has coincided with the growth of ETFs in the small cap space," as pairwise correlations for stocks in that index rose from 5% in 2000 to 25% in 2012. Similarly, the fact that ETFs were disproportionately affected in the Flash Crash of May 6, 2010 (ETFs accounted for 70% of trades ultimately cancelled by exchanges) has fueled discussion regarding ETF flows, return volatility, and systemic risk.[3] The role of leveraged ETFs has also been discussed (see, e.g., Cheng and Madhavan 2009) in the context of end-of-day volatility effects.

2. Sullivan and Xiong (2012) note that "equity betas have not only risen but converged in recent years; also consistent with the accelerating growth and importance of passive investing."

3. See, e.g., Bradley and Litan (2010); Wurgler (2010); Ramaswamy (2010). Ben-David, Franzoni, and Moussawi (2014) argue that ETFs served as "a conduit for shock propagation between the futures market and the equity market during the Flash Crash on May 6, 2010."

15.6. IMPACT OF FLOWS ON UNDERLYING CONSTITUENT RETURNS

15.6.1. Pairwise Correlations

The average correlation coefficient between the returns between any two stocks has increased sharply over the past decade. In that period, as we saw in chapter 1, so has the growth of ETP assets. These two facts have led some commentators to draw a causal connection. The idea is intuitively appealing—ETF flows cause stock prices in the underlying baskets to move more together. For example, Israeli, Lee, and Sridharan (2015) explore the idea that an increase in ETF ownership is accompanied by a decline in pricing efficiency for the underlying component securities.[4] They argue that an increase in ETF ownership is associated with: (a) higher bid-ask spreads and price impact; (b) an increase in what they term "stock return synchronicity" meaning increased co-movement of firm-level stock returns with market and industry returns; and (c) a decline in "future earnings response coefficients" (measured as the predictive power of current returns for future earnings). They conclude, "Collectively, our findings support the view that increased ETF ownership can lead to higher trading costs and lower benefits from information acquisition, a combination which results in less informative security prices for the component firms."

But does this proposition even make sense conceptually or empirically? Madhavan and Morillo (2016) argue that it does not. Arguments attributing the higher correlation environment to ETF growth frame the problem incorrectly in their view. If ETFs were not a viable investment vehicle, investors seeking broad based exposures have many other alternatives, such as active mutual funds or hedge funds. It is possible that new investors enter into ETFs with a mistaken belief that they will have liquidity in all eventualities, but this seems unlikely.

From an empirical viewpoint, Madhavan and Morillo and (2016) show that pairwise correlation is ultimately a secondary statistic, driven by the ratio of factor volatility to specific volatility. Common factor effects are the primary drivers of changes in pairwise correlation because it is unlikely that there would be significant changes in idiosyncratic risk across all equities. So, for example, the results of Israeli, Lee, and Sridharan (2015) may capture the influence of other factors that are coincident with the rapid growth of ETF assets from a low base, but not caused by ETFs per se. Indeed, over the entire period of their analysis, ETFs accounted for less than 3% of individual stock ownership holdings, so it seems economically unlikely that ETFs would increase return correlations or synchronicity as claimed by Israeli, Lee, and Sridharan (2015) and others, even though these facts are not in question.

---

4. See also Chris Flood, "Dark Side of ETFs Erode Active Managers' Outperformance," *Financial Times*, August 9, 2015: "The ability of active fund managers, who aim to beat the market, to pick winning stocks is being eroded by the huge growth in assets controlled by exchange traded funds, according to new academic research . . . the growth in ETFs is resulting in distortions in the share prices of those companies held by such funds and could be a factor in explaining why stockpickers are having difficulty delivering outperformance."

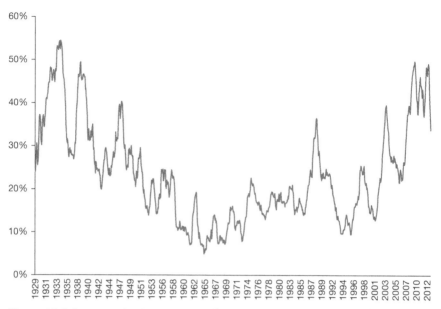

Figure 15-2. Average pairwise return correlations, January 1926 to December 2012.

But how to demonstrate that these effects are merely coincident? Madhavan and Morillo (2016) use data on individual US equities going back to 1926 from the CRSP database to make their point that in the longer historical and macro-economic context the argument ETF flows have increased correlations is not convincing. Indeed, while cross-stock correlations are indeed high today, they are not at unprecedented levels relative to the past, a time well before the rise of passive indexing.

Figure 15.2 illustrates the time series (using daily returns from January 1926 to December 2012) of monthly correlation among the stocks based on daily returns in the month and smoothed with a 12-month moving average. The data source is CRSP for the largest 200 stocks prior to 1958 and the S&P 500 thereafter.

Correlations were very high in the past, well before the growth of index and ETF investing. They also show that correlations and volatility are strongly related—macro uncertainty drives overall factor volatility and hence correlation. Further, asset classes such as currencies also show an increase in correlation despite very limited ETF penetration. This is consistent with the hypothesis that the driver of higher correlations is the macro environment, and not growth in ETFs.[5] As for the purported linkage between stock selection ability and the correlation environment, there is no logical connection. Indeed, at any correlation level, active managers (defined as those who deviate from the cap-weighted distribution of holdings in the universe) must, by definition, have average performance equal to the benchmark return less fees. So, correlation really is not linked to the success of active management and stock selection in particular.

5. See also Mazza (2012).

15.6.2. Impact on Volumes of Underlying Assets

The idea that ETF trading might replace or substitute for trading in the underlying basket securities—be they stocks or bonds—is intuitively appealing. Trading in ETFs typically does not result in trading in the underlying, but it is not clear what the contra-factual proposition is if there were no ETFs. In other words, investors may trade ETFs more frequently and this may result in higher volumes in the underlying assets, versus a substitution effect.

The idea that flows into ETFs take liquidity away from the individual components does not appear to be borne out by the data, meaning there is no evidence of a substitution effect. Madhavan and Morillo (2016) show that volume correlations (using what they term normalized volumes which are scaled and log transformed) are closely related to return correlations. That is not surprising as derivative markets offer opportunities to trade versus single stocks. Most important, even though investors continue to shift from active management into index tracking vehicles (ETFs and index mutual funds), the quantitative impact on volumes is likely minimal. The reason is that there are substantially more assets in active funds, and those funds have greater turnover. Further, much of the volume in developed markets is attributable to high-frequency trading, which is closely linked to volatility. So, the ultimate driver of volumes for single stocks and for ETFs is volatility. As the old saying goes, "differences of opinion make a horse race," and hence volume is intrinsically linked to the divergence in value estimates and to market volatility.

15.6.3. Shock Propagation

Some recent discussion has taken the view that trading in the ETF, possibly quite transitory in nature, leads to a propagation of volatility into the underlying securities. For example, Broman (2013) argues that "ETF mispricing" is only partially mean-reverting. Ben-David, Franzoni, and Moussawi (2014) posit that ETF flows transmit liquidity shocks to their underlying baskets of securities. In their view, creation/redemption activity adds a layer of volatility to the underlying security returns as opposed to our model where arbitrage gaps are self-correcting. Their empirical evidence is based on regressions of NAV returns on the lagged premium, lagged NAV return, and lagged ETF return, or in our notation (assuming all prices and values are in logs):

$$(n_t - n_{t-1}) = \beta_0 + \beta_1 \pi_{t-1} + \beta_2 (n_{t-1} - n_{t-2}) + \beta_3 (p_{t-1} - p_{t-2}) + \varepsilon_t. \quad (15.5)$$

The coefficient on lagged ETF returns is interpreted as shock propagation. Given the decomposition of the premium derived earlier, it is clear that the left- and right-hand side terms both include weighted sums of past returns so the regression estimates are difficult to interpret. In other words, as shown before, the alternative explanation is that price impact reflects shocks to fundamentals, ETFs lead price-discovery, NAV is "stale" and "catches up" over time. The stylized facts from this regression can be interpreted either way, with no evidence of causality in either direction.

15.7. CHAPTER SUMMARY

Flows into and out of ETFs have attracted considerable attention from investors and regulators. These flows reflect primary market creation/redemption activity and are also available on a $T + 1$ basis, meaning they are observed with a one-day lag. As such, flows are a timely and cross-asset class barometer of the market sentiment of sophisticated investors. This chapter shows that flows can be modeled well statistically as functions of past flows and on macroeconomic indicators such as changes in inflation, interest rates, or unemployment.

Flow shifts ultimately reflect changes in investor sentiment, so flow surprises can be informative. Further, flows can be used to gauge the extent of co-movement or crowding, an issue that is especially important for the success of active strategies. Flow analysis has other applications. These include gauging the likely variation in flows, an issue important for asset managers, and stress testing, a critical element for regulators.

The evidence also shows that correlations in individual stock returns of a basket are not driven by flows, but rather by common factor variation. There is also no evidence that flows into ETFs have had detrimental impacts on the underlying securities. Nor is there any evidence of substitution, meaning that volume shocks to the ETF and its underlying or constituent securities are positively correlated. In subsequent chapters, we will deal directly with the concerns about flows in stressed periods, particularly redemptions in ETFs against illiquid sectors such as high-yield bonds.

Leveraged and Inverse Products

16.1. INTRODUCTION

Leveraged and inverse exchange-traded products (LETPs) provide leveraged long or short exposure to the daily returns of various indexes, sectors, and asset classes including equities, volatility, and currencies. The LETP space has seen significant and rapid growth in assets and now comprises leveraged, inverse, and leveraged inverse products offering 2× or 3× long (bull) exposure or short (bear) exposure of –1×, –2×, or –3× the underlying daily index return. Leveraged (sometimes called "geared") ETPs are extensions of leveraged mutual funds that were first introduced in 1993. They are structured as 1940 Act funds with derivative exposures collateralized by treasury bills and cash. As these products contain embedded leverage, I use the term LETP as opposed to the term ETF that refers to a physically backed fund offering no embedded leverage or structural features such as return caps or floors. At year-end 2015, there were 274 LETPs that together account for just over 2% of all assets in US-listed exchange-traded products.

16.2. DRIVERS OF GROWTH

Several factors explain the attraction of LETPs. First, these products offer short-term traders and hedge funds a structured vehicle to express their directional views regarding a wide variety of equity indexes and sectors. Second, unlike traditional ETFs, these products have leverage embedded in their design, so that investors do not need to explicitly use derivatives or margin. That is attractive to investors who might face mandates against the use of explicit leverage. Third, investors, including many hedge funds, are attracted by the convenience and liquidity of these products and increasingly use them to place longer term leveraged bets or to hedge their portfolios. Fourth, investors can gain still more leverage by trading options on levered ETPs. Finally, as with regular ETFs, investors in these products have limited liability; you cannot lose more than you invest. Leveraged products have been controversial for several reasons that I discuss later and—despite their low share of overall fund assets—been the source of continued discussion among regulators concerned about systemic risk.

16.3. COMPOUNDING AND RETURNS

16.3.1. Compounding and Return Decay

An early concern with LETPs is that some investors might not recognize the impact of the compounding of daily leveraged returns over longer intervals.

Case Study: Compounding of Levered Returns

Consider a 2× LETP with an initial net asset value of $100. Suppose the underlying index falls 10% on day one from its initial value of 100 to 90 and then goes up 10% on the subsequent day to 99, for a two-day decline of −1%. While investors might expect the leveraged product to decline by twice as much, or −2%, over the two-day period, it actually declines by −4%. This is because doubling the index's 10% fall on the first day lowers the LETP's value from $100 to $80, which then recovers to $96 (=2 × 10% × $80) the following day, upon doubling the index's 10% gain.

While the simple case study example provides valuable intuition, it is useful to more formally model the underlying return process to better understand return dynamics. Cheng and Madhavan (2009) develop a continuous time model where the benchmark index S_t follows geometric Brownian motion with a non-stochastic drift rate μ and volatility σ. Denote by W_t a Wiener process with a mean of zero and a variance of t:

$$dS_t = \mu S_t\, dt + \sigma S_t dW_t. \tag{16.1}$$

As time intervals shrink and ignoring microstructure frictions (i.e., $u_t = 0$) the instantaneous return on a LETP with leverage x over an interval $[t, t+dt]$ is given by:

$$\frac{dp_t}{p_t} = x\frac{dS_t}{S_t} - (x-1)r_f dt, \tag{16.2}$$

where r_f is the risk-free rate. Leverage x is positive for "bull" funds and negative for "bear" or inverse funds. So, the instantaneous return on the LETP is x times the return on the index, less the interest factor; a result that can be verified by an intraday plot of any actively traded LETP against its benchmark index.

Under Cheng and Madhavan's (2009) assumptions of non-stochastic drift and variance, and with constant interest rates, the LETP's total return from time 0 to T, denoted $r_{0,T}$, can be written as:

$$r_{0,T} = \left(\frac{S_T}{S_0}\right)^x e^{-(x-1)T(r_f+x\sigma^2/2)}. \tag{16.3}$$

Observe in equation (16.3) that the LETP's total return is the product of x-levered index returns, that is, $\left(\dfrac{S_T}{S_0}\right)^x$, multiplied by a term that is strictly less than one that increases with time, implying a decay.

* * *

TRADING OPTIONS ON LETPS

The advantage of the formal model is to demonstrate how a buy-and-hold investor experiences return decay, and to relate that decay explicitly to volatility, leverage, interest rates, and the time horizon. Some hedge funds and active managers use options to bet that both the leveraged ETP and the companion inverse ETP will fall over time. For example, consider the case of a 3× long Natural Gas ETN that lost 57% annually from August 2012 to August 2105. The corresponding −3× product lost 42% annually over the same period.

NOTE: See, e.g., Daisy Maxey, "Fund Reaps Windfall Investing in ETF 'Minefield': One of Catalyst Macro Strategy's Primary Strategies Involves Buying Options Tied to Leveraged Index ETFs," *Wall Street Journal*, August 28, 2015, which cites the use of paired LETP option trades to capture decay.

For short intervals of time, as shown in equation (16.3), time decay is not economically significant, in keeping with arguments made by LETP proponents. Avellaneda and Zhang (2009) and Lu, Wang, and Zhang (2009) empirically examine how close LETPs correlate to reproducing the corresponding multiple of index returns over extended investment horizons. In trending markets, LETPs have delivered multiples of returns over longer periods. It is really the choppiness in price movements that is the source of return erosion. The prospectuses of LETPs explicitly provide warnings about compounding effects over longer horizons.

The model of equation (16.3) also helps us understand how the effects of compounding can be mitigated with a dynamic rebalancing strategy. Indeed, if an investor could continually rebalance, they would avoid the long-term decay. This is essentially the logic behind the portfolio insurance strategies popularized in the 1980s. Hill, Nadig, and Hougan (2015) suggest an investor rebalances using a trigger rule: If the investor's investment has experienced a loss on their leveraged/inverse ETP position beyond a pre-set gap, the investor will invest more. Correspondingly, if the index has declined relative to investor's leveraged/inverse ETF position, the investor will take profits and reduce the position. In practice though, this strategy may result in higher transaction costs and taxes.

16.3.2. Extensions

The model is straightforward to extend to incorporate complexities such as dividends, stochastic volatility, jump diffusions, and fund expenses, but the fundamental insights are not altered. Giese (2010) shows that Cheng and Madhavan's results hold under generalizations for multi-asset portfolios with stochastic volatility. He shows there is an optimal degree of leverage that maximizes the expected future return of the daily rebalanced leveraged investment strategy that depends on observable market parameters. Further insight is provided by Haugh (2011) who shows that an investor with a long position in an LETP is short realized variance and interprets the exposure of a non-leveraged constant-proportion strategy to realized variance as a multiplicative premium. Jarrow (2010) provides a construction with a LETF and riskless bond that characterizes the return distribution of the leveraged ETF over any investment horizon. See also Trainor (2010).

Other suitability concerns beyond tracking error for investors in LETPs include tax efficiency and transaction costs arising from higher turnover, and typically higher management fees than other products. These concerns led to warnings by the SEC in 2009 and a moratorium on new issuers in this space.

EXAMPLE: RETURN DEVIATIONS

A real-world example (Cheng and Madhavan 2009) is the ProShares Ultra Short Oil & Gas –2× inverse product. Between August 2, 2011, and November 15, 2011, the underlying Dow Jones U.S. Oil & Gas Index lost 3.9%. Although a holder of an inverse fund would expect to gain in this case, the actual ETP experienced a loss of –9.9%.

As awareness has grown about the impacts of compounding, the market has matured, and all fund prospectuses are now very clear on the effect of compounding over longer intervals. Indeed, according to ETF.com, the median holding period for LETFs with over $100 million in assets (about a fifth of the universe, as of 2014) is just 9.5 days. That said, there are still many investors, including sophisticated hedge funds, who hold LETPs for substantially longer intervals.

16.4. REBALANCING

16.4.1. Mechanics

Leveraged and inverse exchange-traded products generally rely on total return swaps to produce returns that are a multiple of the underlying daily index returns. These funds typically invest most of their capital in benchmark securities or treasuries (held by a third-party custodian) plus a position in total return swaps or futures. Swaps are negotiated agreements with large investment banks. There is an element of counterparty risk implicit in a swap agreement, but this is mitigated by the fact that most LETP arrangements specify that the fund will true up their profits/losses on a daily basis. This implies, however, that the exposures of total return swaps underpinning LETPs must be rebalanced daily in order to generate the leveraged returns every day. Cheng and Madhavan (2009) show that LETPs (including inverse funds) induce rebalancing activity toward the end of the day in

the same direction of the market. This is, in effect, similar to same-direction trading induced by portfolio insurance in the 1980s. When the underlying index is up,
additional total return swaps exposure must be added; but when the underlying
index is down, the exposure of total return swaps must be reduced. This is always
true whether the products are leveraged, inverse, or leveraged inverse.

Specifically, Cheng and Madhavan (2009) derive an expression for the estimated end-of-day rebalancing aside from creation/redemption activity. Let L_t
represent the notional amount of the total return swap exposure that is required
before the market opens on the next day to replicate the intended leveraged return
of the index for the fund on day $t + 1$. With the fund's total assets under management at the start of day t denoted by A_t (the product of shares outstanding and
net asset value per share), the notional amount of the total return swaps required
before the market opens on day $t + 1$ is given by $L_t = x A_t$.

On day $t + 1$, the underlying index generates a return of r_t and the exposure of
the total return swap position, denoted by E_{t+1}, becomes:

$$E_{t+1} = L_t (1 + r_t) = x A_t (1 + r_t). \tag{16.4}$$

At the same time, reflecting the gain or loss that is x times the index's performance
on the day, the leveraged fund's NAV at the close of day $t + 1$ becomes:

$$A_{t+1} = A_t (1 + xr_t), \tag{16.5}$$

which suggests that the notional amount of the total return swaps required before
the market opens on day $t + 2$ to maintain constant exposure is:

$$L_{t+1} = xA_{t+1} = xA_t(1 + xr_t). \tag{16.6}$$

The difference between L_{t+1} in equation (16.6) and E_{t+1} in equation (16.4) is the
amount by which the exposure of the total return swaps need to be adjusted or re-
hedged at the close of day $t + 1$. Denoting the rebalancing demand by B_{t+1} we get:

$$B_{t+1} = L_{t+1} - E_{t+1} = A_t(x^2 - x)r_t. \tag{16.7}$$

The fund's total rebalancing is the product of the day's dollar returns $A_t r_t$ and a
nonlinear function of leverage $(x^2 - x)$. Interestingly, the latter function is the same
term that appears in the compounding portion of equation (16.3) derived earlier.

From equation (16.7), it is clear that the effects of rebalancing are highly
nonlinear. For example, for a triple-leveraged ETF $x = 3$, and the leverage term
equals 6 (=$3^2 - 3$) meaning that every dollar earned by the fund on a given day
requires $6 of rebalancing. The rebalancing effect of inverse products is even
more pronounced, and because the term $(x^2 - x) > 0$, it implies that inverse
or bear funds also rebalance in the same direction as the market, just like
their bull cousins. For a triple-inverse fund $(x = -3)$, the leverage term is 12 =
$(-3)^2 - (-3)$. Why is the direction of the effect the same for LETPs that are short
the index and why are the leverage factors different? Intuitively, an inverse or

leveraged inverse product's total assets will *increase* if the index *falls*, which requires it to *increase* short exposure still further, generating selling pressure. Conversely, if the index rises, the fund suffers losses, reducing its assets and hence the size of its needed short position. Reducing its short exposure is equivalent to buying pressure, but the rebalancing required not symmetric for bull and bear funds.

EXAMPLE: LEVERAGE REBALANCING

Consider an $-2\times$ inverse ETP with initial NAV of $100. Initially, the required notional amount of the total return swaps is $-$200$ (i.e., short twice the NAV). If the index falls 10% on day one, the fund's NAV increases 20% to $120, and the exposure of the total return swaps goes to $-$180$, reflecting the initial short exposure plus the $20 gain from the day. Now, the required notional amount for the total return swaps is $-$240$, or $-2\times$ $120. So, the fund will need to increase its short exposure of total return swaps. The change in exposure is $-$60$ (= $180 - $240), which the swap counterparty will presumably need to short in turn to avoid undue market risk. I can verify the formula given in Cheng and Madhavan (2009), that the implied rebalance is AUM $\times$ index return $\times$ leverage factor, or, $-$60 = $100 \times (-10\%) \times ((-2)^2 - (-2))$. By comparison, if the fund were a $2\times$ levered fund, the implied rebalance would be $-$20 = $100 \times (-10\%) \times (2^2 - 2)$.

In other words, there is no offset or "pairing off" of leveraged long and short products on the same index. Note that the need for daily rebalancing is unique to LETPs due to their product design. Traditional ETFs that are not leveraged or inverse (whether they are holding physicals, total return swaps, or other derivatives) do not induce such daily rebalance activity.

16.4.2. Impact of Rebalancing Activity

In theory, LETPs' rebalancing activity should be executed as near the market close as possible, given the dependence of the rebalancing amount on the close-to-close return of the underlying index. Whether LETPs rebalance their exposure of total return swaps immediately before or after the market close, however, the counterparties with which they execute total return swaps will want to put on or adjust their hedges while the market is still open, to minimize the risk to their capital and position taking, especially in volatile markets. As LETPs gain assets, there may be a heightened impact on the liquidity and volatility of the underlying index and the securities comprising the index during the closing period of the day's trading session (e.g., the last hour or half-hour), a particular regulatory concern for less liquid or more volatile market segments such as biotech or in some regional markets. As shown above, the rebalancing impact of increased assets is magnified by an increase in leverage and a shift in the asset mix toward inverse products.

Further, as rebalancing flows are always in the same direction as the market movement, LETPs cannot by themselves mechanically cause whipsawing in the market, as the rebalancing induced by their need to keep to their leverage targets is, by construction, in the same direction as the market. Trading in the same direction as the market can, however, result in higher volatility, simply via increasing the overall scale of market moves as a result of the price impact that rebalancing may have into the close.[1]

In the period 2008–2011, when volatility was more pronounced, LETP rebalancing activity accounted for a significant fraction of end-of-day volumes as documented in Cheng and Madhavan (2009). Fund managers have become more aware of the impact of their rebalancing activity and have been more careful in their actions around the close since the SEC first warned about the products in 2009 and imposed a moratorium for new issuers. The share of LETPs in overall assets (just over 2% in 2014) also is small overall and the market has matured considerably. Whether this potential effect is material is ultimately an empirical question that depends on the size of the rebalances (and, in turn, dependent on the size and leverage of these products), the proportion of those rebalances that are actually traded in the market on any one day, and the price impact associated with those trades.

16.4.3. Empirical Evidence on Rebalancing Activity

Recent evidence is presented by Tuzun (2013) who finds that price-insensitive and concentrated trading of LETPs could be destabilizing during periods of high volatility, especially for the stocks of financial firms. See also Haryanto et al. (2013), who conclude the impact was economically significant only during volatile periods. An opposing view is Ivanov and Lenkey (2014), who argue that capital flows reduce the need for ETFs to rebalance when returns are large in magnitude and, therefore, mitigate the potential for these products to amplify volatility. They find that investors take profits from leveraged funds when the funds move up significantly and vice versa, stabilizing the asset base and mitigating the need to rebalance in the direction of the market. Of course, this argument relies on an implicit assumption that any historical contrarian behavior by investors will continue to hold in an extreme market movement. From a financial stability viewpoint, LETPs rebalancing could amplify a large stock market move and trigger a cascade effect through further rebalancing in the event of a jump in volatility.

---

1. Note that the use of leverage itself is not the key issue, as investors have had access to instruments that allow for taking leveraged positions across a wide range of assets well before LETPs were available. The major consideration is that LETPs reset their leverage on a daily basis and, thus, have to mechanically rebalance toward the close of the market. This may not otherwise be the optimal implementation choice for investors interested in long-term positions.

The World's Largest LETF Cannot Take New Cash

As a case study of why the concerns on LETF are not merely academic exercises, the world's largest leveraged exchange-traded fund—Nomura Asset Management Company's Next Funds Nikkei 225 leveraged Index ETF—stopped taking new subscription orders on October 15, 2015, amid growing concerns that rebalancing activity increased market volatility at the end of the day. The fund is still accepting redemptions. The ETF had $6 billion in assets with 2× leveraged exposure of about $12bn. Assets under management had doubled in the previous five months, with flows coming largely from individual investors. The ETF holds futures, not physical equities or swaps. This means when the market moves 1%, the fund (and two related inverse funds that were simultaneously gated) must trade in significant size and in the same direction into the close of Nikkei futures. For example, the Next Funds ETF held 79,855 Nikkei 225 futures contracts on October 14, 2015, accounting for 23% of open interest, according to Bloomberg. The fund will also have to roll its futures contracts quarterly. Some commentators noted that the issues in Japan were a cautionary tale for leveraged funds in sectors such as financials and biotech.

NOTE: See, e.g., Anna Kitanaka and Toshiro Hasegawa, "World's Biggest Leveraged ETF Halts on Liquidity Concern," Bloomberg, October 14, 2015, available at http://www.bloomberg.com/news/articles/2015-10-15/world-s-biggest-leveraged-etf-halts-orders-on-liquidity-concern and Chris Dieterich, "Godzilla-Sized Leveraged ETF Is Wreaking Havoc on Tokyo's Stock Market," Barrons, October 15, 2015, available at http://blogs.barrons.com/focusonfunds/2015/10/15/godzilla-sized-leveraged-etf-is-wreaking-havoc-on-tokyos-market/.

Smaller capitalization stocks in more volatile sectors such as financials, REITs, energy, health care, and biotech are sensitive to rebalancing pressures. Bai, Bond, and Hatch (2015) examine the impact of LETPs on the trading of real estate sector stocks, concluding that rebalancing activity significantly moves the price of component stocks and increases their volatility. Their evidence is consistent with trading on predictable late-day order flow.

In recent years, exposure using levered and inverse ETPs on volatility—such as the VelocityShares Daily 2x VIX ETN (TVIX) and VelocityShares Daily Inverse VIX ETN (XIV)—has grown considerably relative to unlevered VIX futures-based ETPs such as the iPath S&P 500 VIX Short-Term Futures ETN (VXX). As with all leveraged and inverse ETPs, these funds rebalance in the same direction as the market, selling VIX futures as volatility falls and buying VIX futures as volatility rise. Further, volatility is strongly inversely related contemporaneous market returns, with a correlation coefficient in daily VIX returns and S&P 500 returns is about −0.89. Could volatility rebalancing activity affect volatility? Is it possible that a volatility shock affect the equity market itself? These are open questions but ones well worth further research.

16.5. CHAPTER SUMMARY

There are a few key points to keep in mind with leveraged and inverse products. First, these products offer investors a way to obtain a multiple of the day's return in a given index. They can be useful tools for short-term hedging or tactical exposures. Longer run investors, particularly in markets that are not trending, need to be aware of the effects of compounding. The good news is that most investors have received the message (which is clearly stated in the fund prospectus) and the average holding period is relatively short. Second, the mechanics of rebalancing mean that rather counterintuitively, both bull and bear funds will rebalance by buying if the underlying index is up and selling if it is down.

The effects of rebalancing are highly nonlinear because these funds have embedded leverage. Leveraged/inverse funds often hold stocks in physical form in addition to swaps/futures but offer multiples of the returns of their underlying index, which distinguishes them from conventional ETFs. Although empirical evidence to date is inconclusive, it is possible that LETPs may have a disproportionate impact in narrower, niche markets. For this reason, regulators are watchful, even though LETPs are still small relative to overall ETF assets.

Systemic Risk

17.1. INTRODUCTION

Regulators and policymakers around the globe are trying to understand the impact of ETF flows from a systemic risk perspective. We need to distinguish between systemic risk and extreme return events because the two are often conflated, causing confusion. Systemic risk refers to the notion that the entire financial system itself may collapse, as opposed to any individual entity or component failing in isolation. By contrast, extreme negative returns ("Black Swan" events) are common in financial markets, examples that include the crash of October 1987 and the crash in China A stocks in July 2015, neither of which imperiled the entire system.

In terms of systemic risk, regulators have focused on the impact of ETF flows on the volatility of the underlying securities, as well as larger questions about liquidity and capital formation. Reports from leading global bodies such as the International Monetary Fund (IMF) and Bank of International Settlements have raised a variety concerns. These include the complex eco-system of ETPs (with a possibility of domino effects via their reliance on banks), the dependence on a few APs to make markets in times of stress, possible fire sales as ETFs are created against less liquid assets. Beyond the rapid growth in assets under management, the complexity of newer structures outside of traditional index based ETF structures using forwards, options, swaps, and so on is a source of unease. In Europe, for example, many ETPs are actually notes or hold swaps issued by the same banks that are their issuers, raising counterparty risk concerns.[1]

Here I consider these issues in detail, beginning by describing concerns about the ecosystem of ETFs and related dependencies, and then turn to policy issues around stressed markets. In the subsequent chapter, I will cover broader concerns about herding, contagion, and agency conflicts, and discuss with some concrete actions that policymakers can take to reduce systemic risk and increase financial market stability.

---

1. Although passive turnover is roughly 3% versus 33% for active managers (eVestment, Goldman Sachs Research), ETF volumes are 30% of total equity volumes, a figure that rises in times of stress as measured by the VIX index. Note that these figures are for the United States because, until regulatory change in the form of MiFID II the reporting of ETF transactions in Europe is voluntary and hence greatly understated.

Table 17.1 Select Policy Issues and Implications

Policy Question	Implications for Regulation
What is the contribution of fund size/asset manager to systemic risk?	• Evidence to date suggests no relationship between asset manager size and a fund's contribution to systemic risk • This means that policy should emphasize the specific risks of products, not just size
What possible problems are created by manager incentives?	• Is there evidence of excessive risk taking, herding, and spillovers of redemption within fund a family? • Externalities may include fire sales, contagion, and elevated volatility that require regulatory focus
Can asset managers' behavior amplify risks?	• Financial stability risks from mutual funds could stem from many small funds taking similar positions, meaning regulation should not just focus on the positions of large funds • What is the potential impact on market volatility and systemic risk from rebalancing activity by Leveraged Exchange-Traded Products (LETPs) following major market movements?
Do fund flows affect asset prices?	• If fund flows affect aggregate asset prices, then regulators need to focus on concentration and price-impact analysis • Mutual funds' concentration in ownership, especially in less liquid asset classes, is a focus
What are the sources of liquidity risk?	• Pricing-in the cost of liquidity may reduce the first-mover advantage for funds with large liquidity mismatches • Regulators should examine the benefit of flexible NAV pricing rules (such as swing and dual pricing) and illiquid asset valuation rules to adequately reflect liquidity risk costs

17.2. REGULATORY ISSUES AND POLICY IMPLICATIONS

The increased popularity of ETFs with institutional and retail investors has led to increased attention from policymakers.[2] The salient policy matters under investigation by the International Monetary Fund (2015), Office of Financial Research (2013), and other regulatory bodies with respect to open-end mutual funds and ETFs are summarized in table 17.1.

---

2. In the United States, ETF assets represent only 12% of open-end mutual fund assets as of mid-2015, but are increasing in market share.

17.3. POSSIBLE RISKS AND DEPENDENCIES

17.3.1. Visualizing the Ecosystem

In comparison to traditional mutual funds, the so-called ecosystem of ETFs is much richer with many more players. In a traditional fund, the investor interacts directly with the fund, which in turn interacts with the market. In the ETF structure, however, there are multiple players (including authorized participants) as visualized in figure 17.1 in a creation (a redemption is the opposite).

From the viewpoint of a regulator, there are several possible risks and dependencies in the ecosystem in figure 17.1. For example, the asset manager may be a large financial institution. The authorized participants (large financial institutions like JP Morgan or Goldman Sachs) may be deemed Systematically Important Financial Institutions (SIFIs), and their ability to transact in the underlying markets may be challenged in times of low liquidity.

17.3.2. Dependence of Authorized Participants

A concern often voiced about the ecosystem of ETFs is the dependence on a relatively small number of APs to provide primary market liquidity. There are a handful of well-known cases when APs sharply curtailed their activities. For example, Citigroup Inc. ceased to act as an agent of redemption on June 20, 2013, citing internal limits. In 2012, Knight Trading Group, a large market maker in several hundred ETFs, experienced operational losses that forced it to restrict its activities. Regulators seek answers to some basic questions: Are trades at risk should an AP, perhaps an SIFI, fail? What happens when an AP withdraws or ceases to provide for creation/redemption?

Let's deal with these issues in turn. First, consider normal safeguards and protections. Note that APs are US-registered self-clearing broker-dealers and as such can process trade submission, clearance, and settlement trades for themselves and for their own account. This means that creations and redemptions are processed

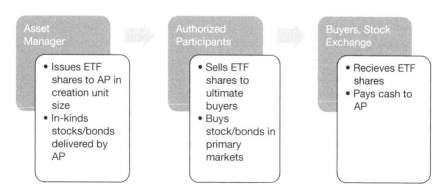

Figure 17.1 ETF ecosystem—share creation.

through the National Securities Clearing Corporation (NSCC) with the same safeguards and protections as a trade in a domestic stock. For ETF trades that fall outside the purview of the NSCC, ETF managers will typically require the AP to post collateral, again mitigating risk. So, failure of an AP itself is not a source of systemic risk any more than a failure of a broker-dealer.

Second, the failure to distinguish between primary (underlying markets) and secondary markets (exchange trading of the ETF shares) is the source of much confusion. Liquidity in the primary market refers to the ability of APs to acquire the underlying assets and transfer them in-kind (or vice versa) to the ETF manager for shares in the fund. Should an AP withdraw or cease to trade a particular ETF, nothing will happen unless the other APs who are also providing primary market liquidity also withdraw. There is also a conflation of several different issues, most important, confusing overall market liquidity with fund liquidity. Market liquidity refers to the ability to buy or sell without substantial price changes. By contrast, fund liquidity refers to the structural features of a fund and the conditions under which redemption can occur. These include redemption frequency (e.g., daily or monthly) and provisions (e.g., notice periods, gates, fees). While market liquidity may vary over time, dropping in times of market stress, this does not necessarily impair fund liquidity.

Could any of these events be the source of systemic risk? A comprehensive analysis of 931 US funds covering $1.8 billion of AUM by the ICI (see Antoniewicz and Heinrichs 2015) shows that the largest ETFs (assets over $790 million) that are of most concern from a systemic risk viewpoint have an average of 38 APs. Across the whole sample of ETFs, the average number is 36 APs, a robust figure.

In figure 17.2, I plot the median number of APs (line, left scale) and total assets under management (in billions of dollars, right scale) for various types of ETFs based on ICI data. The smallest median number of APs is for emerging market bonds, a tiny category in terms of total assets and again, less of a concern from a systemic risk viewpoint.

Another informative statistic is the number of APs who are *actively* engaged in primary market activity. An AP for a given ETF was considered active in the ICI study if it had conducted at least one creation or redemption a particular ETF's shares in the previous six months. The largest ETFs have upward of seven active APs. Only very new or smaller funds have fewer than four APs, examples being emerging market bond funds where specialized trading skills are needed. Even so, there is competition between active APs and there are many others who can and will step in to provide liquidity if one backs away. It is often the case that products with fewer "active" APs reflects a number of market makers choosing one clearing broker as AP for their primary market activity. However if that clearing broker were to exit the AP business, market makers could easily redirect their business to another AP that has not been active in the product, but is set up to process orders. The market share of an AP is more representative of pricing rather than dependency, with strong competition between active and non-active firms.

In the very unlikely event that all APs jointly cease their activities at the same time, the ETF will trade like a closed-end fund with possibly wider premiums or discounts. This is, however, a *primary* market phenomenon that may or may not

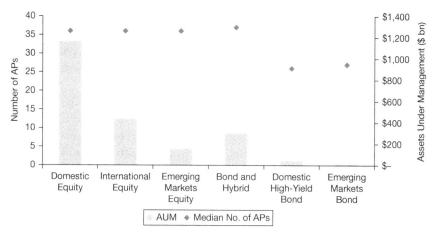

Figure 17.2 Median number of APs by type of ETF.
SOURCE: Antoniewicz and Heinrichs (2105, figure 2), Investment Company Institute.

impact *secondary* market liquidity where investors use organized exchange and other venues to trade ETF shares among themselves or with market makers.

WHAT ACTUALLY HAPPENS WHEN AN AP BACKS AWAY?

A good case study of the primary market is when Citigroup Inc. ceased to act as an agent of redemption to ETFs with foreign underlying securities on June 20, 2013, citing internal capital ceilings. Citi did continue market-making activities in the secondary markets and other APs continued to take redemption orders providing primary market liquidity. Similarly, Knight Trading Group experienced technological problems on August 1, 2012, that caused severe losses. Knight also was an active AP for most ETF managers, and its ability to create and redeem ETF shares was severely compromised. Other APs quickly stepped in to facilitate primary liquidity, and Knight's difficulties had little impact on bid-ask spreads in the secondary market. In both cases, the primary and secondary markets functioned efficiently and there was no disruption of pricing.

NOTE: See, e.g., Christopher Condon and Michelle Kaske, "ETF Tracking Errors in Rout Shows Access Comes with Risks," *Bloomberg Business*, June 23, 2013.

The liquidity (measured by dollar volume) in the secondary market can be many times that of the primary market, as discussed earlier. In the bond markets, roughly $1 is traded in the primary market for the underlying bonds for every $4 traded in the ETF secondary market. As the liquidity of the primary market is the liquidity of the underlying securities, the ETF liquidity in the secondary market (via the creation/redemption mechanism of arbitrage) is always greater than or equal to the liquidity of the underlying assets. That is to say that ETFs add a layer of incremental liquidity. From a financial stability viewpoint, this buffer is highly additive.

For there to be broader systemic risk implications, that is a chain reaction, arising from a withdrawal of all APs (primary market phenomenon), it would imply that liquidity providers and market makers (secondary market phenomenon) would be affected by widening of premiums or discounts. That is possible, but these events have yet to be observed.

It is worth emphasizing though the advantage of ETFs relative to the underlying bonds in the extreme situation of a complete liquidity crisis in bonds. In the bilateral OTC market, dealers are not required to make firm bids or offers, and they did in fact back away during the crisis. This is in contrast to the role of designated market makers on organized exchanges such as NYSE specialists who have an affirmative obligation to maintain "fair and orderly markets." In an extreme case, the physical portfolio underlying a bond ETF is subject to the same "step-away" liquidity risk of liquidity providers simply refusing to trade. However, investors in a bond ETF can access incremental liquidity on an organized exchange even if dealers in individual bonds step-away, albeit at a price that could reflect the diminished liquidity and ability to transfer risk in the OTC market. Compared with the OTC market, a market determined price for the ETF is at least an option compared with either a much lower price in the component securities or no price point whatsoever.

17.4. FIRE SALES AND REDEMPTION RISK

Regulators across the globe have voiced concerns about so-called run risk regarding ETFs and open-ended mutual funds that hold illiquid underlying assets, especially in fixed income. In a stressed market, the argument goes, investors who redeem early may have a first mover advantage, creating an incentive to sell early. (See also Golub and Tilman [2000] for a discussion of risk management in fixed income markets including stress testing.) Such a "fire sale" could create a chain reaction that spreads to related asset classes, possibly even creating the perception of risk at the asset manager level.

FIRST MOVER ADVANTAGE—MONEY MARKET FUNDS

Money market funds invest in short-term cash equivalents such as Treasury bills, commercial paper, and certificates of deposit. In the financial crisis of 2009, money market funds experienced major runs and challenges with liquidity. Money market funds in the United States offered constant NAV (mutual fund price per share) at $1 per share. However, this induced a first-mover advantage because (with a couple of notable exceptions that "broke the buck") funds honored the $1 per share convention even though NAV was below this figure because of losses. As investors withdrew at a higher valuation than true valuation, this increased the risk of loss for the remaining investors. By contrast, with open-ended mutual funds and ETFs, the NAV is not fixed but floats mitigating such a scenario.

Indeed, the diversity of asset managers in funds and models has been a focus for regulators who believe their activities should be analyzed in aggregate, particularly with respect to the transmission and amplification of a shock. The lack of data organized by related activities is a major driver of this concern.

ETFs and Destabilization

On January 26, 2015, federal prosecutors arrested a Russian citizen, who was posing as a banker, on grounds of economic espionage. The arrested man, along with two other Russians who left the United States, was charged with working secretly for Russian intelligence. The alleged spies had expressed curiosity about ETFs and market stability. Specifically, a transcript of an intercepted phone call revealed that the supposed spy had wanted to know more about ETFs: "how they are used, the mechanisms of use for destabilization of the markets." While this event fed media concerns about ETFs and systemic risk, some have interpreted this interest in reverse as an attempt by the Russian government authorities to learn more about preventing the manipulation of the Russian equity market, following unusual movements in Russian ETFs in the recent past.

In an important report, the International Monetary Fund (2015) warns of possible fire sales if investors seek to withdraw massively from mutual funds and ETFs focused on relatively illiquid high-yield bonds or leveraged loans. The mechanism as posited is similar to that of a bank run, where the lack of liquidity confers a first-mover advantage (see also Financial Stability Board 2011). Similarly, the Office of Financial Research (2013) of the US Treasury notes that ETFs "could also potentially accelerate or amplify price movements in markets during market turbulence, thus reducing market liquidity."

The Bank of Canada (Financial System Review 2014) notes that "if a run on an ETF is triggered, it could amplify selling pressure in the underlying asset market and on other similar funds." The risk is in their view that: "a liquidity shock can originate in the ETF itself; as APs provide their services to multiple ETFs, a redemption halt could affect a number of funds simultaneously. In a worst-case scenario, this could trigger investor runs on the ETFs and similar funds (e.g., mutual funds). These events could then feed back to the underlying asset markets, amplifying the initial shock and propagating beyond the ETF market."

Examples often cited in recent regulatory reports, press articles, and academic studies include fixed income ETFs (especially emerging market debt and high-yield bonds), bank loan funds, and proposed ETFs based on virtual currencies. For example, Goldstein, Jiang, and Ng (2015) find that while the relation between flows and performance for equity funds is convex (based on analysis from 1992 to 2014), it is concave for bond funds. In other words, bond investors react more negatively to market declines than do equity investors. They argue that this finding shows bond funds are more fragile. Illiquidity in underlying assets could amplify the reaction of investors to poor performance. Regulators focused on the impact of massive redemptions in bond funds often refer to this concern.

This kind of study misses one important point though: While investors might leave a manager, they are less likely to leave an entire asset class. For example, Pacific Investment Management Company (PIMCO) saw billions of dollars of redemptions from its Total Return Bond Fund after star manager and co-founder William H. Gross abruptly left for Janus Funds in September 2014, but these assets flowed to other bond funds, not out of the entire asset class. Further, in the event of a large sell-off in any asset class—say high-yield bonds—there are many other entities who will likely step in to provide liquidity at the right price. The key point to note is that these entities need not be designated APs but can be other market participants such as hedge funds or market makers who seek opportunity when prices are distressed.

17.5. POLICY TOOLS

17.5.1. Swing Pricing

What can policymakers actually do to reduce systemic risk and promote financial stability? We advocate a solutions-based approach based on intended consequences of regulation. Let's begin with the key issue around flows. Some fund structures externalize transaction costs associated with redeeming investors, including ETFs. When combined with a floating NAV, the risk of first mover advantages leading to fire sales of assets is greatly mitigated. One of the more important solutions in the "tool kit" to mitigate first-move advantage is "swing pricing." This adjusts the NAV to the bid or offer side depending on net flows, essentially externalizes any fund transaction costs to the redeeming investors. For example, UCITS and AIFs can use swing pricing, dual pricing, or other mechanisms to allocate transaction costs to redeeming investors. In the United States, 1940 Act Open-End Mutual Funds do not currently have the ability to externalize transaction costs when redeeming in cash through pricing mechanisms such as swing pricing or dual pricing. Note though that more than 40% of US mutual fund assets are held in retirement accounts (401(k) and IRA accounts) that are infrequently rebalanced. Further, 1940 Act mutual funds can provide redemptions in-kind for large institutional investors.

Here is an example of how swing pricing might work to externalize transaction costs versus a traditional 1940 Act open-ended mutual fund. A fund begins with assets of $100 million and a million shares outstanding. The bid-ask spreads of the underlying assets are assumed to be 0.20% on average, so one-way transaction costs are 0.10%. Suppose on a given day there are $5 million of inflows (subscriptions) and –$20 million of outflows (redemptions) for a net flow of –$15 million. Say fundamental values remain constant over the day. In the traditional open-ended mutual fund example, subscriptions and redemptions occur at the NAV of $100 and the fund manager must sell $15 million of the underlying assets. These sales occur at the bid price of the underlying assets and hence an average discount of 0.10% to NAV. At the start of the following day NAV is—assuming no change in fundamentals—equal to $84.985 (=$100 – $15 × (1 – 0.10%)). The fund's remaining investors thus bear the costs of the transaction costs incurred by the participants who redeemed or subscribed. That is why NAV in this hypothetical case is lower than $85. This would have been the fund's value had the investors that bought or sold actually borne the costs associated with their transactions.

By contrast, with swing pricing, both subscription and redemption activity is evaluated on the bid-side (that is $100 \times (1 - 0.10\%)$ of the market because there are net outflows. (Had there been positive net flows, we would use the ask price in swing pricing and execute the purchases at a premium to NAV.) This means that subscribers (new investors) benefit because instead of buying at $100 they actually are able to buy at the bid, meaning a lower price than NAV of $99.90. Sellers (who collectively account for $20 million) also trade at the swing price of $99.90. What is the net impact on a fund that uses swing pricing? Exactly zero because all the transaction costs of the fund are fully externalized to the investors who transact, preserving the value of the remaining fund investors.

17.5.2. The Fund Managers' Tool Kit

Beyond swing pricing, fund managers (UCITS funds have more flexibility than traditional 1940 Act funds in this regard) have at their disposal a tool kit to handle redemptions. These include lines of credit (i.e., the ability to borrow in times of stress), gates (that limit redemptions), the use of in-kind redemptions versus cash payouts for institutional participants, cash buffers, and holdings of liquid assets.

It is important to understand that unlike a conventional mutual fund, where investor redemptions will trigger a sale, most ETFs can always resort to in-kind redemptions instead of cash. For example, if a fund has 1,000 units outstanding and an AP redeems 10 units, the fund can choose to give the AP a 1% slice of its holdings instead of cash. So, in general, ETFs need not carry cash balances to handle redemptions like conventional mutual funds. There are some exceptions such as in particularly illiquid markets where redemptions are all in cash.

In reality, ETFs do typically have a cash buffer, but this is not because of redemption risk per se but rather to handle settlement mismatch issues. For example, while settlement for US equities is generally on a $T + 3$ basis, some foreign equities (e.g., South African stocks with $T + 5$ settlement) may take much longer to settle. Similarly, stocks on loan may take longer than $T + 3$ to be recalled. Intangibles such as tax refunds/credits offer a good example of mismatched settlement cycles; in some countries (e.g., Switzerland), tax refunds may only be available to a manager after a lag of at least a year.

A related issue is redemption timing, and the possible mismatch between the liquidity offered by funds versus their underlying basket securities. In one sense, this is a regulatory issue regarding "suitability" of investment. I will come back to the basic thesis that mutual fund structures and ETFs both allow investors to gain access; at the end of the day, ETF investors have an additional layer of liquidity because their transactions do not necessarily imply a transaction in the underlying securities. So ETFs are always at least as liquid as the underlying. But in some cases, there may be a mismatch between ETF or mutual fund settlement and that of the underlying instruments. One take-away for regulators from this discussion is that empowering funds with tools like swing pricing can mitigate concerns regarding fire sales and run risk.

17.5.3. Example: Leveraged Loans

Let's consider the popular and high-yielding leveraged loan ETFs in more detail as a poster child example of the issues pointed to by regulators. The largest bank-loan ETF is the $7.2 billion PowerShares Senior Loan Portfolio (BKLN), and there are significant assets in correspondingly structured mutual funds. Bank loans, also called leveraged loans or senior loans, are akin to junk bonds. They are floating-rate loans to companies with below-investment-grade credit offering higher yields than investment grade bonds to compensate for the higher risk of default. As bank loan rates in theory adjust upward as interest rates rise, they have been attractive to investors concerned with a rise in interest rates; in reality, there are thresholds so investors may not get the interest rate sensitivity they desire.

However, bank loans are not conventional securities like stocks and bonds. They are traded using physical loan documents and require the approval of the borrowing company. This manual process takes an average of 22 day versus $T + 3$ for equities, including ETFs. The concern is that faced with heavy withdrawals, ETF prices will fall much more than the underlying loans themselves. In a worst case scenario, the mismatch in settlement period means that ETF investors will potentially not get their money back within the conventional $T + 3$ settlement period. Bank loan funds manage this risk by keeping a liquidity buffer to meet redemptions, which can induce a cash drag, as well as investing in junk bonds with conventional settlement periods. Nonetheless, the optimal ratio of these more liquid assets is determined by fund managers and has not been tested in a severe market disruption. Ultimately the challenge is one of expectations management. Investors should be aware of the potential for delay in receiving funds and should, as always, exercise judgment in trading at steep discounts or at wide bid-offer spreads.

17.6. DO ETFS DRIVE PRICES OF UNDERLYING ASSETS?

The major public policy issues center around the implications of passive flows on prices in underlying markets, an issue distinct from contagion and financial stress risk. Previously, we showed that ETF flows do not affect correlations in securities. But can flows affect the prices of illiquid assets? Just as with a settlement mismatch, physical commodity based ETFs have been cited as the source of additional volatility. Zhang (2015) examines the SPDR Gold Trust exchange-traded fund (GLD), an ETF that holds physical gold. She finds that soon after the introduction of GLD, the liquidity of gold stocks declined and bid-ask spreads increased. She concludes that uninformed traders migrated away from gold company stocks, causing a decrease in underlying stock liquidity and a decline in prices.

However, it is difficult to separate out the effects of a one-time introduction of an ETF from other macro-events. Hamm (2014) provides an information asymmetric story where ETF introduction can increase the adverse selection at the stock level as more liquidity traders migrate to the basket. She finds a positive association between the percentage of firm shares being held by ETFs and a measure of illiquidity in the market for the underlying stocks. Consistent with her hypotheses, this "liquidity deprivation" is less for stocks with high quality earnings.

On a related point, Dannhauser (2015) argues that corporate bond ETFs lower the yield of constituent bonds. ETF activity has no impact on bond liquidity in the high-yield market, but appears to increase the transaction costs of investment grade bonds. In both markets, however, the proportion of retail volume decreases with ETF activity. Her results, like Zhang (2015), are consistent with the idea that liquidity trading migrates from the underlying securities to a basket security when it is introduced.

17.6.1. Imputed Flow

We define the imputed impact of flows into ETFs based on their holdings of stocks. To fix ideas, consider Boston Properties, Inc. (BXP), a real estate investment trust (REIT) that is an owner and developer of office properties.[3] According to public data as of May 1, 2015, BXP has a market capitalization of just over $20.6 billion. The REIT is held by 77 domestic ETFs as well as other internationally listed ETFs. Those funds (which include broad funds as well as niche funds focusing on real estate) are listed on sites such ETFChannel.com. The collective weight of the 77 ETFs is 5.75% of BXP's market capitalization, much higher than the stock's weight in the US equity market (which at the time had a total market capitalization of approximately $24 trillion).

By contrast, International Business Machines (IBM) is held by 91 ETFs whose collective holdings account for 3.6% of its market capitalization of $171 billion. The top five domestic ETFs that hold IBM and their respective weights are shown in table 17.2 as of May 1, 2015.

I define the imputed flow in a particular stock on a given day as the product of the collective weight of flows into all ETFs holding the stock. Formally, suppose a particular stock i is held by J different ETFs, where ETF j (where $j = 1, \ldots, J$) has weight $w_{i,j}$ in stock i. In the example of IBM, if j is XLK, then $w_{i,j} = 0.0378$. The primary market flows into ETF j on a given day (where the time subscript is omitted for notational simplicity) is the change in shares outstanding times the value of the fund, or $f_j = \Delta o_j n_j$, so the ETF will in theory have flows in the individual stock of $w_{i,j} f_j$. In the example above, suppose hypothetically that XLK sees a flow of $100 million in a given interval, this would imply flows into IBM of $3.78 million.

---

3. This stock was chosen purely as an illustrative example and this in no way is meant to be an endorsement for investment, business model, or other purposes.

Table 17.2 Top Five Domestic ETFs Holding IBM Equity by Value

ETF Name (ticker)	Weight in Fund (%)	Value of IBM ($ millions)
SPDR S&P 500 (SPY)	0.85	1,523
Vanguard Dividend Appreciation (VIG)	4.02	1,007
SPDR Dow Jones (DIA)	6.39	751
Shares S&P 500 (IVV)	0.85	597
Technology Select Sector SPDR (XLK)	3.78	503

SOURCE: Based on data from ETFChannel.com, May 1, 2015.

Adding over all *j* ETFs that hold stock *i* gives imputed flow:

$$I_i = \sum_{j=1}^{J} w_{i,j} f_j. \tag{17.1}$$

As an example, if the flows into the top five funds in table 17.2 are $100 million each, and there were no flows into any other funds holding the stock, the total imputed flow into IBM would be $158.9 million.

The really interesting point about imputed flows is that we can aggregate over *any* set of stocks to get imputed flows for a thematic basket. For example, we may be interested in flows into baskets with exposure to particular countries (e.g., China), regions (e.g., BRICs), sectors (e.g., technology stocks), or investment themes (e.g., income). Simply using the stated focus of an ETF (e.g., growth) might not really capture the effect of flows into ETFs that hold these stocks but do not declare this as an objective. Consider investors' search for income in the low interest rate environment post the financial crisis. Investors may invest in high dividend yield ETFs with the objective of higher income or may buy many of the same stocks indirectly. They do so by purchasing ETFs that hold higher dividend yield stocks but are not dividend focused. In the example above, IBM with its approximately 3% dividend yield may see inflows through different ETF channels including S&P 500 oriented funds, dividend appreciation funds, and technology sector funds. The overall impact of these flows is not immediately obvious without imputed flow.

17.6.2. Concerns about Differential Weighting and Flows

Should we be concerned that a stock's weight in total ETF assets is very different from its share in overall market capitalization? A recent report by Goldman Sachs[4] argues that creation and rebalancing activity in ETFs can increase

4. See Chris Dietrich, "ETFs May Be Moving Stocks in Unseen Ways," Barron's, April 18, 2015. The Goldman Sachs report is Katherine Fogertey and Robert D. Boroujerdi, "ETFs: The Rise of the Machines," Goldman Sachs Investment Research, April 2015.

stock and sector correlation. As an example, they cite Boston Properties, Inc. (BXP), arguing that flows into the ETFs holding smaller stocks like BXP, particularly those that weight the stock highly, may result in imputed impact in the primary market.

Tail Wagging the Dog?

In April 2015, BXP was the ninth-largest holding of the iShares U.S. Real Estate Sector ETF (IYR) with about a 2.5% weight. This ETF has daily volume of $873 million (in the three months prior to April 2015) versus BXP's daily volume of $116 million. The Goldman study assumes primary market activity is 50% of total trading, which implies that APs will trade about $11 million daily ($11m = 50% × 2.5% × $873m) in Boston Properties' shares for IYR, or about 9.5% (=$11m/$116m) of BXP's transaction volume. Aggregating across all 77 ETFs that hold BXP, nearly 20% of the BXP dollar volume is, by this calculus, driven by ETF flows. These flows are not reflective of investors who have specific views on BXP fundamentals.

Of course, the key here is the framing of the question: If investors trade exposures for beta, then some fraction of flows in an individual stock will necessarily be driven by factors that are not fundamentally related. But the assumption of 50% primary activity is also high: Using a figure of 9% (see, e.g., Antoniewicz and Heinrichs 2014) will make the figures much lower. As a final point, note that, there is no evidence that flows in ETFs drive return correlations over any period of time beyond an immediate price impact, as we have already seen. Indeed, ETFs despite their growth represent than a third of all indexed assets, less than fifth of US mutual fund assets, and less than a thirtieth of outstanding US public debt and equity.

Example: Manager Discretion

In evaluating discussions around systemic risk, it is important to understand that ETF managers have many tools at their discretion to help protect investors: First, ETFs can use the create/redeem baskets to manage liquidity. Second, ETFs can increase the share of their portfolio in out-of-index securities, although this may result in more tracking error. Third, so-called NAV+ creation (where the manager charges investors a fee) is a way to mitigate transaction costs. So, creation and redemption is a relatively flexible process with human oversight.

17.6.3. Governance and Passive Flows

The basics of fund governance are quite straightforward. A fund signs an investment management agreement with an asset management company, which manages the portfolio, controls risk, executes trading and securities lending. Although investors are shareholders and ultimately own the fund's assets, they do not actually control the fund or the key activities of the fund such as buying or selling securities. Rather, the fund's board will represent and protect shareholder rights vis-à-vis the asset manager, under the applicable regulation as described earlier. Specifically, ETFs must comply with the provisions of the 1940 Act that also apply to mutual funds or unit investment trusts. Like all regulated investment companies under the 1940 Act, ETFs that are open-end investment companies, like mutual funds, must:

- Have a Board of Directors consisting primarily of directors that are legally "independent" of the sponsor and from time to time elected by shareholders; and
- Have their fees approved annually by the Board of Directors, which is empowered to negotiate such fees on behalf of shareholders.

Governance is an important issue that occasionally becomes highly prominent due to exceptional or systemic events when standard procedures do not apply. Commonly asked questions center on whether the assets backing an ETF can ever be frozen or exchange ever be suspended. The answer in general to all such questions is that, like all funds, the board of directors ultimately governs an ETF. The board is charged with the responsibility to make decisions in the interests of the fund holders. For example, in the case of an event such as sanctions (e.g., restrictions on investing in certain countries or companies as was the case against Russia in 2014), the board must ultimately decide on the best course of action, which may involve taking on tracking error due to an inability to invest within the confines of the law. The same applies to more common events such as ETF closures, suspensions, and so on, where existing investors may be told their fund is closed and receive securities upon delisting.

There is also the question of who votes the ETF's shares in proxy fights. Typically, the asset manager will vote the underlying shares, usually in line with clear guidelines that are previously disclosed. For example, I served for many years on BlackRock's Americas Corporate Governance Committee. The Committee has a well-documented set of guidelines regarding governance issues such as director attendance and over-boarding (i.e., being represented on the boards of too many companies), "say on pay," CEO succession planning, proxy contest guidelines, and many other criteria that are publicly posted. BlackRock will typically engage with companies on these issues and then vote its shares appropriately. Lastly, a word on the safeguards against fraud. If an investor holds shares directly in their brokerage account, then they have SIPC protection (not against adverse performance, but against fraud) up to a certain dollar amount. These protections also apply to ETFs and mutual funds held in a brokerage account.

Passive institutional investors account for a growing share of equity ownership and their influence on firm-level governance is widely debated. Index investing is in the minds of some also associated with a passive approach to governance. For example, Norges Bank Investment Management, the Sovereign Wealth Fund of Norway, accounts for 2% to 3% of ownership of individual global equities, and it has varied over time in its approach to governance and level of activism. But evidence on the impact of passive owners has been difficult to evaluate.

Appel, Gormley, and Keim (2015) provide empirical evidence on whether passive investors influence firms' governance structures. They find that passive investors play a key role in influencing firms' governance choices. In particular, passive ownership by institutions is associated with more independent directors, the removal of poison pills and restrictions on shareholders' ability to call special meetings, and fewer dual class share structures. Passive investors exert influence through large voting blocs; they provide less support for management proposals and more support for shareholder-initiated governance proposals. They find that passive ownership is associated with better performance, which is consistent with the prior empirical literature on the benefits of improved governance.

17.7. CHAPTER SUMMARY

Are there systemic risks arising from the rapid growth of exchange-traded products that regulators should be monitoring? The standard classification scheme for ETPs introduced earlier in the book is important; the dialogue needs to shift to focus on the relatively small segment of funds that are the source of most discussion. Regulatory enhancements should make it easier for funds to manage periodic liquidity challenges. This can be achieved by promoting a uniform tool kit including mechanisms to suspend redemptions and externalize transaction costs. Finally, as in the case of fixed income funds, market structure modernization can be sped up and guided by forward-looking regulation, enhancing financial stability. Governance affects financial stability; there is no evidence that passive investing styles lead to weaker governance.

Public Policy Issues

18.1. OVERVIEW OF CONCERNS

The previous chapter considered issues of systemic risk, where the entire financial system could potentially be endangered. I discussed how many of these concerns are based on misconceptions regarding the operation of ETFs. Institutional detail does matter, and especially so when there is a conflation of concepts that apply to banks, open-ended mutual funds, and ETFs. But this is not to say that there are not broader public policy considerations regarding the growth of passive investing, and ETFs in particular.

In this chapter, I turn to public policy issues that extend beyond systemic risk, dealing first with some common myths around ETFs including excessive shorting, counterparty risk, settlement failures, and the Flash Crash of May 2010. The Flash Crash, although a potentially systemic event, is one that has attracted considerable attention concerning the role of ETFs. The market turmoil of August 2015 also saw disruption in the prices of many ETFs causing many of the same concerns to be raised once again. In my view though, the underlying causes were not to do with the ETP wrapper but rather with the nature of market structure, particularly greater fragmentation.

18.2. COMMON MYTHS

18.2.1. Excess Shorting

Several commentators (e.g., Bradley and Litan 2010) have argued that when ETFs are sold short, aggregate long and synthetic long positions can exceed in total the actual number of outstanding ETF shares. If investors simultaneously redeem their shares in an ETF at the same time, some argue that this could theoretically "bankrupt" the fund as redemptions would exceed available assets to be redeemed. In reality, on the settlement day, ETF managers only release redemption proceeds against actual delivery of the ETF shares, that is, Delivery versus Payment (DVP) settlement. An *attempt* to redeem by a party that does not actually physically have ETF shares to deliver (usually because they have lent their shares to a short seller) will simply fail to settle. It is possible that the failure of a large number of such attempted "redemptions" could itself result in market disruption, such as a short squeeze. This scenario seems highly unlikely. The failure of redemptions would not result in real costs to the ETF but in accounting entries that are later cancelled.

CASE STUDY: RUSSELL RECONSTITUTION, JUNE 2007

In June 2007, the annual rebalancing of the Russell indexes was accompanied by significant redemptions from the US iShares Russell 2000 Index ETF (IWM) from APs who chose to handle the tracking (basis) risk themselves. Redemptions from IWM essentially equaled the ETF's assets, but were reversed within a few days. Even with massive redemptions during the rebalance period, at the extremes the index only moved with a 1% band of NAV. Today, the redeeming AP must certify that it has access to ETF shares to deliver upon settlement of the redemption.

18.2.2. Securities Lending and Counterparty Risk

A closely related issue is securities lending and counterparty risk. Securities lending is the temporary transfer of a security by its owner (e.g., a pension fund) to another party (e.g., a hedge fund), typically for shorting. The lender remains the owner and so is exposed to any security price movement over the life of the loan. The borrower usually provides collateral (typically in excess of the security's value ranging from 102% to 112%) to compensate the lender if, in the extremely rare case, the borrower fails to return the borrowed security. Mechanically, the steps involved in securities lending of ETFs are illustrated in figure 18.1. The specific steps are as follows:

- The owner (lender) engages a lending agent (such as the asset manager for the ETF) who negotiates a loan with a borrower;
- The borrower delivers collateral (cash or securities) and simultaneously[1] the lending agent releases securities to the borrower;
- The lending agent invests the collateral into an approved cash investment vehicle to generate additional return. This is first given as a rebate to the borrower and the residual earnings are split between the lender and the lending agent as previously specified;
- Every day, the lending agent makes sure the collateral exceeds the market value of the security, collecting (or delivering) any difference;
- The borrower forwards any distributions from the security (such as dividends/interest) that occur during the loan; and

---

1. Simultaneous settlement is achieved through Delivery versus Payment (DVP).

- The borrower or lender can end the loan at will. The borrower returns the securities if recalled by custodian/lender (or if they are no longer needed) and again simultaneously the custodian returns collateral.

The key benefits to securities lending are (1) incremental income for investors at relatively low risk given the loan is over-collateralized; and (2) additional liquidity that keeps asset bubbles from forming, enhancing global market efficiency. Securities lending is significant in dollar terms (over $1.7 trillion), but is modest at the individual ETF level where, on average, less than 10% of ETF holdings are on loan. There is presently a 50% aggregate statutory limit on securities lending for ETFs in the United States. For ETFs, securities lending safeguards include the ability to recall loans from borrowers to cover standard and unexpected redemptions and possibly even the liquidation of the borrower's collateral to "buy-in" the non-delivered securities from the market.

Securities lending can enhance ETF returns when safeguarded as above, while greater loan activity improves liquidity and price efficiency by reducing the costs of expressing negative views through short selling. Although securities lending is prevalent and economically significant, there is little academic literature on securities lending. Cheng, Massa, and Zhang (2013) argue that ETFs engage in cross-subsidization and cross-trading within fund families increase fund revenues. But their sample consists of (non-US) synthetic ETNs sponsored by a bank, where there is counterparty risk, and not physically backed ETFs.

Blocher and Whaley (2015) look at US ETFs and claim that ETFs use securities lending as an additional source of revenue. Securities lending revenues are large relative to the expense ratios of ETFs, and the authors argue for greater transparency about lending revenues that accrue to fund managers. They argue that less transparent ETFs make more securities lending revenue. Portfolio weights in ETFs that use sampling/optimization diverge from the underlying index weights in a manner that over-weights stocks that are profitable to lend. Consistent with the view above, tracking difference is positively correlated with securities lending income. However, Blocher and Whaley (2015) do not have actual securities lending revenues but draw their conclusions from an indirect measure. Further, asset managers have legal obligations to adhere to their lending contracts, which mandate a pre-specified split of securities lending revenues between the manager and the fund, after costs are considered. Managers do not have the discretion to retain revenues or not share them with fund clients.

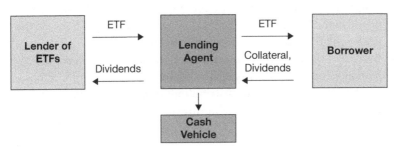

Figure 18.1 Mechanics of a securities loan transaction.

18.2.3. Settlement Failures

The rise in ETF volumes has been accompanied by increased ETF settlement failures at the clearing corporation. Stratmann and Welborn (2012) document a positive relationship between daily ETF settlement failures and short sale volume and cost to borrow ETFs, which they argue is consistent with market makers failing to deliver to avoid paying borrowing costs associated with their short sales. They also argue that ETF settlement failures Granger-cause higher market index volatility as market makers close-out fails positions by trade date plus six days ("$T + 6$"), concluding that ETF fail-to-deliver "are not inconsequential for market stability."

Securities lending is generally done with multiple collateralized borrowers, and ETF managers have the option of handling AP redemptions in whole or partly with cash. In the extremely unlikely event of massive redemptions that exceed the ETF's available securities (not on loan) and loan reallocations are infeasible, the securities are recalled from the borrower. Under standard lending agreements, if the shares are not returned within the standard market settlement cycle, the borrower is in technical default of the lending agreement. Typically for US equity-based iShares ETFs that clear through Continuous Net Settlement System at NSCC (National Securities Clearing Corporation), the custodian fronts the cash to the iShares funds as if the settlement had occurred. Any positive rebate rate to the borrower gets reduced to zero. The fund and lending agent continue to share interest earned on the collateral, thus continuing to benefit.

The AP receives cash plus the available deliverable securities from the fund. If the AP has a contractual right to redeem fully in-kind for this particular ETF, they may choose to purchase the shares and pass on all related charges to the lending fund (this would generally be done after settlement date, not within the settlement cycle). Those charges are covered by collateral seized from the borrower. Alternatively, given that the borrower is in technical default of the lending agreement, the lending agent may seize the borrower's collateral in order to liquidate it and purchase the securities for delivery to the AP.

18.2.4. Synthetics

Unlike physical ETFs that hold unlevered baskets of securities, synthetic ETFs derive exposure through derivative contracts and face counterparty risk. Synthetics can be appropriate products (e.g., if exposures cannot be accessed physically) and if structured (using multiple counterparties, collateral, etc.) well to minimize counterparty risk. Some synthetic ETFs created by banks in Europe use a single affiliated counterparty which reduces funding costs but also is a potential conflict of interest. For example, an equity ETF can enter into a total return swap with an affiliated bank (which swaps the total return on the invested portfolio with the return on the underlying index). Normally, the swap counterparty will deliver the index return, but if the affiliated bank defaults, the investor will face a very different exposure. Variation in the issuer's risk (manifested in credit spreads of the underlying counterparty) will then be reflected in the secondary market price and hence the investor's return.

18.2.5. Fund Closures

ETF closures, like the closures of mutual funds, are not uncommon. Anywhere from 50 to 80 funds close each year, based on industry figures gathered by the Investment Company Institute (ICI). In 2014, for example, the ICI reports that 57 out of 1,339 funds were liquidated or merged, while 174 were created. Yet, despite the attention in the media, an ETF closure does not create investment risk, meaning the fund's assets are safe. Part of the confusion comes from a natural tendency to equate ETFs with operating firms. When a firm fails, its equity price falls in theory to a level that shareholders might reasonably expect to receive after bondholders are paid in bankruptcy. When a physical ETF closes, however, its price should converge to its NAV. The exception is an ETN whose issuer declares bankruptcy, as did Lehman Brothers in 2008, because the fund is really an unsecured debt obligation.

Investors in a fund to be closed may experience unanticipated taxes, lack of liquidity, and some costs depending on the nature of closure. The two types are:

- **Liquidation**—If the asset manager chooses to liquidate an ETF, a prospectus supplement will be sent to investors stating the last trading date and date of liquidation. Investors will typically receive a cash distribution equal to NAV, which is possibly a taxable event, or an in-kind share distribution, which can be better from a tax perspective. The fund will halt creations and prepare to convert to cash, which may cause performance to diverge from the underlying index. In the time from announcement to the last trading date, net asset values are still available, but the one-sided nature of trading (i.e., on the bid side with sellers greatly dominating buyers) may create transitory price pressure. Lack of liquidity combined with a one-sided market may widen bid-ask spreads.
- **Delisting**—An issuer may also choose to delist the ETF, which is likely to be more costly to investors than a straight liquidation of the portfolio. This is because investors who choose not to sell their shares before the last trading date have to trade in the opaque and costly OTC market versus on a transparent, organized stock exchange. This type of closure is not common.

In both cases, investors who either sell their shares or receive cash may realize capital gains and possibly incur an unanticipated tax burden.

What types of funds are closed? Asset managers must ultimately make rational decisions on whether or not to continue to offer a fund whose economics do not make sense. Most funds are launched with AUM below what is economically viable in terms of the explicit costs of portfolio management, fees, and the implicit costs associated with possible operating errors, franchise risks, and so on. Typically when a fund is launched it is with modest seed capital and the asset manager is willing to incubate the fund even if the costs of operation outstrip revenues. But ultimately if AUM does not grow, the manager may be forced to close the fund.

What is the cutoff point? Industry professionals usually point to a range of $50–$100 million; doing the math, if the costs of operating a fund including both explicit (compensation for the portfolio managers, data feeds, etc.) and implicit costs (the asset manager bears the burden in the event of an operating error) are, say, at least $300,000 a year, this means a fee of at least 30–60 basis points to break even, hence the rough rule of thumb. Issuer size and strength is a major factor too. In the cost calculus, a small niche player without economies of scale may have a much higher break-even level than a large manager with dozens of similar funds all managed by a small team. Past clusters of ETF closures have occurred when asset managers withdrew entirely from the industry, rather than from the selective closure of unprofitable funds. This is also true of managers with undifferentiated products facing large, global competitors.

In summary, for a physically backed ETF, there is no concept of bankruptcy. An unlevered fund is just a pool of assets with no real liabilities, and should the fund be redeemed in full, the assets will just be given back in kind. The exceptions are ETNs, which are really debt obligations, and some synthetic ETPs, where there is counterparty risk from swap positions with investment banks. Counterparty risk, however, is offset by diversification rules that spread the risk across multiple swap counterparts. It is extremely unlikely that a leveraged fund's losses could exceed its assets because a leveraged fund is collateralized with cash and securities. Plain vanilla ETF closures are normal and pose no real risk to investors.

18.3. FLASH CRASH

18.3.1. Theories of the Flash Crash

The "Flash Crash" of May 6, 2010, was a potentially serious systemic risk event that warrants a detailed discussion. The event saw the Dow Jones Industrial Average drop almost 1,000 points in 20 minutes. Many well-known stocks traded at clearly unreasonable prices including some that traded at pennies. Notable was the disproportionate representation of exchange-traded funds among the securities most affected (see Borkovec et al. 2010), with prices diverging widely from their underlying net asset values. Despite its short duration, the Flash Crash affected many market participants. Exchanges ultimately cancelled trades at prices below 60% of the 2:40 p.m. price, but many retail investors with market stop loss orders still had orders executed at prices well below prevailing market levels earlier in the day. Professionals who bought at distressed prices and hedged by short-selling similar securities or futures contracts incurred steep losses as their long positions were ultimately cancelled while the assets they had shorted rebounded in price.

A repeat event, especially at the close, could dramatically erode investor confidence and participation in the capital markets and ETFs as an investment vehicle. That loss of confidence in turn could reduce liquidity and increase transaction costs for many years to come.[2] Further, a repeat event could cause some systemically important firms to suffer extreme losses, damaging the financial system.

Initial speculation for the cause of the Flash Crash included so-called "fat finger" trading error, a software bug, or a malicious "denial of service" type attack. Yet, no evidence for these explanations has since come to light, although authorities recently allege a market manipulation scheme may have been the cause. Even so, the question arises as to why any trigger would have such a large impact on asset prices.

HAS THE FLASH CRASH MYSTERY BEEN SOLVED?

Almost five years after the Flash Crash on April 21, 2015, Scotland Yard investigators arrested a sole UK-based trader to face criminal and civil charges in the United States for contributing to the 2010 Flash Crash. The Commodities Futures Trading Commission (CFTC) added in a civil complaint "Defendants have engaged in a massive effort to manipulate the price of the E-mini S&P by utilizing a variety of exceptionally large, aggressive, and persistent spoofing tactics."

The disproportionate impact of the Flash Crash on ETPs led some commentators to draw a connection between the sharp market moves on May 6 to the pricing and trading of these instruments.[3] In a controversial report by Bradley and Litan (2010), the authors conclude that ETF pricing poses risks to the financial system, noting "the proliferation of ETFs also poses unquantifiable but very real systemic risks of the kind that were manifested very briefly during the 'Flash Crash' of May 6, 2010." The authors proposed ETF-related reforms and note that in the absence of such rules, "We believe that other flash crashes . . . potentially much more severe than the one on May 6, are a virtual certainty." Ben-David, Franzoni, and Moussawi (2014) conclude that ETFs served as "a conduit for shock propagation between the futures market and the equity market during the Flash Crash on May 6, 2010."

2. See, e.g., Colin Barr, "Progress Energy Joins Flash Crash Crowd." *Fortune*, September 27, 2010 who writes: "Whatever their cause, the frequent market outages only feed the sense that the entire market is either a casino rigged by the money never sleeps crowd or a house of cards on the verge of collapse. Neither view, it seems safe to say, is apt to restore investors' dwindling confidence."

3. See, e.g., Wurgler (2010). Ramaswamy (2010) examines the operational frameworks of exchange-traded funds and relates these to potential systemic risks. The role of leveraged ETFs has also been discussed (see, e.g., Cheng and Madhavan 2009) in the context of end-of-day volatility effects.

18.3.2. Flash Crash and Fragmentation

The joint report of the Commodities Futures Trading Commission (CFTC) and Securities and Exchange Commission (SEC) provides a chronology of events on May 6, 2010, and identified the catalyst for the Flash Crash. Faced with increased volume, the NYSE entered "slow trading mode" while stocks continued to trade in electronic venues, such as BATS, resulting in price distortions. Liquidity providers began to withdraw their liquidity, given concerns that some trades would be cancelled under the "erroneous trade rule," resulting in some market sell orders, including stop loss orders, being executed at pennies. The notion that the Flash Crash arose from an unlikely confluence of factors is reassuring and consistent with the absence of widespread and rapid price declines in any asset class or region in recent decades. However, there have also been recent instances where individual stocks experienced "mini" Flash Crashes. For example, on September 27, 2010, Progress Energy fell almost 90% in price before recovering in the next five minutes for no obvious reason. Unlike May 6, these "mini" Flash Crashes do not cluster in time and affect only individual stocks. Nonetheless, they are recent phenomena and suggest the presence of more systematic factors.

It seems likely that prices are more sensitive to liquidity shocks in fragmented markets because imperfect inter-market linkages effectively "thin out" (see also O'Hara and Ye 2011) each venue's limit order book. Madhavan (2012) finds strong evidence that securities that experienced greater prior fragmentation were disproportionately affected on May 6, 2010. Zhang (2011) reports that high frequency trading accounts for up to 70% of dollar trading volume in US equities, including ETPs. The increase in high frequency trading has raised concerns, especially given order cancellation rates in the region of 90% and the fact that these strategies are not well understood.

TREASURY MARKET VOLATILITY ON OCTOBER 15, 2014

On October 15, 2014, the yield on the 10-year US Treasury note—one of the safest and most liquid securities—experienced a sharp 34 basis point drop to 1.86% before reversing to 2.13%, all within a 15-minute time interval. The intraday yield movement was unprecedented, almost 8 standard deviations greater than normal, yet there was little fundamental news. One report noted: "The volatility of the US Treasury market that day has been pored over by regulators, traders and exchanges, but no definitive reason has been found for the wild fluctuations." The New York Fed and others have attributed the speed and size of the yield changes to the evolving structure of the Treasury market, including the role of automated trading.

NOTE: See, e.g., Robin Wigglesworth, "Fed Official Warns 'Flash Crash' Could be Repeated," *Financial Times*, April 14, 2015.

Kirilenko, Kyle, Samadi, and Tuzun (2010) examine the behavior of the e-mini S&P 500 stock index futures market on the day of the Flash Crash using audit-trail transaction data. They conclude, "High Frequency Traders did not trigger the Flash Crash, but their responses to the unusually large selling pressure on that day exacerbated market volatility." The analysis provides insight into why ETPs were differentially affected (ETPs accounted for 70% of equity transactions ultimately cancelled on May 6), even though ETP trading is less fragmented than that of other equities. For ETPs whose components are traded contemporaneously, widespread distortion of the prices of underlying basket securities prices can confound the arbitrage pricing mechanism for ETPs, thus delinking price from value.

THE ISHARES RUSSELL 1000 GROWTH ETF (IWF)

The iShares Russell 1000 Growth ETF (IWF) provides an illustrative case study of an ETF on May 6, 2010. Prior to the Flash Crash, the ETF price closely tracks the intraday net asset value of its constituent stocks, reflecting the smooth operation of the intraday creation-redemption arbitrage mechanism. The tight relationship of price and intraday net asset value holds until about 2:45 p.m., at which point, the constituents of the underlying basket themselves cannot be correctly priced. The uncertainty causes a temporary delinking price and value. The ETF then experiences a sharp price decline at one point trading down −60%, but recovers rapidly with price again closely tracking intraday net asset value by 3:10 p.m.

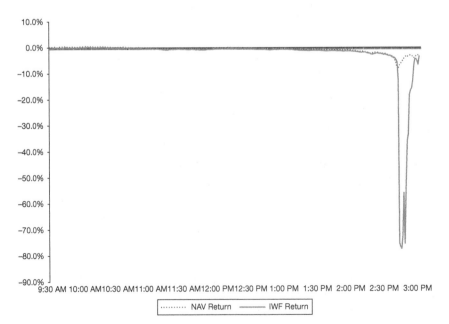

Figure 18.2 iShares Russell 1000 Growth ETF on May 6, 2010.
SOURCE: Madhavan (2012).

Figure 18.2 shows the cumulative returns of the iShares Russell 1000 Growth ETF (IWF) on the day of the Flash Crash beginning at the opening of trading. The extreme nature of the Flash Crash is evident, as is the close tracking to NAV throughout the day and post-recovery.

From the public policy viewpoint, the fact that fragmentation is now at its highest level (as shown by Madhavan [2012] using daily tick data from 1994 to 2011) ever may help explain why the Flash Crash did not occur earlier in response to other liquidity shocks. Madhavan (2012) concluded: "The safeguards and reforms that have been implemented in the US equity markets should help slow down a potential future market disruption similar to the Flash Crash. But they have not eliminated the possibility that another Flash Crash would occur, albeit with a different catalyst or possibly in a different asset class."

18.4. FLASH BACK

18.4.1. Market Disruption of August 2015

Five years after the original Flash Crash on August 24, 2015, the equity market experienced an eerily similar disruption. Unlike a single market-wide event, a series of mini-Flash Crashes occurred on Monday, August 24, 2015, in the second most active trading day ever recorded in US equities.[4] Following market volatility over the prior weekend, S&P 500 futures suggested the open would be sharply lower, down over 7%. Exchanges enacted "extreme market volatility" rules, and as a result, 43% of US equities did not open in the first 10 minutes of trading. When markets opened, extreme imbalances caused large price declines of over 22% in well-known, large stocks such as General Electric, JP Morgan, and KKR.

The prices of many ETFs deviated substantially from the estimated values of their holdings. Examples included many multi-billion dollar popular ETFs such as the Guggenheim S&P 500 Equal Weight (RSP), that dropped 42%, the iShares Core S&P 500 ETF (IVV), down 26%, and the Vanguard Dividend Appreciation ETF (VIG), which declined 37%. These steep declines in a short period should be viewed in the context of declines in their constituents of about 8%, meaning that their prices were delinked from underlying fair value. Within the first hour of trading, 361 different ETFs experienced trading halts. Across all exchanges and including stocks and ETFs, there were 1,278 instances of a security halted during the day. What explained these unusual events? Were they another illustration of the perils of ETF investing, as some have argued? Specifically, why were some ETFs affected while others, sometimes on the same underlying index, trading normally? Why didn't ETF arbitrage work to keep prices in line with value?

---

4. See, e.g., Todd Frankel, "Mini Flash Crash? Trading Anomalies on Manic Monday Hit Small Investors," *Washington Post*, August 27, 2015.

18.4.2. ETFs in the August 2015 Flash Event

The key point is that the August Flash Event was not only an ETF incident, but affected many equity instruments traded on organized exchanges. Nor was any one ETF issuer or market maker differentially affected. Foreign markets and ETFs traded abroad that were focused on the United States functioned well. In the Flash Event of August 2015, US-domiciled equity focused funds experienced the most disruption. This suggests that the events of August 24, like the Flash Crash, were related to US equity market structure. Ironically, exchange rules intended to quell panic trading implemented post the Flash Crash led to the temporary suspension of information dissemination on prices and order imbalances. The ETF arbitrage mechanism discussed in chapter 2 relies on APs and market makers who in turn need reliable pricing information about stocks in the index and the price of ETF shares. With limited price transparency at the chaotic opening of trading and unreliable quotes for delayed or halted stocks, the arbitrage mechanism did not work efficiently for a period of time. Automated systems may shut-down (or be turned off) if the underlying data is suspect, limiting normal arbitrage.

Non-automated (that is human) liquidity providers were also afraid, as in the Flash Crash, that some paired trades subsequently would be cancelled by the exchanges under rules about "clearly erroneous trades." For example, consider an ETF on the S&P 500 that is trading at $150 when the underlying basket has an intrinsic value of, say, $193. In theory, an arbitrager would buy the ETF at $150 while simultaneously selling the basket securities or, if these were not available, short selling E-Mini futures contracts, thereby locking in a profit of $43 per share traded less transaction costs. But if there is uncertainty over whether the ETF purchase at $150 would ultimately be cancelled by the exchange because the rules are vague, the arbitrager has the risk that their hedged trade is actually unhedged. If futures were to rally, the one-sided short position could lead to large losses for the arbitrager.

The cessation of normal arbitrage contributed to unusually wide bid-ask spreads, and ETF prices were driven by order flows rather than a link to intrinsic value. Sharp price declines, as in the case of the Flash Crash, were triggered by investors using market orders or by stop loss orders without a price limit. These orders guarantee execution, but possibly at very unfavorable prices. In terms of our model, the liquidity shock u_t was extremely negative leading to a large gap of price from value while the arbitrage parameter ψ was, for a brief time period, effectively 1 implying that pricing errors were not being corrected.

To understand why some funds experienced dislocation while others did not, I analyzed all US-domiciled ETFs (above $10 million in assets, $100,000 in volume, and above $5 in price) that traded on August 24, 2015. This yields a universe of 890 ETFs. For each of the 890 funds, I compute a measure of price dislocation or drawdown defined as the maximum price decline from the previous close on Friday. So, if an ETF closed on Friday, August 21, 2015, at a price $100 and experienced an intraday low on August 24, 2015, of, say, $60, the drawdown is 40%. If the fund traded up on August 24, the drawdown is negative. Over all US-domiciled, equity-focused ETFs the drawdown was 21% versus a decline in

E-mini futures of less than 8%. But some ETFs were greatly affected, with some experiencing drawdowns of ~90%. As noted above, US-focused funds traded in foreign markets had average drawdowns in line with the futures market.

I also compute for each fund the signed order flow for that day based on trade-by-trade (or tick) data. Signed order flow is a measure of net buying pressure. For example, suppose after the open, the bid and ask quotes for an ETF at 9:35:04 are $100.2 and $100.5, respectively when 1,000 shares are traded. If the trade price were 100.5, we would reckon this as a buy and say that signed order flow for this trade was $100,500. If a few seconds later the quotes were the same and we saw a trade for 100 shares at $100.2, we would reckon this as a sell, with signed volume of −$10,020. Adding up the signed volume for every trade gets the day's signed volume for that asset, which is scaled by the average daily volume in the previous 20 days so that each fund's buying or selling pressure is reflected as a pure number for comparability.

I then sort the 890 funds into deciles by drawdown. For each decile, I compute the average signed order flow. The result is shown in figure 18.3. Each point represents a portfolio of 89 ETFs. On the vertical axis is the drawdown in percent where higher numbers indicating more price dislocation. On the horizontal axis is the average order imbalance scaled by volume, with positive numbers representing buying pressure over the day and negative numbers indicating selling pressure. The straight line in figure 18.3 is a linear regression, and the negative relation (the correlation is −0.91) between flow pressure and price dislocation measured by drawdown is very evident. This statistically significant relation is confirmed in a more formal cross-sectional regression using all 890 data points, and controlling for attributes such as size, asset type, issuer, lead market maker, and other variables.

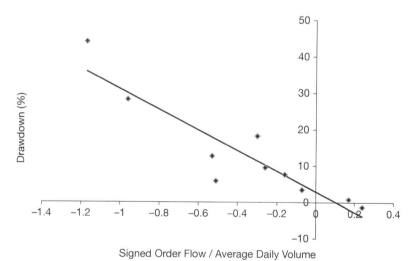

Figure 18.3 Plot of drawdown against signed order flow on August 24, 2015.
SOURCE Author's estimates based on TAQ and Bloomberg data for August 24, 2015. The universe consists of all US-domiciled ETFs with prices above $5, AUM above $10 million, and 20-day average daily volume above $100,000.

On a normal day, when price is in line with NAV and volatility is minimal, the negative relation shown in figure 18.3 is not evident and the regression line is nearly flat. The statistical analysis explains the variation across funds in the Flash Event of August 24. Of course, other factors such as the composition of flow, lead market maker identity and so on also play a role.

Ironically, exchange rules imposing trading halts for stock prices experiencing volatility slowed the recovery to equilibrium. Trading halts for five minutes kick in when prices move beyond specified ranges, either Limit-Up or Limit-Down. There were many cases in which ETF prices moved sharply down and were halted under the limit-down rule, only to be halted under limit-up rules as they tried to recover to the intrinsic value of the underlying index. Ironically, exchange rules imposing trading halts for stock prices experiencing volatility slowed the recovery to equilibrium. Trading halts for five minutes kick in when prices move beyond specified ranges, either Limit-Up or Limit-Down. There were many cases in which ETF prices moved sharply down and were halted under the limit-down rule, only to be halted under limit-up rules as they tried to recover to the intrinsic value of the underlying index. The lessons learned echo those of the original Flash Crash. First, education so that investors do not assume their order will necessarily execute near previous prices. Rather, investors should use limit orders as a default. Special care is needed near openings and closings when volatility is higher. Second, advisors need to place limits with stop loss orders that otherwise may trade through the limit book and result in large losses. Third, regulators have an important role to play in reforming market structure and the effects of fragmentation that caused the original Flash Crash. Those reforms, including better intermarket linkages, improvements to current rules about halts, harmonization of rules across venues, clear guidelines on "erroneous trades" and a consolidated audit trail tape will help prevent future occurrences.

18.5. CHAPTER SUMMARY

The benefits of ETFs are relatively clear and—as proved by their continuing and growing adoption worldwide—are economically significant. But the costs and risks of these products are much less clear. There is no evidence that ETFs played a role in the Flash Crash or in subsequent Flash Events such as August 24, 2015. Rather, the dislocation to ETFs arise largely from underlying US equity market fragmentation. Similarly, there is no evidence that ETFs have exacerbated volatility in the underlying markets. Nor do any of the other concerns voiced about ETFs contributing to systemic risk have demonstrable validity on an empirical basis, and several claims appear to stem from confusion about how ETFs operate and differ from open-ended mutual funds. There is also a conflation of several different issues, most important, confusing overall market liquidity with the liquidity of a given fund. Market liquidity refers to the ability to buy or sell securities without substantial price changes. By contrast, fund liquidity refers to the structural features of a fund and the conditions (timing, gates, etc.) under which redemption can occur. While *market* liquidity may sharply decline in times of extreme stress, this does not necessarily impair *fund* liquidity.

This said, some caveats are in order. First, we have yet to see how market participants will behave in times of extreme stress. Some of the arguments against ETFs come from concerns about suitability and whether investors understand the nature of liquidity in these products. It is hard to come up with counter-factuals to hypothetical scenarios, but that said, investor education should continue to be a top focus of regulators and policymakers. Further, as emphasized throughout, it is important to distinguish between plain vanilla physically backed funds (conventional ETFs) and more exotic structures involving synthetics or leverage. Most of the concerns cited in recent policy papers actually refer to only a relatively small set of ETPs. Regulators are correctly taking a more holistic approach today, evaluating not just individual funds as independent products but also considering the broader market implications.

Future Opportunities

19.1. INTRODUCTION

Is the trend to passive investing sustainable or will active management experience resurgence? Are ETFs truly an innovation? Will the dramatic growth in assets in ETFs slow or taper? Speculating about the future is inevitably prone to error. Nonetheless, the fundamental drivers behind passive investing and the adoption of the ETF wrapper are now discernible and, in the view of the author, are likely to continue for decades. This is not to say there is no room for differentiated active management. There is, as noted earlier, growing interest in active strategies including those that are more passive, rule-based in nature or so-called "Smart Beta" products. The result is a "barbell" effect where passive managers and active managers who add diversified alpha experience asset growth, while closet-indexers and active managers/hedge funds that offer exposure to well-known factor risk premiums at a high cost experience outflows.

There are other, more fundamental shifts, under way in the industry. One theme throughout this book is the growing importance of technology and analytics to broaden and deepen the asset base. New technology and regulation is offsetting some of the disadvantages facing ETF adoption. For example, model portfolios and robo-advisors offer ways for investors to automate rebalancing and diversification using a single ticker that maps to multiple ETFs. In the final chapter, I try to give a sense of how the industry is changing and evolving, along with some speculations regarding what the future may bring.

19.2. LONG-HORIZON DRIVERS

Starting with early adopters, passive investing through ETFs has grown rapidly in the last few decades. Newer investors—with diverse needs and uses—such as pension funds, financial advisors (FAs), registered investment advisors (RIAs), self-directed investors and others have become comfortable with ETFs and passively managed portfolios. In many cases, this has taken considerable education and changes in the legal and regulatory environment. For example, until relatively recently, insurance companies could not invest in bond ETFs as they were classified as equities, not fixed income instruments. That kept a major segment of potential investors away from the benefits of diversification at low cost. Similarly, defined-contribution or 401(k) plans are typically not set up to handle ETFs in retirement accounts, although such funds offer many advantages to savers. The growth in the user base is likely to continue for years to come. This is not to say that the growth will come at the expense of active management.

In my view, there is clearly a role for active management that offers true alpha that is excess return over and above the benchmark. To return to a key theme, the trick here is to define the benchmark. Is it simply a benchmark index return or a factor-based based return? In a simple example, an active manager whose benchmark is say the Barclays Aggregate Bond Index may have excess returns by incorporating foreign or high-yield bonds. Those bonds may carry some credit or duration risk, so although the manager may "outperform" the index that was selected, they may in actuality not earn an excess return on a risk-adjusted basis. Many active mutual funds or hedge-funds fall into this category: their excess return is really only a risk premium to factors that they "load" upon. Holdings based style analysis can help attribute the portion of a manager's return in excess of their benchmark to genuine skill in timing and stock selection, as opposed to simply maintaining a tilt towards a factor such as value. As investors gain greater understanding of factor based approaches (see, e.g., Ang 2014), I would expect the continued disintermediation of this type of manager toward the true generators of alpha and also toward more passive investment styles.

19.3. TECHNOLOGY

19.3.1. The Growing Importance of Technology and Analytics

The growing role of technology and analytics in asset management requires special mention, as does its intersection with behavioral finance. Digital advisors— that automate much of financial and investment planning—are gaining assets very quickly, and typically offer portfolios using ETFs. These advisors offer ways to overcome some of the biases and cognitive errors individuals make that have been identified by behavioral finance, including loss aversion and home bias. Advances in Data Sciences (also referred to as "Big Data") offer investment advisors new insights into how retail investors think and act. This makes it easier to identify those the barriers to greater ETF adoption by ordinary investors. For example, some investors may be unfamiliar with bond ETFs, choosing individual bonds, paying high hidden fees and failing to diversify adequately across issuers. Bid data offers asset managers the opportunity to better understand how best to reach these types of investors through marketing or educational efforts. Trading technology—both in terms of ease of access and the growing movement toward electronic trading venues—are major forces.

19.3.2. Digital Advisors

Digital Advisors, sometimes called robo-advisors, are automated financial planners that provide a technology solution to investment advice. Although digital advisors (such as Betterment, Wealthfront, and Schwab Intelligent Portfolios) are a relatively recent phenomenon, these firms have seen rapid growth and now have tens of thousands of clients. Robo-advisors offer low fees based on the individual's assets or as a flat monthly fee, and often recommend portfolios comprised solely of ETF assets. The fact that these advisors are compensated on assets (versus commissions, which can be sizable for traditional mutual funds) is favorable to ETFs. Unlike high-touch financial advisors, robo-advisors typically do not offer services outside of portfolio management such as estate or retirement planning, although they may offer tools such as retirement calculators. They are consequently most used by individual investors who are comfortable with technology and do not feel they need the personal services of a financial advisor. Most digital advisors are attempting to broaden their client base by targeting wealthier, traditional investors.

Digital advisors offer three basic types of portfolio management services to clients, as explained below. These services are valuable to investors because they can help overcome well-documented behavioral biases. First, digital advisors provide model-based portfolio solutions to clients using low-cost ETFs and index funds. As seen earlier, most individual investors struggle to identify managers who can consistently add alpha above fees, so limiting the opportunity set to low-cost vehicles may enhance returns over the long haul. Individuals may also exhibit counter-productive behaviors—such as home bias, loss aversion, and trend chasing—whose impact can be mitigated with an automated, model-based solution. Model portfolios are selected for the client when the account is first established, based on answers to questions regarding risk aversion, horizon, and financial goals. A systematic approach to portfolio construction ensures, at least in theory, that clients with similar risk tolerances, goals, and horizons will have similar (but not necessarily identical) portfolio allocation.

Second, robo-advisors automate routine rebalancing by buying assets that have declined in price while selling assets that have appreciated. Automated rebalancing helps overcome the natural tendency of individual investors to let their portfolios to drift, especially in the face a strong market returns. In this sense, robo-advisors help overcome a well-documented behavioral finance bias where investors are reluctant to buy assets that have declined in value. Similarly, automated rebalancing also acts as a counter to trend chasing, where individuals invest more in assets that have increased in value.

Third, digital advisers will perform tax loss selling to harvest any tax losses that have been accrued because of declines in price, in some cases on a daily basis. They also automate tax-aware location-based investing, meaning that a client located in New York does not invest solely in California municipal bonds. Again, this helps overcome known behavioral biases on the part of individual investors (such as investing in local securities that are familiar) as well as offering considerable convenience. For example, individual investors are well known to exhibit *loss aversion*, meaning they hold on to losers too long (they are reluctant to realize losses) and sell their winners too quickly. Robo-advisors automate the process of realizing a loss while taking a position in a similar asset (e.g., selling an emerging markets ETF such as EEM and buying a highly correlated, but not identical basket such as VWO) without triggering the IRS Wash Sale rule.

19.3.3. Data Science and Behavioral Finance

The term "big data" refers to large and complex data sets (high volume, variety and velocity) that are not amenable to analysis using traditional data processing applications. Issues in data science include the capture, storage, curation, visualization, and analysis of big data. New sources of data from search engines, social media, wearables (e.g., fitness trackers), and satellite imagery have been married to new technologies, providing additional opportunities for understanding economic behavior. Extracting insight from complex, often large data sets requires combining old and new ideas, and using innovative techniques. An additional challenge in asset management is *veracity* because data quality can vary dramatically across different sources. Some key big-data-related technologies are:

- Scientific data visualization (summarizing information in new ways);
- Natural language processing (reading text such as broker reports);
- Machine learning (allowing computers to identify patterns in the data); and
- Distributed computing paradigms (to scale platforms).

Most applications of data science to date have been in the realm of social media and Internet advertising, but it should not come as a surprise that investors and asset managers are looking to such techniques for new products (e.g., identifying investment themes), alpha generation, understanding investor behavior, and better marketing.

An important element of whether digital advisors can expand their offerings to wealthier individuals who are used to dealing with a human advisor is whether they can offer a "high touch" service in an automated manner. Data science, together with behavioral finance insights, offers such a possibility. For example, a robo-advisor that records all logins and mouse clicks might find that some clients check their accounts much more in volatile periods. By sending these investors personalized messages at such times, the advisor might prevent these types of investors from making common errors such as selling after a sharp market decline. Similarly, a client that updates some information (e.g., retirement age or employment status) might receive materials targeted at sustainable retirement income or be directed to online retirement calculators that allow clients to target particular savings goal given their horizon.

19.3.4. Individual Investors

As ETFs gain in popularity, some have questioned whether intraday liquidity has encouraged over-trading, shorter investment horizons, and entry into new (and perhaps unsuitable) asset classes by individual investors. Such activity might, in the view of some commentators, increase transaction costs and returns, while adding to risk. Behavioral finance (see, e.g., Barber and Odean 2000) has documented several such cases where investors seek risk, including some interesting gender differences.

But what does the evidence show about ETFs versus index mutual funds? A study by Ameriks, Dickson, Weber, and Kwon (2012) examined 3.2 million transactions conducted by self-directed, individual investors in more than 500,000 positions held in the mutual fund and ETF share classes of four different Vanguard funds from 2007 through 2011. They conclude that both ETF and traditional mutual fund shareholders were long-term, buy-and-hold investors, and although investors were more active in ETFs than in traditional mutual funds, more than 40% of the variation can be explained by differences in personal (e.g., age, gender) and account characteristics (assets, account type, tenure, premium service level) between ETF and traditional fund shareholders. There are interesting gender differences in the data (see also Barber and Odean 2001) with mutual fund owners much more likely than ETF owners to be female at 39% versus 28%. Those figures are consistent with other studies using different data sources.

Ameriks, Dickson, Weber, and Kwon (2012) conclude "it is not valid to assume that the so-called ETF temptation effect explains the higher-observed trading in ETFs relative to mutual funds, nor is it a reason for long-term individual investors to avoid using appropriate ETF investments as part of a diversified investment portfolio." Of course, these results hold only for the funds studied, all of which are from one asset manager, but there is no reason to believe the results do not generalize.

Beyond these analyses of trading patterns at the account level, one might imagine additional insight into individual behavior through textual analysis of social media, broker commentary, and other data that might easily run into billions of records. Market sentiment engines can read text such as broker reports, newspaper articles, regulatory filings, patent applications, tweets, and so on and extract some sense of the underlying sentiment. These are useful to financial advisors in many ways. For example, a large advisory firm may use sentiment signals to time factors or shift between asset classes in their model portfolios, or to provide market color to their clients. ETF managers, for example, might also use data science to target the buyers of their products, data that is not readily available unlike for a mutual fund, making it easier for asset managers to reward the distributors of their funds for their work on education and marketing.

19.4. FINAL REMARKS

ETFs have grown substantially in diversity and size in recent years, reflecting a broader shift toward passive, index investing. As a consequence, there is increased attention by investors, regulators, and academics who seek to assess and understand the implications of this rapid growth. Substantively, ETFs represent a disruptive financial innovation that we have explored in this book.

This book provides a framework based on arbitrage to understand liquidity and price dynamics. I use the framework to analyze several aspects to the pricing and trading of ETFs including their role in price discovery, the nature of premiums and discounts, performance and tracking relative to benchmark, return autocorrelations, transaction costs, and liquidity sourcing in underlying and secondary markets.

The framework is also applied to understand some of the issues related to so-called "Smart Beta." I prefer the term "factor based investing," which utilizes model-driven, quantitative portfolio construction techniques and attempts to outperform a market capitalization weighted benchmark index. Factor investing, like the ETF wrapper itself, is an *innovation* in that it offers clients exposures that were previously very expensive (or simply unavailable) at relatively low cost, helping to complete markets. It is also a *disruptive* innovation to the asset management industry because some traditional active managers and hedge funds deliver a significant fraction of their active returns via static exposures to factors like value/growth.

In essence, the debate is not about active versus passive management; it is where to *pay* for active and passive investing. How one chooses active or passive managers is a critical driver of returns. This book takes the view that there is room for both types of managers, implying that investors should anchor their portfolios with high value active strategies and efficient ETFs or other passive vehicles. Logic also supports the view that a fully passive market cannot be in equilibrium—how will price discovery take place if everyone is a price taker?

Active management makes sense for investors seeking specific outcomes or strategies that cannot be replicated easily with passive vehicles. Many active managers use ETFs to implement their strategies (e.g., asset allocation) accomplish specific objectives—establishing factor tilts for instance. Active management may also make sense for relatively less informed investors in complex and opaque markets that are difficult to replicate with an index. Active management can potentially take advantage of illiquidity, where the manager can add value by sourcing assets (e.g., high-yield bonds) that might not be readily available. It also makes sense at the overall asset allocation level since the notion of market capitalization weighting across all asset classes—and even the definition of an asset class—is yet to be agreed upon. The requirement though is high conviction in a manager's ability to beat a benchmark (net all fees and taxes) and a sufficiently long holding period (it may take years to capture a full cycle of some factors), as timing alpha is virtually impossible. Investors need to be aware of the challenges in identifying such active managers; simple metrics such as Active Share are unlikely to be useful in identifying outperformers, although they can help in screening against high cost closet indexers.

ETFs offer convenient passive access in lieu of securities selection and can be used for core "style box" exposures, asset allocation building blocks, and relatively shorter term investments. In the middle of the spectrum, investors are migrating away from traditional long-only equity active funds. Some of these funds charge active fees but are content to deliver performance that can be replicated with a handful of low-cost factors such as value or momentum, while others add true alpha by superior securities selection or timing.

An important element of the future growth of ETFs is the externalization of distribution fees. The movement toward a compensation model based on external fees has helped the ETF industry grow. In this model, financial advisors are paid directly by the client for their services typically based on the total amount of assets managed. For advisors, ETFs are attractive because distribution, account servicing, or maintenance fees are not included in the expense ratio. In Europe, the trend toward eliminating retrocessions (i.e., commission payments to financial advisers for recommending products to clients) puts ETFs and mutual funds on par from a compensation perspective. Again, that change should also increase incentives for advisors to offer their clients ETFs as an element of portfolio construction. Finally, model portfolios using ETFs and the rise of robo-advisors are also longer term trends that favor ETF use and adoption.

I also review public policy debates regarding ETFs and passive indexing more generally, including concerns about systemic risk, flash events, and liquidity.[1] The evidence presented here strongly supports the conclusion that ETFs have extended significant benefits to investors and to the functioning of markets, and that concerns over their operation are largely due to misconceptions about pricing and liquidity.

---

1. Golub et al. (2013) provide a comprehensive overview of the benefits of ETF ownership and dispel many of the myths concerning index products more generally.

Accrued Interest—Interest earned by a bond investor that has yet to be paid; most bonds pay semi-annually or even monthly.

Active Share—A measure between 0 and 1 corresponding to the deviation of a fund's holdings from its benchmark; higher figures correspond to more active management while lower figures correspond to index-type investing.

Alpha—Return in excess of a pre-specified benchmark; a measure of the performance of active managers who seek to outperform the benchmark return.

Alternatives—Generic term for non-traditional asset classes (e.g., private equity) or hedge fund strategies (e.g., merger arbitrage) previously difficult or costly for investors to access.

Authorized Participant (AP)—A large financial institution that enters into a legal contract with an ETF distributor to create and redeem shares of the fund. APs are the only investors allowed to interact directly with the fund.

Backwardation—A state where the futures (or forward) price of a commodity is lower than the expected spot price (the opposite of **Contango**).

Balance Sheet—An accounting statement that reflects a company's assets and liabilities at a particular point in time.

Beta—A measure of how a security's return moves with the overall market in a linear single factor model. Beta also refers to portfolios that seek to mimic an existing index without active security selection.

Bid-Ask Spread—The difference between the quoted price for an immediate sale (bid) and an immediate purchase (ask). The bid-ask spread is a commonly used metric for liquidity and the transaction cost. Bid and ask quotes are usually good for pre-specified quantities or depth.

Broker-Dealer—A firm in the business of buying and selling securities.

Closed-End Mutual Funds—A type of mutual fund whose shares are in fixed supply. Closed-end funds may trade at prices that are different from Net Asset Value.

Contango—A state where the futures (or forward) price of a commodity is higher than the expected spot price (see also **Backwardation**).

Creation/Redemption—The process by which shares of ETFs are added or subtracted from a fund in order to meet market demand.

CUSIP—A CUSIP (Committee on Uniform Securities Identification Procedures) is a nine-character alphanumeric code that identifies most securities, including stocks, for the purposes of facilitating clearing and settlement.

Debt Issuance—Corporations and governments offer debt issues as a means of raising funds. In return, lenders generally receive payments from these corporations and governments in return.

Delta One—Refers to instruments that offer 1:1 exposure to the returns of the underlying benchmark; leveraged funds or those with embedded options are not Delta One products.

Digital Advisors—Automated financial planners, offering a systematized technology solution to investment advice (see also **Robo-Advisors**).

Exchange-Traded Fund (ETF)—A fund that combines features of mutual funds and stocks, ETFs are diversified mixes of assets managed by experienced professionals. ETFs typically offer low overall costs, tax benefits, and the ability to buy and sell throughout the day as long as the market is open.

Exchange-Traded Note (ETN)—An unsecured debt obligation; unlike an ETF, an ETN is not physically backed but is backed by the issuer's credit which may or may not be collateralized.

Exchange-Traded Product (ETP)—A generic term for any portfolio exposure product that is traded on an exchange. ETPs include as subsets ETFs that are physically backed and ETNs, as well as exchange-traded commodity funds.

Information Ratio—Performance measure defined as the ratio of active return beyond a stated benchmark to active risk measured by the standard deviation of returns in excess of benchmark (see also **Sharpe Ratio**).

In-Kind Transfer—The exchange of ETF shares for shares of the underlying securities. It is this transfer that enables ETFs to create/redeem shares of the ETF without undergoing a taxable event.

Leveraged Exchange-Traded Product (LETP)—An exchange-traded product offering a multiple of the day's return in a specified index. Inverse funds offer a negative multiple. Unlike traditional ETFs that are physically backed, LETPs are based on swap contracts.

Liquidity—The extent to which an asset can be bought or sold in the market without substantially affecting the asset's price. Assets that exhibit high liquidity are those that can be easily bought or sold at prices close to prevailing quotes.

Market Maker—A provider of liquidity that stands ready to buy or sell on demand. The term traditionally referred to designated market makers who profit from trading at the bid-ask spread, but can be informally used to refer to any entity that profits from supplying liquidity.

Mutual Fund—A type of professionally managed fund that pools money from investors to purchase securities.

Net Asset Value (NAV)—The per share dollar value of a fund, reflecting the value of the securities in a portfolio divided by the number of shares outstanding.

Open-End Mutual Funds—A type of mutual fund without restrictions on the amount of shares the fund can issue. The vast majority of mutual funds are open-end.

Over-the-Counter (OTC)—A security that is not listed or traded on an organized exchange such as a secondary market.

Price Discovery—The forces of supply and demand that determine the equilibrium price for a specific security in the market.

Price Transparency—The level of information available to investors regarding the quantity of assets being offered in the market (the supply) and the bids at various price levels (the demand). Greater transparency means investors have more clarity around what an asset is currently worth in the market.

Primary Market—The market for new issues of securities including both stocks and bonds. In the ETF context, primary market liquidity refers to accessing the underlying stock and bond markets in order to facilitate a creation or redemption.

Proprietary Trading—The practice of a firm trading for its own gain rather than to merely process customer trades.

Redemption—The process of exchanging shares in an ETF for cash or a basket of securities.

Robo-Advisors—Automated financial planners (see **Digital Advisors**).

Secondary Markets—Markets, such as the New York Stock Exchange, where investors buy and sell securities, including ETFs, from other investors and from market makers.

Securities Lending—The process by which securities are lent for short sale; these securities are usually over-collateralized.

Sharpe Ratio—Ratio of a portfolio's excess return over the risk-free rate to its **volatility**, measured by the standard deviation of returns (see also **Information Ratio**).

Systemically Important Financial Institution (SIFI)—A bank, insurance company, or other financial institution whose failure would pose a serious risk to the economy, as designated by the US Federal Reserve.

Total Expense Ratio (TER)—The explicit fee on the assets under management (AUM) charged by the ETF issuer to manage the fund, expressed usually in basis points; AUM is the market value of the assets managed by the fund.

Tracking Difference—The difference between an ETF's NAV returns and the returns of the underlying index, net of the ETF's expense ratio.

UCITS—Undertakings for the Collective Investment in Transferable Securities, a set of European Union (EU) Directives to allow collective investment schemes to operate freely across all EU nations, provided that the fund and fund managers are authorized by one member state.

Volatility—Measure of risk of an asset measured by the standard deviation of returns over a particular interval of time.

Volume—The number of shares of a security or those that comprise a market that trade during a period of time. Broadly, the higher the volume the more liquid the security or market.

Yield-to-Maturity—The annualized internal rate of return an investor would receive if he or she held a particular bond until maturity. Yield-to-maturity should not be confused with the total return of the bond.

Abner, David. 2010. *The ETF Handbook: How to Value and Trade Exchange Traded Funds*. New Jersey: Wiley.

Agapova, Anna. 2011. "Conventional Mutual Index Funds versus Exchange Traded Funds." *Journal of Financial Markets* 14, no. 2: 323–343.

Alexander, Carol, and Dmitris Korovilas. 2013. "Volatility Exchange-Traded Notes: Curse or Cure?" *Journal of Alternative Investments* 16, no. 2: 52–70.

Ameriks, John, Joel M. Dickson, Stephen Weber, and David T. Kwon. 2012. "ETFs: For the Better or Bettor?" Vanguard research, July.

Ang, Andrew. 2014. *Asset Management: A Systematic Approach to Factor Investing*. New York: Oxford University Press.

Antoniewicz, Rochelle, and Jane Heinrichs. 2014. "Understanding Exchange-Traded Funds: How ETFs Work." ICI Research Perspective 20, Investment Company Institute, Washington, DC, September. Available at http://www.ici.org/pdf/per20-05.pdf.

Antoniewicz, Rochelle, and Jane Heinrichs. 2015. "The Role and Activities of Authorized Participants of Exchange-Traded Funds." Investment Company Institute, Washington, DC, March. Available at http://www.ici.org/pdf/ppr_15_aps_etfs.pdf.

Appel, Ian R., Todd A. Gormley, and Donald B. Keim. 2015. "Passive Investors, Not Passive Owners." Working paper, Wharton School of the University of Pennsylvania.

Arnott, Robert D., Jason C. Hsu, and Philip Moore. 2005. "Fundamental Indexation." *Financial Analysts Journal* 61, no. 2: 83–99.

Avellaneda, Marco, and Stanley Jian Zhang. 2009. "Path-Dependence of Leveraged ETF Returns." Working paper. Available at http://ssrn.com/abstract=1404708.

Bai, Qing, Shaun A. Bond, and Brian Hatch. 2015. "The Impact of Leveraged and Inverse ETFs on Underlying Stock Returns." Working paper, University of Cincinnati.

Barber, Brad M., and Terrance Odean. 2000. "Trading Is Hazardous to Your Wealth: The Common Stock Investment Performance of Individual Investors." *Journal of Finance* 55, no. 2: 773–806.

Barber, Brad M., and Terrance Odean. 2001. "Boys Will Be Boys: Gender, Overconfidence, and Common Stock." *Quarterly Journal of Economics* 116, no. 1: 261–292.

Barr, Colin. 2010. "Progress Energy Joins Flash Crash Crowd." *Fortune*, September 27. http://finance.fortune.cnn.com/2010/09/27/progress-energy-joins-flash-crash-crowd/.

Ben-David, Itzhak, Francesco Franzoni, and Rabih Moussawi. 2014. "ETFs, Arbitrage, and Contagion." Dice Center WP 2011-20, Ohio State University.

Bessembinder, Hendrik, William Maxwell, and Kumar Venkataraman. 2006. "Market Transparency, Liquidity Externalities, and Institutional Trading Costs in Corporate Bonds." *Journal of Financial Economics* 82, no. 2: 251–288.

Black, Fischer. 1972. "Capital Market Equilibrium with Restricted Borrowing." *Journal of Business* 45: 444–455.

BlackRock, 2016. "BlackRock Global ETP Landscape: December 2015." Available at http://www.iShares.com.

Blocher, Jesse, and Robert Whaley. 2015. "Passive Investing: The Role of Securities Lending." Working paper, Vanderbilt University.

Borkovec, Milan, Ian Domowitz, Vitaly Serbin, and Henry Yegerman. 2010. "Liquidity and Price Discovery in Exchange-Traded Funds: One of Several Possible Lessons from the Flash Crash." White paper, ITG Inc.

Bradley, Harold, and Robert E. Litan. 2010. "Choking the Recovery: Why New Growth Companies Aren't Going Public and Unrecognized Risks of Future Market Disruptions." Kauffman Foundation.

Broman, Markus S. 2013. "Excess Co-movement and Limits-to-Arbitrage: Evidence from Exchange-Traded Funds." Working paper, York University.

Carhart, Mark M. 1991. "On Persistence in Mutual Fund Performance." *Journal of Finance* 52: 57–82.

Chacko, George, Sanjiv Das, and Rong Fan. 2014. "Excess Co-movement and Limits-to-Arbitrage: Evidence from Exchange-Traded Funds." Working paper, York University.

Cheng, Minder, and Ananth Madhavan. 2009. "The Dynamics of Leveraged and Inverse Exchange-Traded Funds." *Journal of Investment Management* 7, no. 4: 43–62.

Cheng, Si, Massimo Massa, and Hong Zhang. 2013. "The Dark Side of ETF Investing: A Worldwide Analysis." Available at http://ssrn.com/abstract=2224424.

Chow, Tzee-man, Jason Hsu, Vitali Kalesnik, and Bryce Little. 2011. "A Survey of Alternative Equity Index Strategies." *Financial Analysts Journal* 67, no. 5: 38–57.

Clarke, Roger G., Harindra de Silva, and Steven Thorley. 2006. "Minimum-Variance Portfolios in the U.S. Equity Market." *Journal of Portfolio Management* 33, no. 1: 10–24.

Cremers, Martijn, and Antti Petajisto. 2009. "How Active Is Your Fund Manager? A New Measure That Predicts Performance." *Review of Financial Studies* 22, no. 9: 3329–3365.

Da, Zhi, and Shive, Sophie. 2013. "Exchange-Traded Funds and Equity Return Correlations." Working paper, University of Notre Dame.

Dannhauser, Caitlin D. 2015. "The Equitization of the Corporate Bond Market: ETFs Impact on Bond Yields and Liquidity." Working paper, Carroll School of Management, Boston College.

Downing, Christopher, Ananth Madhavan, Ajit Singh, and Alex Ulitsky. 2014. "Portfolio Construction and Tail Risk." *Journal of Portfolio Management* 42, no. 1: 85–102.

Edwards, Amy K., Lawrence E. Harris, and Michael S. Piwowar. 2007. "Corporate Bond Market Transparency and Transactions Costs." *Journal of Finance* 62: 1421–1451.

Elton, Edwin J., and Martin J. Gruber, George Commer, and Kai Li. 2002. "Spiders: Where are the Bugs?" *Journal of Business* 75, no. 3: 453–472.

Engle, Robert F., and Debojyoti Sarkar. 2006. "Premiums-Discounts and Exchange Traded Funds." *Journal of Derivatives* 13, no. 4 (Summer): 27–45.

Fama, Eugene F., and Kenneth R. French. 1993. "Common Risk Factors in the Returns on Stocks and Bonds." *Journal of Financial Economics* 33: 3–56.

Fama, Eugene F., and Kenneth R. French. 2016. "Dissecting Anomalies with a Five-Factor Model." *Review of Financial Studies* 29, no. 1: 69–103.

Financial Stability Board (FSB). 2011. "Potential Financial Stability Issues Arising from Recent Trends in Exchange-Traded Funds." Financial Stability Board, Basel, Switzerland.

Financial System Review. 2014. "Exchange-Traded Funds: Evolution of Benefits, Vulnerabilities and Risks." Bank of Canada, December, 37–46.

Fisher, Jeffery, David M. Geltner, and R. Brian Webb. 1994. "Value Indices of Commercial Real Estate: A Comparison of Index Construction Methods." *Journal of Real Estate Finance and Economics* 9: 137–164.

Frazzini, Andrea, Jacques Friedman, and Lukasz Pomorski. 2015. "Deactivating Active Share." White paper, AQR Capital Management.

Gastineau, Gary. 2010. *The Exchange-Traded Funds Manual.* 2d ed. Chichester: John Wiley & Sons.

Giese, Guido. 2010. "On the Performance of Leveraged and Optimally Leveraged Investment Funds." Working paper. Available at http://ssrn.com/abstract=1510344.

Goetzmann, William N., Zoran Ivković, and K. Geert Rouwenhorst. 2001. "Day Trading International Mutual Funds: Evidence and Policy Solutions." *Journal of Financial and Quantitative Analysis* 36, no. 3: 287–309.

Goldstein, Itay, Hao Jiang, and David T. Ng. 2015. "Investor Flows and Fragility in Corporate Bond Funds." Working paper, Wharton School of the University of Pennsylvania.

Goldstein, Michael A., Edith Hotchkiss, and Erik R. Sirri. 2007. "Transparency and Liquidity: A Controlled Experiment on Corporate Bonds." *Review of Financial Studies* 20: 235–273.

Golub, Bennett W., Barbara Novick, Ananth Madhavan, Ira Shapiro, Kristen Walters, and Mauricio Ferconi. 2013. "Viewpoint: Exchange Traded Products: Overview, Benefits and Myths." BlackRock Investment Institute.

Golub, Bennett W., and Leo M. Tilman. 2000. *Risk Management: Approaches for Fixed Income Markets.* New York: Wiley Frontiers in Finance.

Green, Richard C., Burton Hollifield, and Norman Schürhoff. 2007. "Financial Intermediation and the Costs of Trading in an Opaque Market." *Review of Financial Studies* 20: 275–314.

Grégoire, Vincent. 2013. "Do Mutual Fund Managers Adjust NAV for Stale Prices?" Working paper, University of British Columbia.

Grinold, Richard, and Ronald Kahn. 2000. *Active Portfolio Management.* 2d ed. New York: McGraw-Hill.

Grossman, Sanford J., and Joseph H. Stiglitz. 1980. "On the Impossibility of Informationally Efficient Markets." *American Economic Review* 70, no. 3: 393–408.

Hamilton, James D. 1994. *Time Series Analysis.* Princeton, NJ: Princeton University Press.

Hamm, Sophia J. 2014. "The Effect of ETFs on Stock Liquidity." Working paper, Ohio State University. Available at SSRN: http://ssrn.com/abstract=1687914.

Harris, Lawrence E., and Michael S. Piwowar. 2006. "Municipal Bond Liquidity." *Journal of Finance* 61, no. 3: 1330–1366.

Haryanto, Edgar, Arthur Rodier, Pauline M. Shum, and Walid Hejazi. 2013. "Intraday Share Price Volatility and Leveraged ETF Rebalancing." Working paper, University of Toronto.

Hasbrouck, Joel. 2003. "Intraday Price Formation in US Equity Index Markets." *Journal of Finance* 58, no. 6: 2375–2399.

Haugh, Martin. 2011. "A Note on Constant Proportion Trading Strategies." Working paper, Department of Industrial Engineering and Operations Research, Columbia University, New York.

Hendershott, Terrence, and Ananth Madhavan. 2015. "Click or Call? Auction versus Search in the Over-the-Counter Market." *Journal of Finance* 70, no. 1: 419–447.

Hill, Joanne M., Dave Nadig, and Matt Hougan. 2015. "A Comprehensive Guide to Exchange-Traded Funds." CFA Research Institute.

Hong, Gwangheon, and Arthur Warga. 2000. "An Empirical Study of Bond Market Transactions." *Financial Analysts Journal* 56, no. 2: 32–46.

Huang, Jennifer C., and Ilan Guedj. 2009. "Are ETFs Replacing Index Mutual Funds?" Available at SSRN: http://ssrn.com/abstract=1108728.

International Monetary Fund. 2015. "Global Financial Stability Report: The Asset Management Industry and Financial Stability." Washington, DC, April.

Israeli, Doron, Charles M. C. Lee, and Suhas Sridharan. 2015. "Is there a Dark Side to Exchange Traded Funds (ETFs)? An Information Perspective." Stanford University Graduate School of Business Research Paper No. 15–42.

Ivanov, Ivan T., and Stephen L. Lenkey. 2014. "Are Concerns about Leveraged ETFs Overblown?" Federal Reserve Board, Working paper 106.

Jacobsen, Brian. 2015. "The Big ETF Charade." *Journal of Portfolio Management* 41, no. 3: 3–4.

Jarrow, Robert A. 2010. "Understanding the Risk of Leveraged ETFs." *Finance Research Letters* 7: 135–139.

Kahn, Ronald N., and Michael Lemmon. 2014. "The Asset Manager's Dilemma: How Strategic Beta Is Disrupting the Investment Management Industry." Working paper, BlackRock.

Karolyi, G. Andrew. 2015. *Cracking the Emerging Markets Enigma*. New York: Oxford University Press.

Kirilenko, Andrei, Albert S. Kyle, Mehrdad Samadi, and Tugkan Tuzun. 2010. "The Flash Crash: The Impact of High-Frequency Trading on an Electronic Market." Working paper, University of Maryland, College Park, MD.

Koesterich, Russ. 2008. *The ETF Strategist: Balancing Risk and Reward for Superior Returns*. New York: Portfolio Press.

Lu, Lei, Jun Wang, and Ge Zhang. 2009. "Long Term Performance of Leveraged ETFs." Working paper. Available at http://papers.ssrn.com/sol3/papers.cfm?abstract_id=1344133.

Madhavan, Ananth. 2004. "Implementing Fair Value Pricing." *Journal of Investing* 13, no. 1: 14–22.

Madhavan, Ananth. 2012. "Exchange-Traded Funds, Market Structure, and the Flash Crash." *Financial Analysts Journal* 68, no. 3: 20–35.

Madhavan, Ananth. 2014. "Exchange-Traded Funds: An Overview of Institutions, Trading and Impacts." *Annual Review of Financial Economics* 6: 311–341.

Madhavan, Ananth, Ursula Marchioni, Wei Li, and Daphne Du. 2014. "Equity ETFs vs. Index Futures: A Comparison for the Fully-Funded Investor." *Journal of Index Investing* 5, no. 2: 66–75.

Madhavan, Ananth, and Daniel Morillo. 2016. "The Impact of Flows into Exchange-Traded Funds: Volumes and Correlations." Forthcoming in the *Journal of Portfolio Management*. Available at SSRN:

Madhavan, Ananth, and Aleksander Sobczyk. 2016. "Price Dynamics and Liquidity of Exchange-Traded Funds." Forthcoming in the *Journal of Investment Management* (www.joim.com). Available at SSRN: http://ssrn.com/abstract=2429509.

Mazza, David B. 2012. "Do ETFs Increase Correlation?" *Journal of Index Investing* 3, no. 1: 45–51.

Morillo, Daniel, Nelson Da Conceicao, Jessica Hamrick, and Solomon Stewart. 2012. "Index Futures: Do They Deliver Efficient Beta?" *Journal of Index Investing* 3, no. 2: 76–80.

Office of Financial Research. 2013. "Asset Management and Financial Stability." US Department of Treasury, Washington, DC. Available at http://www.treasury.gov/ofr.

O'Hara, Maureen, and Mao Ye. 2011. "Is Market Fragmentation Harming Market Quality?" Working paper, Cornell University.

Pedersen, Niels, Sébastien Page, and Fei He. 2014. "Asset Allocation: Risk Models for Alternative Investments." *Financial Analysts Journal* 70, no. 3 (May/June): 34–45.

Perold, André F. 2007. "Fundamentally Flawed Indexing." *Financial Analysts Journal* 63, no. 6: 31–37.

Perold, André F., and Evan C. Schulman. 1988. "The Free Lunch in Currency Hedging: Implications for Investment Policy and performance Standards." *Financial Analysts Journal* 44, no. 3: 45–50.

Petajisto, Antti. 2013a. "Inefficiencies in the Pricing of Exchange-Traded Funds." Working paper, New York University.

Petajisto, Antti. 2013b. "Active Share and Mutual Fund Performance." *Financial Analyst Journal* 69, no. 4: 73–93.

Poterba, James, and Lawrence Summers. 1988. "Mean Reversion in Stock Prices." *Journal of Financial Economics* 22: 27–59.

Ramaswamy, Srichander. 2010. "Market Structures and Systemic Risks of Exchange-Traded Funds." Bank of International Settlements, BIS Working paper No. 343.

Schoenfeld, Steven. 2004. *Active Index Investing: Maximizing Portfolio Performance and Minimizing Risk through Global Index Strategies.* New Jersey: Wiley.

Sharpe, William F. 1991. "The Arithmetic of Active Management." *Financial Analysts Journal* 47, no. 1 (January/February): 7–9.

Staal, Arne, Marco Corsi, and Christopher Woida. 2015. "A Factor Approach to Smart Beta Development in Fixed Income." *Journal of Index Investing* 6, no. 1: 98–110.

Stratmann, Thomas, and John W. Welborn. 2012, "Exchange-Traded Funds, Fails-to-Deliver, and Market Volatility." Working paper 12–59, George Mason University.

Sullivan, Rodney, and James X. Xiong. 2012. "How Index Trading Increases Market Vulnerability." *Financial Analysts Journal* 68, no. 2: 70–85.

Trainor, William J. 2010. "Do Leveraged ETFs Increase Volatility?" *Technology and Investment* 1, no. 3: 215–220.

Tucker, Matthew, and Stephen Laipply. 2013. "Bond Market Price Discovery: Clarity through the Lens of an Exchange." *Journal of Portfolio Management* 39, no. 2 (Winter): 49–62.

Tuzun, Tugkan. 2013. "Are Leveraged and Inverse ETFs the New Portfolio Insurers?" Board of Governors of the Federal Reserve System.

Wermers, Russ. 2000. "Mutual Fund Performance: An Empirical Decomposition into Stock-Picking Talent, Style, Transaction Costs, and Expenses." *Journal of Finance* 54, no. 4: 1655–1695.

Wimbish, W. 2013. "Serious Health Warnings Needed for Some ETFs." *Financial Times*, June 23.

Wurgler, Jeffrey. 2010. "On the Economic Consequences of Index-Linked Investing." NBER Working Paper 16376, National Bureau of Economic Research, Cambridge, MA.

Zhang, Frank. 2011. "High-Frequency Trading, Stock Volatility, and Price Discovery." Working paper, Yale University, New Haven, CT.

Zhang, Yue. 2015. "The Securitization of Gold and Its Potential Impact on Gold Stocks." *Journal of Banking and Finance* 58, (September): 309–326.

Ananth Madhavan is a Managing Director and Global Head of Research for BlackRock's iShares division. He is responsible for advancing thought leadership and innovation for iShares, the world's largest provider of Exchange-Traded Funds. Madhavan's service with the firm dates back to 2003, including his years with Barclays Global Investors (BGI), which merged with BlackRock in 2009. At BGI, he was the Global Head of Trading Research and Transitions and CEO of BGI's affiliate broker. He also worked closely with the alpha and trading teams to design and implement trading strategies to capture short horizon market opportunities.

Prior to joining BGI, Madhavan was a Managing Director of Research at ITG and a member of the firm's management and executive committees. Previously, he was the Charles B. Thorton Professor of Finance at the Marshall School of Business at the University of Southern California and an Assistant Professor of Finance at the Wharton School of the University of Pennsylvania. Dr. Madhavan earned a BA degree from the University of Delhi, MA degree from Boston University, and a PhD in economics from Cornell University.

DISCLOSURE STATEMENT

The views expressed here are those of the author alone and not necessarily those of BlackRock, its officers, or directors. This work is intended for educational purposes and is not a recommendation to trade particular securities or of any investment strategy. Information on particular funds/securities is provided strictly for illustrative purposes and should not be deemed an offer to sell or a solicitation of an offer to buy shares of any funds that are described in this book.

The performance quoted represents past performance and does not guarantee future results. Investment return and principal value of an investment will fluctuate so that an investor's shares, when sold or redeemed, may be worth more or less than the original cost. Current performance may be lower or higher than the performance quoted. Index returns are for illustrative purposes only. Index performance returns do not reflect any management fees, transaction costs, or expenses. Indexes are unmanaged and one cannot invest directly in an index. Investing involves risk, including possible loss of principal. The author may own some of the funds mentioned in the book, but again mentions of particular funds are not in any way a recommendation to purchase or sell those securities.

This material is not intended to be relied upon as a forecast, research or investment advice, and is not a recommendation, offer, or solicitation to buy or sell any securities or to adopt any investment strategy. The opinions expressed are those of the author and may change as subsequent conditions vary. The information and opinions contained in this material are derived from sources deemed reliable, are not necessarily all-inclusive, and are not guaranteed as to accuracy. Past performance is no guarantee of future results. There is no guarantee that any forecasts made will come to pass. Reliance upon information in this material is at the sole discretion of the reader.

AUTHOR INDEX

SUBJECT INDEX

Note: Page references followed by *f* and *t* denote figures and tables, respectively. Numbers followed by n indicate notes.